PLATO'S *REPUBLIC* AND SHAKESPEARE'S ROME

PLATO'S *REPUBLIC* AND SHAKESPEARE'S ROME

A Political Study
of the Roman Works

Barbara L. Parker

DELAWARE
Newark: University of Delaware Press

©2004 by Rosemont Publishing & Printing Corp.

All rights reserved. Authorization to photocopy items for internal or personal use, or the internal or personal use of specific clients, is granted by the copyright owner, provided that a base fee of $10.00, plus eight cents per page, per copy is paid directly to the Copyright Clearance Center, 222 Rosewood Drive, Danvers, Massachusetts 01923. [0-87413-861-2/04 $10.00 + 8¢ pp, pc.]

Other than as indicated in the foregoing, this book may not be reproduced, in whole or in part, in any form (except as permitted by Sections 107 and 108 of the U.S. Copyright Law, and except for brief quotes appearing in reviews in the public press).

Associated University Presses
2010 Eastpark Boulevard
Cranbury, NJ 08512

The paper used in this publication meets the requirements of the American National Standard for Permanence of Paper for Printed Library Materials Z39.48–1984.

Library of Congress Cataloging-in-Publication Data

Parker, Barbara L.
  Plato's Republic and Shakespeare's Rome : a political study of the Roman works / Barbara L. Parker
    p. cm.
  Includes bibliographical references (p.   ) and index.
  ISBN 0-87413-861-2 (alk. paper)
  1. Shakespeare, William, 1564-1616—Knowledge—Rome. 2. Shakespeare,
William, 1564-1616—Political and social views. 3. Politics and literature—Great Britain—History—16th century. 4. Politics and literature—Great Britain—History—17th century. 5. Political plays, English—History and criticism. 6. English drama—Roman influences. 7. English drama—Greek influences. 8. Politics in literature. 9. Rome—In literature. 10. Plato. Republic. 11. Plato—Influence. I. Title.
  PR3069.R6P37 2004
  822.3'3—dc22
                                                          2003020616

PRINTED IN THE UNITED STATES OF AMERICA

For John

Contents

Acknowledgments 9
References and Abbreviations 11

1. Introduction 15
2. *The Rape of Lucrece* 31
3. *Coriolanus* 54
4. *Julius Caesar* 74
5. *Antony and Cleopatra* 92
6. *Titus Andronicus* 110
Conclusion 130

Notes 139
Bibliography 167
Index 179

Acknowledgments

IT IS WITH PLEASURE AND GRATITUDE THAT I ACKNOWLEDGE THE debts I have accrued during my eight years of work on this project. I wish first to thank William Paterson University for its support in the form of two sabbatical leaves and released class time; Georgianna Ziegler of the Folger Shakespeare Library, George Thompson of the New York University Library, and Susan Palmer, Archivist of Sir John Soane's Museum, London, for their invaluable help; Orlando Saa for the translation of Latin passages; and the University of Delaware Press and Associated University Presses—exemplified by Donald Mell, Julien Yoseloff, and Christine Retz—for the care and professionalism they accorded the manuscript from the outset.

I wish next to thank those who have read the manuscript in whole or in part and whose counsel has immeasurably strengthened the final product: Anthony Low, Maurice Charney, and the superb anonymous reader at the University of Delaware Press; and, in particular, John Velz, who painstakingly critiqued two separate drafts of the manuscript and also saved me from assorted blunders. I want also to stress my indebtedness to the work of the many scholars acknowledged in the notes.

I am grateful to the following presses for generously granting me permission to include material from previously published or forthcoming work: The Johns Hopkins University Press for permission to use "'A Thing Unfirm': Plato's *Republic* and Shakespeare's *Julius Caesar*," *Shakespeare Quarterly* 44 (1993), which comprises portions of Chapter 1 and the bulk of Chapter 4; Routledge/Taylor & Francis Books, Inc., for permission to quote or draw from "*Julius Caesar* among Shakespeare's Roman Works," forthcoming in *Julius Caesar,* edited by Horst Zander; and New York University Press for permission to include brief excerpts from *A Precious Seeing: Love and Reason in Shakespeare's Plays,* © 1987 by New York University. Preliminary versions of portions of this study have been presented as papers at various meetings of the Shakespeare Association of America, where they benefited greatly from the feedback of colleagues. The responsibility for any remaining errors, omissions, or gaffes is strictly mine.

References and Abbreviations

REFERENCES TO SHAKESPEARE ARE TO *THE COMPLETE WORKS OF SHAKEspeare*, ed. David Bevington, updated 4th ed. (New York: Addison Wesley Longman, 1997). Scriptural references are to the Geneva Bible (1560; reprint in facsimile, Madison: University of Wisconsin Press, 1969). Abbreviated titles of Shakespeare's works follow C. T. Onions, *A Shakespeare Glossary*, 3d ed., revised and enlarged by Robert D. Eagleson (Oxford: Clarendon Press, 1986).

Other frequently cited works are identified by the following abbreviations:

Bullough   Geoffrey Bullough, ed., *Narrative and Dramatic Sources of Shakespeare*, vols. 5 and 6 (London: Routledge and Kegan Paul; New York: Columbia University Press, 1964, 1966).

FQ   Edmund Spenser, *The Faerie Queene*, ed. Thomas P. Roche, Jr. (1978; reprint, London: Penguin, 1987).

Governor   Sir Thomas Elyot, *The Book Named the Governor*, ed. S. E. Lehmberg (London: Dent; New York: Dutton, 1962).

OED   *The Oxford English Dictionary*, 20 vols., 2d. ed., prep. J. A. Simpson and E. S. C. Weiner (Oxford: Clarendon Press, 1989).

Rep.   Plato, *The Republic*, vol. 1 of *The Dialogues of Plato*, trans. B. Jowett, 3d ed. (1892, 1920; New York: Random House, 1937).

PLATO'S *REPUBLIC* AND SHAKESPEARE'S ROME

1
Introduction

ACTORS, HAMLET TELLS POLONIUS, "ARE THE ABSTRACT AND BRIEF chronicles of the time" (2.2.524). In his ensuing instructions to the players, Hamlet famously elaborates the concept: "the purpose of playing . . . is to hold . . . the mirror up to nature, to show virtue her feature, scorn her own image, and the very age and body of the time his form and pressure" (3.2.20–24). He accordingly proposes to stage *The Murder of Gonzago*—"the image of a murder done in Vienna" (3.2.236), which images an actual crime committed in Urbino as well as the murder of Hamlet's father in Denmark—in order to "catch the conscience of the King" (2.2.606).[1] At the heart of these passages are two commonplace and interrelated English Renaissance practices. The first is the use of drama as a vehicle for political criticism or counsel; Hamlet's referentially unspecific "King" alludes not only to Claudius but also to the reigning English monarch who may be similarly engaged in viewing this "mirror" of his time (here, *Hamlet*) and, very likely, of his policies.[2] The second practice, implicit in the first, is the use of history to gloss contemporary political issues, thereby to "catch" the royal conscience and induce reform in policies deemed pernicious to the state. On the public stage, history served a similar function: to mold—likewise in the national interest—popular opinion and behavior. Both practices inform the five works in this study.

The politicization of history was a primarily Renaissance phenomenon. The Augustinian view of history, which dominated the Middle Ages, posited history as linear, providential, and universal, a sequence of irreversible, nonrecurring events that began with the Creation and ended with the Last Judgment. Progress was measured in supernatural terms, as a pilgrimage whose goal of salvation was exterior to space and time.[3] In the Renaissance, however, several things conspired to alter the nature of historiography, moving it decisively into the realm of practical action. One was the recovery of ancient historical texts, which fostered a view of history as ameliorative and nonlinear; what had interested classical writers about history was its utility. Another was the emergence of territorial and national states, which gave rise to a "clear perception of the state or the nation as the unit of historical development."[4] As Joseph Mazzeo observes, to new historians like Bruni and Machiavelli, "History was not the story of mankind, nor was it the story of God's dealings with mankind. It was, rather, the tale of the gain and loss of human liberty in one's own city and state. . . . When they looked to the ancient past they looked to it for guidance concerning their own specific problems, for clues to action which would enable them to master events and achieve political progress."[5] "[T]he increasing popularity of the two most 'politic' of ancient historians, Tacitus and Polybius, helped spread a 'Machiavellian' attitude to politics and thus, incidentally, his attitude to history as the guidebook of political life," rendering history particularly instructive for statesmen.[6] Hence the Renaissance bent for writing national rather than universal histories, and the confidence in the power of human reason to effect great and momentous change.

Concurrently restored to Renaissance historical thinking was the Greek theory of cycles or "tides." Integral to the politicization of history and among the most widely held historical theories in the Renaissance, this concept asserted that nations and governments (like all organisms in nature) exhibit a process of birth, flourishing, and decline, a process that does not cease upon completion but recurs again and again. Alternatively, civilizations ebb and flow in a continuously recurring process.[7] Hence history as ameliorative: since events and phenomena repeat themselves, the past informs and instructs the present. In addition to growing and declining, types of government tended to change into others;[8] monarchy might pass into oligarchy, for instance, or oligarchy into democracy. This Platonic notion, modified by Aristotle and recast by Polybius, will be treated more fully below.

These two theories—the cyclical and that of constitutional change—were utilized, often in tandem, by Renaissance writers to explicate and assess historical events. For Sir Thomas Elyot, history concerned "not only . . . acts of princes" but "the forms of sundry public weals

1 / INTRODUCTION

with augmentations and decays and occasion thereof." In Elyot's largely orthodox view, the razing of Rome's monarchy precipitated a progressive political decline culminating in the ruinous democracy of the Republic, thus proving that monarchy was the best form of government.[9] In his *Augustus,* Peter Heylyn invoked the Polybian *anacyclosis* in order "to demonstrate that monarchy was the first and final point in a cycle which could be repeated at any place or time."[10] And Machiavelli showed how both cycles of change effect progress:

> In the changes that are incident to all governments, they often degenerate into anarchy and confusion; and from these emerge again to good order and regularity. For since it is ordained by Providence that there should be a continual ebb and flow in the things of this world; as soon as they arrive at their utmost perfection, and can ascend no higher, they must of necessity decline: and on the other hand, when they have fallen, through any disorder, to the lowest degree that is possible, and can sink no lower, they begin to rise again. And thus there is a constant succession of prosperity and adversity in all human affairs. Virtue is the mother of peace: peace produces idleness; idleness, contention and misrule; and from thence proceed ruin and confusion. This occasions reformation and better laws; good laws make men virtuous; and public virtue is always attended with glory and success.[11]

Both in England and on the Continent, the politicization of history inevitably extended to theology, owing to the fusion of politics and religion wrought by the war between Protestantism and Rome. In England this conflict gave rise to a revolutionary, Protestant view of history; its foundation was the book of Revelation, which the Reformers interpreted historically. Its basic premise, established by John Bale's *Image of Both Churches,* held that the Whore of Babylon (Rev. 12, 17) and the Chaste Woman Clothed with the Sun were "prophetic figures for conflict between the 'true' church [identified with Protestantism] and the 'false' church governed by the papal Antichrist." To quote Roy Strong, "all the great religious changes of the century had been predicted in *Revelation*; Rome was the Beast of the Apocalypse against which each nation had revolted, and the result was a chaotic struggle between the forces of darkness and light." The "hordes of the Roman Antichrist were only kept at bay while God's holy handmaiden [Elizabeth] ruled. Chaos would be let loose if ever she ceased to guide the realm of England."[12] Influencing most major Elizabethan poets, the apocalyptic view of history reached its height following the defeat of the Armada, resulting in the conviction of "England's unique role as God's elect nation," and of Spain "as the epitome of evil."[13]

The study of history was considered particularly relevant for monarchs. In language strikingly reminiscent of Hamlet's,[14] Richard Reynoldes describes history as "the glasse of Princes, the image most lively bothe of vertue and vice, the learned theatre or spectacle of all the worlde, the councell house of Princes, . . . [and] a witnes of all tymes and ages."[15] History was essential for statesmen as well. The Elizabethan chronicler Richard Grafton, for instance, urged the rising Robert Dudley in 1563 to read history for (among other things) the lessons "in polecie" it furnished. Thomas Blundeville dedicated his *True Order and Methode of Wryting and Reading Hystories* (1574) to the Earl of Leicester, his aim being "as well to direct your priuate actions, as to giue Counsell lyke a most prudent Counseller in publyke causes, be it matters of warre, or peace."[16] As I suggest in the next chapter, Shakespeare's *Lucrece* served a similar function with respect to the Earl of Southampton.

THE MATTER OF ROME

In the political lessons it afforded, England's history was rivalled only by Rome's, particularly that of the late Republic and early Empire,[17] which significantly paralleled England's own history while mirroring in pertinent respects her contemporary milieu.[18] England's dynastic wars, still fresh in the national consciousness, recalled the broils that had toppled the Republic: in both instances, monarchic collapse or impotence had initiated power struggle and faction, and the attendant democratic impulses culminating in potential or actual popular rule.[19] Now another civil war appeared imminent, and for similar reasons: a monarchy undermined by an unsettled succession and the growing inefficacy of an aging queen, situations boding a coup preceding Elizabeth's death or a contest for the crown after it. Indeed, a scanning of relevant state papers of the time conveys an impression of plots, and of brewing sedition and political assassination.[20] Paramount was the fear of popular insurrection, on which a coup—as well as the success of a foreign invasion—largely depended. The charges (unproven) against Roderigo Lopez, Elizabeth's physician—that he conspired to kill the queen, incite rebellion, and overthrow the state—are indicative of the temper of the time, as are similar charges against the Earl of Essex following his revolt. Under the divisive and despotic policies of James I, civil unrest intensified. Nicolo Molin, Venetian Ambassador in England in 1605, remarked on persons "vigorously plotting against the life of the sovereign and of the state," and on the imminence of "a great revolution," a situation causing the ministers to "live in anxiety and suspicion, for they do not understand from what quarter nor from whom the blow is to come." Following the Northampton peasant revolt against the gentry in 1607, Venetian Ambassador Zorzi Giustinian observed that popular unrest in western England was "growing to such an extent that they only require a leader to make it a formidable and open rebellion."[21] It is no accident that the "[s]ocial conflict which developed by 1642 into organized rebellion, which produced by 1649 a regicide, and which culminated in the Commonwealth, . . . had its beginnings in the sixteenth century."[22]

That monarchic collapse was a prelude to civil war was an axiom deriving from Plato. The king, as the embodiment of reason, was the agent of unity and order and hence of the state's survival. The criticality of a single, rational ruler will be apparent when we recall that the state was considered a macrocosm of the soul; in the soul, vitiation of the governing faculty of reason loosed the fractious, power-hungry passions (the correlative of the masses), the ensuing battle for sovereignty sundering the soul's unity and incurring the equivalents of civil war, anarchy, and mob rule.[23] English historians, accordingly, almost unanimously endorsed monarchy, "in which the king governed with the advice of his nobles and people but did not in any sense share sovereignty, except insofar as parliamentary statutes constituted law."[24] In this view concurred not only the age's statesmen but even the Puritans, who "however much they might dislike the official hierarchy, did not question the queen's rule, the reality of degree, or the universal order of which both men and society must be reflections."[25]

The Roman republic perfectly illustrated the perils of monarchic collapse, along with the constitutional decline such collapse incurred. Fulke Greville, whose poetic treatise *Of Monarchy* contains many early-seventeenth-century ideas concerning ancient Rome, sees "the expulsion of the kings as a disaster, the consequence of the first Brutus having mistaken the sins of one tyrant, Tarquin, for the faults of a system."[26] Greville recounts Rome's lapse into a "many-headed Pow'r," the realm eventually coming "'To such descent of anarchie' through the pretensions of the tribunes that she finally succumbed to civil war." William Fulbecke condemns Rome's expulsion of the kings for the same reasons.[27] The sequence of decline this expulsion actuated is elaborated by Elyot: the people "more and more encroached a license" until they compelled the Senate to institute the Tribunate: "under whom they received such audacity and power that they [eventually] obtained the highest authority in the public weal. . . . Finally, until Octavius Augustus had destroyed Anthony, and also Brutus, and finished all the Civil Wars . . . , the city of Rome was never long quiet from factions or seditions[,] . . . so much discord was ever in the city for lack of one governor."[28]

Elyot articulates what was conventionally deemed the fatal flaw of republicanism: multiple sovereignty. As survival lay in unity, so ruin lay in plurality, which led to faction (precipitating the sundering of the state), a battle for supremacy and thus perpetual strife, and to the attendant rise of the irrational masses. As Elyot observes, "by the multitude of sovereign governors" are "all things . . . brought to confusion." Christopher Marlowe, likewise invoking Rome's example, reiterates the point: "Dire league of partners in a kingdom last not. . . . / Dominion cannot suffer partnership."[29] Shakespeare makes the point again and again, but nowhere more explicitly than in *Coriolanus*: "when two authorities are up, / Neither supreme, how soon confusion / May enter twixt the gap of both and take / The one by th' other" (*Cor* 3.1.112–15), an axiom, as we will see, borne out by the play. Relatedly, *Lear*'s Regan asserts the near impossibility of concord among the inhabitants of "one house. . . under two commands" (*Lr* 2.4.242–43). The remark refers simultaneously to household and realm, the former of which was conventionally construed as a microcosm of society-at-large.[30] Regan's remark additionally invokes Christ's warning that "Euerie kingdome deuided against it self, shalbe broght to naught: & euerie . . . house, deuided against it self, shal not stand" (Matt. 12.25).

In razing the monarchy, therefore, the Republic planted the seeds of its own demise, its ensuing broils rendering Rome an archetype of civil strife.[31] This perception of Rome is reflected not only in the preponderance of English plays on Rome dealing with civil war,[32] but also in the fact that no fewer than fifteen of them invoke the stereotype of Roman 'factiousness,' many as early as the opening scene: in *Catiline*, for instance, the rebels are committed to "contention" and "faction" (4.3.19–26); and in *Sejanus* the Romans malign the "factious" "traitor[s]" (3.350–52).[33]

In Shakespeare, factiousness initiates all four of the Roman plays. *Coriolanus* opens on a disordered citizenry plotting vengeance on their patrician oppressors; the situation brings Rome to the brink of civil war. *Julius Caesar* opens on a similarly disordered citizenry whose power and contempt for authority have, however, ominously increased; civil war follows. Despite the routing of Caesar's assassins, the Rome of *Antony and Cleopatra* remains racked by "faction" and "civil swords" (*Ant* 1.3.48, 45), the consequence of the continuing power struggle between Rome's rulers. In *Titus Andronicus*, the theme of factiousness is suggested even before the action begins, in the stage directions prefacing the opening scene: "*[E]nter Saturninus and his followers at one door, and Bassianus and his followers [at the other]*." Dissension is rife, as is the threat of civil war: Bassianus exhorts the people to "fight for freedom in your choice" (1.1.17); Saturninus exhorts them to back him with "arms" and "swords" (1.1.2, 4). Significantly, the play concerns the issue of succession, and the object of contention is the crown.

While Elizabethan and Jacobean drama both implement this tradition of political criticism, their focuses differ according to the concerns of their respective ages. In contrast to Jacobean drama, which often deals with court depravity, licentiousness, and corruption, Elizabethan drama attests an overwhelming concern with the succession.[34] This was so not only because the unsettled succession was the gravest crisis of Elizabeth's reign but also because drama furnished one of the few venues for purveying—albeit indirectly—opinions on that forbidden subject with reasonable impunity from royal wrath. Lawyers, for instance, prohibited from broaching in Parliament the topics of the succession and the queen's marriage, turned to drama as their advocacy medium. "Their plays," writes Marie Axton, "dealt with issues and situations rather than personalities, and while leaving themselves latitude to escape censure, they expected their audience [would] . . . provide the relevant contemporary context for an allegory." Tacitly reflecting the age's faith in the stage's instructional potential, "the London theatre of the late eighties and nineties [thus became] perhaps the freest forum for speculation about the future succession to the throne."[35]

The drama, therefore, was also addressed to society at large. It seems clear that besides contriving to promote reform, these playwrights were also seeking—likewise in the national interest—to influence public behavior and opinion. As Thomas Heywood declared, drama aimed "to teach the subjects obedience to their King, to shew the people the untimely ends of such as have moved tumults, commotions, and insurrections, to present them with the flourishing estate of such as live in obedience, exhorting them to allegiance, [and] dehorting them from all trayterous and fellonious strategems."[36] Hence the profoundly topical nature of these plays, which, as Margot Heinemann demonstrates, exploited not only the audience's intense interest in history but also their political anxieties, grievances, and resentments. In thus "[f]using the popular dramatic tradition with new humanist or 'politique' history," these works "helped both to create a consensus of support for a powerful monarchy and, paradoxically, to undermine it" through their potentially subversive portrayals of the dangers, and abuses, of royal policy.[37]

The Role of Plato

As mentioned above, one factor instrumental in the Renaissance politicization of history was the revival of classical theories of constitutional change. While the principal texts for these theories were Plato's *Republic* (along with his *Laws*) and Aristotle's *Politics* (which sought to emend Plato's constitutional views), I shall argue that the decline informing the works under discussion is Platonic, deriving primarily from the *Republic*.[38]

That the *Republic* should inform what are fundamentally political works should not surprise. As James Holly Hanford observed in an essay demonstrating the concurrence of Ulysses' speech on degree with precepts propounded in the *Republic,* Ulysses asserts "not simply that the state must have a single head, but that stability depends upon the preservation [of class hierarchy].... The need of a firm government and of a strict preservation of social ranks was given special emphasis in Shakespeare's day owing to recent tendencies in England toward democratic thought," and, along with *The Politics,* "*The Republic*... furnished... [Tudor] theorists with their best arguments and their chief authorities in their attempt to justify by reason what was already in practice the established social order."[39] Relatedly, the *Republic* was one of the great influential treatises on princeship, providing, with the *Laws*, the basic ideas of most subsequent essays of this genre.[40] Scholars have, in fact, noted correspondences with the *Republic* in a number of Shakespeare's plays, including *Troilus and Cressida*, *The Tempest*, *Henry V*, *Richard III*, *Coriolanus*, and *The Merchant of Venice*, nearly all of which contain prominent political themes.[41]

Central to the *Republic* is the founding of the State on reason. Because rational government is achievable only by rational men, or philosophers, democracy is to be eschewed; rulership must be founded on a knowledge of truth, which knowledge the blind, irrational masses are incapable of attaining. Plato's republic is accordingly rigidly stratified, comprised of three great hierarchically ordered classes: the workers at the bottom, the Auxiliaries or militia over them, and the Guardian or Guardians at the top. The State's integrity lies in the due subordination of the lower classes to the higher, justice—the real subject of the *Republic*—residing in each class maintaining its bounds and function. Injustice, conversely, consists in one class infringing the bounds and vocation of another. The result is the ruin of the State. These three classes correspond to the reason, the will, and the appetites in man, who must similarly be ruled by reason if he is to achieve that internal justice on which his preservation depends.

Because the State's felicity is contingent on its ruler, the ideal guardian possesses a harmoniously ordered soul in turn perfected by a rigorous education whose purpose is "to detach the mind from appearances,"[42] thereby enabling him to effect corresponding justice in the State. Thus he is a guardian in the fullest sense: armed against the "enchantments" that seduce baser minds and, consequently, against ambition, boastfulness, and greed, he can preserve the State against its enemies and maintain peace at home (*Rep.* 3.413–14, 6.486).

The polity thus mirrors the ethos of its ruler, and Plato devotes Books 8 and 9 of his *Republic* to the corresponding perversions of rulership in the State. The best form of government is monarchy. What prompts its perversion is self-interest, especially economic or material self-interest, which incurs the first stage of constitutional decline, timocracy.[43] The desire for wealth leads in turn to impoverishment of the people and thus to the class struggle characterizing oligarchy (the rule of the rich); and to the attendant danger of civil war. The people then procure a champion and eventually expel the rich to establish democracy, i.e., freedom which is synonymous with lawlessness. But the inordinate love of liberty that characterizes democracy leads by way of reaction to tyranny as the power-seeking champion discards pretence and effects a coup d'état.[44] Thereafter, individual warfare supplants class warfare as the ruler strives to retain control of the state.

The substitution of historical for compositional chronology attests this sequence in four of the works under discussion. The sequence is initiated in *Lucrece*: the rapaciousness of the ruling dynasty incurs abolishment of the monarchy, which, together with the instatement of the consulate, paves the way for the empowerment of the masses. In *Coriolanus*, Rome has lapsed into oligarchy, with consequences paralleling those described in the *Republic*. Since, according to Plato, rulership is founded on wealth, "inevitable division" results; "such a State is not one, but two . . . , the one of poor, the other of rich men; and they are living on the same spot and always conspiring against one another" (*Rep.* 8.551). Thus in *Coriolanus*, the famished and seditious masses seek revenge on the surfeiting patricians, who enact "piercing statutes daily to chain up and restrain the poor" (*Cor* 1.1.15–21, 81–82). With the advent of the tribunate, democracy progressively supplants oligarchy as the people continue to amass power. In *Julius Caesar*, the degenerative process is complete, popular empowerment having culminated in mob rule.[45] *Antony and Cleopatra* portrays Rome in an advanced stage of tyranny, her rulers continuing the battle for supremacy by means of treachery and betrayal in a realm now wholly devoid of law. Each of these works, therefore, depicts a separate stage of political decline and of an ever-widening power struggle ultimately waged for control of the world. Power struggle and decline are thus inextricably linked, the inevitable consequences of a polity shorn of monarchic rule.

Fused with this Platonic sequence of constitutional decline is a cyclical view of history, which encompasses both persons and events.[46] Collectively, these four works disclose a movement from monarchy to tyranny and (with the triumph of Augustus) back to monarchy. The cyclical movement also inheres in the metamorphosis of one tyrant (and one triumvirate) into another. The movement informs individual plays as well. In *Julius Caesar*, it underlies the rise and fall that defines each character in turn, a pattern instated even before the play opens, with the vanquishing of Pompey by Caesar who then supplants Pompey as Rome's champion and idol. Caesar is in turn displaced by Brutus, who is displaced by Antony, who is displaced by Octavius, a reincarnation of Caesar. Relatedly, Brutus reembodies Caesar (note the dual import of Third Plebeian's cry, "Let him [Brutus] be Caesar" [*JC* 3.2.51]).[47] In *Coriolanus*, Marcius reincarnates the oppressive, tyrannical Tarquins he fought to destroy; banished and destroyed in turn, he reemerges in the figure of Aufidius. On a still broader cyclical level, events in this Roman "tetralogy" repeat themselves in the English tetralogies and are in the process of recurring yet again in Shakespeare's England.

Titus Andronicus, unlike each of these other works, is ahistorical, not only in its characters and events but in the depiction of Rome itself, which exhibits elements of both a monarchy and a republic. It is nonetheless linked to these works both politically and Platonically in its concern with the consequences of a "headless" state. As in *Lucrece*, kinglessness derives from dissolution of the monarchy, here, however, in the form of a rulerless interregnum produced by an unsettled succession. The resulting power struggle, schism, and descent into what the play terms "a wilderness of tigers"—a movement from monarchy to tyranny—encapsulates a decline analogous to that traced by the other four works. Also like those works, *Titus* addresses the opportunity for seizing power that headlessness affords the unqualified and unscrupulous politician. *Titus* additionally makes use of the apocalyptic view of history, which underlies the play's concern with the danger of a Catholic alien on England's throne.

Of these five works, three, I will argue—*The Rape of Lucrece, Julius Caesar,* and *Titus Andronicus*—concern the Elizabethan succession, while *Coriolanus* and *Antony and Cleopatra* address issues of Stuart absolutism and excess. All five thus employ political allegory. Although generically mixed—one is a poem and four are plays—they are linked by a single overriding theme: the threat to the state of a destabilized monarchy. I will further argue that *Lucrece, Coriolanus, Caesar,* and *Antony and Cleopatra* form a tetralogy in that they collectively trace a continuous span of history coupled with a progressive constitutional decline; that this decline is prefigured and encapsulated in *Titus Andronicus*; and that all five derive their thematic interrelatedness from political concepts articulated in the *Republic*.[48] As applied to the subject works, the term "tetralogy" thus refers not to compositional sequence (the sequence generally informing each of Shakespeare's so-called English tetralogies) but to the political and historical continuum these works collectively evince, i.e., the Platonic constitutional decline they demonstrate and the continuous span of history they collectively encompass, which begins with the expulsion of the Tarquins and concludes with the triumph of Augustus.[49]

Lest it be objected that Shakespeare's political philosophy follows Aristotle rather than Plato, we should note the differences between the two. The chief distinctions between their constitutional theories are (1) the types of government they postulate (for Plato, five: Monarchy, Timocracy, Oligarchy, Democracy, and Tyranny; for Aristotle six: Monarchy, Aristocracy, and Polity (the desirable forms), and Tyranny, Oligarchy, and Democracy (their corresponding perversions [*Politics* 3.7, see also *Nic. Eth.* 8.10]);[50] (2) their theories of constitutional change (Plato links these five constitutional regimes in an evolving, progressively degenerating chain, Monarchy constituting the noblest regime and Tyranny the most debased; Aristotle disputes this sequence, contending that reverse situations are equally possible—for instance, that democracy can pass into oligarchy, or tyranny into democracy [*Politics* 5.12.10–17]; he also disputes Plato's claim that oligarchy entails two separate, economically opposed states [*Politics* 5.12.15]); (3) the psychological component (for Plato, the state ethically images the soul of its ruler; for Aristotle, it does not necessarily); and (4) their concepts of justice (for Plato, justice consists in maintaining hierarchy, both in the state and in the soul, which ensures the unity and order on which preservation depends; for Aristotle, justice consists in awarding the most rights to those contributing the most to the state's good [*Politics* 3.9], entailing as well that course of action which the moral aim of the state requires [*Politics* 3.10]). Most significant for this study, Plato considers the masses inherently unfit to govern and without exception condemns multiple rule as a prelude to mob supremacy. Aristotle does neither; since the "ideal" monarch cannot exist, Aristotle advocates (depending on the circumstances) both Aristocracy (the rule of many good men) and Polity, in the latter of which "there naturally exists a warlike multitude able to obey and to rule in turn by a law which gives office to the well-to-do according to their desert." Polity is thus roughly equivalent to rule by the middle class.[51] This is not to say that Shakespeare was uninfluenced by the political thought of Aristotle.[52] His constitutional theory, however—which is the subject of this study—is Platonic.

1 / INTRODUCTION 27

Given Shakespeare's putatively slim credentials in classical tongues—a notion born of Ben Jonson's famous reference to his "small Latin and less Greek"—the question of Shakespeare's familiarity with the *Republic* naturally arises. We have already remarked Plato's centrality in Tudor thought. The Platonic concept of the state as a structure governed by a sovereign authority and composed of stratified, functionally determined classes was a cultural commonplace.[53] Plato's constitutional theories were likewise well known. Shakespeare could have gained further familiarity with these concepts from such Platonic theorists as Cicero, Erasmus, and Elyot—not to mention Plutarch. Thus he need not have gotten them from the *Republic*.

Yet, given Shakespeare's unarguably keen interest in matters of state (he wrote nine plays on English monarchs in the 1590s alone), it is unlikely that he would have been unread in one of the two most significant political theorists of his time. Supporting this view are the numerous Platonic elements contained in the works under discussion—elements in addition to those noted above, that appear in the *Republic* but in none of Shakespeare's known sources. It is thought that Shakespeare might have possessed some knowledge of Greek but that it would have been inadequate to permit him to access texts in Greek, except possibly portions of the Bible.[54] Could he therefore have read a translation of Plato's work?

While there is no known sixteenth-century English translation of the *Republic*, Marsilio Ficino's well-known complete Latin translation of Plato's works was widely available.[55] An Italian translation of the *Republic* was published in Venice in 1554; a complete French translation, published in Paris, did not appear until 1600, although portions had been published earlier. Thus Shakespeare could almost certainly have obtained the work in Latin—which brings us back to Shakespeare's "small Latin and less Greek."

The curriculum of the sixteenth century English grammar school—which, scholars generally agree, Shakespeare attended—was predominantly Latin-based, owing to the passionate humanist conviction of the relevance of the classics to contemporary endeavor. Shakespeare, accordingly, would have had a rigorous grounding in Latin, learning not only to read it but to write and speak it as well. As Russ McDonald points out, he would have begun with the Latin Grammar of William Lyly, along with supplementary manuals calculated to teach the fundamentals of rhetoric and style. Moving to translation, he would have rendered Latin texts into English and the English back into reinvented Latin, doing this "for most of the day, six days a week, for about ten years" until full translational mastery was achieved. His graduated reading curriculum would have started with the relatively easy Latin of Caesar and Aesop (translated from Greek), in preparation for the works of (among others) Cicero, Virgil, Sallust, Ovid, Horace, Suetonius, and Livy; the *Bucolica* of Battista Spagnuoli (Mantuan); and the plays of Terence. Less studied were the plays of Plautus and Seneca, "but Shakespeare clearly read them, perhaps on his own." By the time Shakespeare had completed the Upper School, he would have read most of the canonical Latin corpus.[56]

It is not surprising, therefore, that modern scholarship on classical influences in Shakespeare points to a verdict substantially opposed to Jonson's. "We now know," for instance, "that while Shakespeare often used translations, he could and did read sources in Latin, French, and probably Italian."[57] Nor is Shakespeare's competence in Latin open to question. As McDonald points out, "Jonson was one of the most learned men of his age, a master of ancient and modern languages, a proud scholar who larded his classically derived tragedies with marginal quotations from and footnotes to the models and originals that he imitated. Compared to Jonson's mastery of Latin, Shakespeare's was perhaps 'small.' But considered on its own terms, Shakespeare's classical learning was respectable for the age in which he lived, and for the age in which *we* live, it was formidable."[58]

That Shakespeare was schooled in the above texts is strongly suggested by their implementation in his works—an implementation on which the revised view of his Latinity ultimately rests. Scholars have inferred direct indebtedness to (among other texts in Latin) Ovid's *Metamorphoses* (Prospero's speech renouncing his magic in *The Tempest* [5.1.33–57] and portions of *Titus Andronicus* [direct indebtedness to Sophocles' *Ajax* is also proposed for *Titus*]),[59] Ovid's *Fasti* (portions of *Lucrece*),[60] and Plautus's *Menaechmi* (*The Comedy of Errors*).[61] T. W. Baldwin, in his landmark study of Shakespeare's classical learning, argues indebtedness to a plethora of sources.[62] Scores of other scholars have argued the influence of classical texts but stop short of asserting direct attribution.[63] As for the works of Plato (which Shakespeare presumably would have read in Latin), direct indebtedness has been suggested for the *Phaedo* (the death of Falstaff [*H5* 2.3.20–25])[64] and the *Republic*,[65] and probable indebtedness to or the influence of these and other Platonic texts copiously proposed.[66] It seems likely, therefore, that Shakespeare would have been able to—and, as the following chapters suggest, probably did—know the *Republic* directly.

Lest it be questioned whether Shakespeare's audience would have understood the political theory informing these Roman works, it should be borne in mind that the issues these works reflect were of vital interest to that audience. As Phillips points out, political actualities in England—not least including the succession crisis and James's absolutism—

> vitally touched the welfare of every Englishman. . . . The popular concern with theories of government which such issues aroused was nourished by dissemination of political ideas through a number of popular channels; . . . sermons, pamphlets, and other media served to familiarize the general public with the concepts and terminology of political thinking. Among the manifestations of this lay concern with political theory the drama . . . was one of the most significant. . . . [Thus] drama came to reflect the active contemporary interest in political theory and to embody the concepts and doctrines involved in that interest.[67]

Why, it may justifiably be asked, would Shakespeare risk the wrath of James, who was his patron as well as his king? As with the Elizabethan stage, politics permeated—often overtly—the theatre at every level, possibly encouraged by the sporadic and apparently lax censorship both at Whitehall and in the public playhouses.[68] The Jacobean period in particular witnessed flagrant and pervasive violations; for some years following James's accession, according to E. K. Chambers,

> the freedom of speech adopted by the stage, in a London much inclined to be critical of the alien King and his retinue of hungry Scots, was far beyond anything which could have been tolerated by Elizabeth. The uncouth speech of the Sovereign, his intemperance, . . . his inordinate devotion to the chase, were caricatured with what appears incredible audacity. . . . "Consider for pity's sake," writes . . . the French ambassador on 14 June 1604, "what must be the state and condition of a prince, whom the preachers publicly from the pulpit assail, whom the comedians . . . bring upon the stage, whose wife attends these representations in order to enjoy the laugh against her

husband.". . . [As one Samuel Calvert wrote to one Ralph Winwood,] "the play[er]s do not forbear to represent . . . the whole course of this present time, not sparing either King, state, or religion, in so great absurdity, and with such liberty, that any would be afraid to hear them."[69]

In addition, censorship was hampered by the non-English settings of many of these plays. Rome, an acknowledged "glass" for England, was yet sufficiently removed temporally and spatially to blur allusions to contemporary persons and events; so were France and Spain, the realms of Greek mythology, and the sundry Italianate locales so dear to Jacobean playwrights. As Thomas Heywood explained regarding the aims of drama: "If wee present a forreigne History, the subject is so intended, that in the lives of Romans, Grecians, or others, either the vertues of our Country-men are extolled, or their vices reproued. . . ."[70] Shakespeare was also writing in something of a tradition: according to Woolf, "Many medieval historical works were composed for the express purpose of instructing the powerful; a parallel tradition existed of non-historical advice books, from John of Salisbury's *Policraticus* through the *specula* or 'mirrors of princes' of the late Middle Ages to Erasmus' *Education of a Christian Prince* and More's *Utopia* at the beginning of the sixteenth century." Renaissance historians in particular increasingly saw their role as one of political guidance, using the device, for example, of criticizing a past prince in order to induce reform in the behavior of a present one without causing offense.[71] As Sir Walter Ralegh states in his preface to *The History of the World*, "in speaking of the past, I point at the present, and tax the vices of those that are yet living, in their persons that are long since dead." Similarly, in Samuel Daniel's *Tragedy of Cleopatra*, the doomed Cleopatra proclaims herself "A fit memoriall for the times to come, / To be example to such Princes good / As please themselves, and care not what become."[72] Nor was Rome as a political exemplum a Renaissance innovation; recounting the background of Rome's civil war and addressed to the Council during Henry VI's minority, John Lydgate's *Serpent of Division* (1422?) "is a plea for national unity, the lack of which, it is stressed, brought about Rome's downfall."[73] Finally, it should be remembered that the aim of these writers was not sedition or revolution but reform, and that the stakes—certainly for Shakespeare, as the following chapters suggest—were nothing less than the survival of the state.

2
The Rape of Lucrece

When *Lucrece* opens, Rome is still a monarchy. It is ruled, however, not by the philosopher king of Plato's ideal state but by a tyrannical usurper. Nevertheless, Rome is not, constitutionally speaking, a tyranny. In Plato, tyranny as a constitution is the outgrowth of democracy; as discussed more fully in chapter 4, it comes into being when the masses, having achieved control of the state, procure a champion whom they nurse into greatness and who then seizes absolute power, thereafter murdering rivals and opponents to retain supremacy. Rome's political situation in *Lucrece* accords more closely with what Plato calls timocracy, the first stage of constitutional decline.

As a mean between aristocracy and oligarchy,[1] timocracy retains elements of the ideal state: the rulers are still respected, and the boundary between workers and auxiliaries remains unbreached (*Rep.* 8.547). But the quality of the rulers has degenerated (*Rep.* 8.546–547), along with a concern for the common good, and a martial ethos has replaced one founded on reason.

The transition from the ideal state to timocracy is rooted in the cause of all revolution, division within the ruling class (*Rep.* 8.545). Thus begins the breakdown of unity, of the principle of specialization essential to the realm's preservation,[2] and of the preeminence of reason that marks the ideal state. With its sovereignty eroded, reason succumbs to the spirited element (the faculty of will), of which the warrior class is the embodiment. Power, therefore, is no longer the province of the philosopher, but of "passionate and less complex characters, who are by nature fitted for war rather than peace"; and owing to the value now placed on martial endeavor, the state is dedicated to "the waging of everlasting wars" (*Rep.* 8.547–48).

Because honor is the motive of the spirited element, timocracy is "the government of honour" (*Rep.* 8.545), the "admired type" now being "the man of high spirit and courageous temper" devoted to the pursuit of honor. Thus the realm has become a military state, "and it promotes to the highest office those of its members who have won honour in war." But the timocrat also covets power and wealth because the spirited element inclines toward the affections. Thus justice, which is predicated on the adherence of each class to its vocation and bounds, is beginning to vanish; "The wise man has lost the reins of office: the soldier has taken the place of the ruler; and even the . . . producing class loses its right position," for, owing to the timocrat's desire for wealth, "[i]ts property is seized, and its members are depressed into serfs by the new rulers."[3]

How the Rome of *Lucrece* conforms to Plato's timocracy will fully emerge after a study of the poem. It will accordingly be useful to begin with some background on the story of Lucrece, for it will assist in contextualizing Shakespeare's work.[4]

The rape of Lucrece had been linked with politics for sixteen centuries, with writers as disparate as Ovid and Henry Bullinger expounding its political significance.[5] "Tarquin and his brood were banished," asserts Ovid, and "A consul undertook the government for a year. That day was the last of kingly rule." Because "Tarquinius had perforce ravished Lucretia," writes Henry Bullinger, "the kings were expelled out of the city of Rome." Sir Thomas Elyot elaborates the connection: under the monarchy, the Romans were well governed, and discord and sedition unheard of. Following the rape, not only were the Tarquins banished but the people determined never again to have a king. The people, in consequence, "more and more encroached a license," eventually amassing "such audacity and power" that they attained "the highest authority" in the realm. The result was continuous faction, sedition, and civil strife.[6]

Not surprisingly, the story furnished copious fodder for political allegory, the use of which became especially pronounced during periods of national turmoil. Bullinger's play *Lucretia* (1533), for instance, "reflects the current political situation in Switzerland after the guilds had seized power: Brutus, drawing up the new democratic constitution of Rome, would have reminded the play's audiences of Bullinger's friend Zwingli, who had been similarly occupied in Zurich." During France's Revolutionary period, Lucius Junius Brutus emerged as a hero, "the father of revolution, not merely in his own country but wherever people are oppressed."[7] In England, Holinshed likened Richard III to Tarquin; later writers equated the exiled Stuarts with the banished Tarquins.[8] By Shakespeare's day the tale of Lucrece had for generations been identified with the Wars of the Roses, with Rome's post-monarchic disorders being compared to the York-Lancaster broils.[9] Thus the story was copiously allegorized, tending to be read in terms of current political events.[10]

Allegory inhered in the story itself: in many versions, Lucrece stands for violated Rome, with the rape epitomizing the wider tyranny of the Tarquins.[11] She thus partakes of the age-old metaphor of the raped nation. As we will see, Shakespeare uses that metaphor in *Titus Andronicus*—a work roughly concurrent with *Lucrece*—in which the raped Lavinia is a synecdoche for Rome.[12]

The Rape of Lucrece contains three levels of allegory. First, the events culminating in Lucrece's rape replicate transpiring political events in Rome. This level additionally encompasses the Platonic correspondence between soul and state that informs the poem, the integrity of the state Platonically imaging that of its ruler; hence the parallel between political events and the rape. The Troy-piece furnishes the second level of allegory: the events culminating in the ruin of Troy prefigure Lucrece's rape and its aftermath, the ruin of Rome, which will be the focus of *Julius Caesar*. The correspondence between the poem's milieu and England's constitutes the third level of allegory. Troy had for centuries been equated with England as well as with Rome, both "second" Troys; Rome was also a political exemplum for England. The three realms were thus in some measure analogous, and they are conflated in the figure of Lucrece. Lucrece additionally represents Elizabeth as does, less prominently, Priam, each character figuring a different aspect of her rulership. Tarquin, Sinon, Paris, and Brutus figure Essex. The technique is similar to Spenser's, that which Spenser terms "mirrours more then one" (*FQ* 3.proem.5); Britomart, for instance, stands for England, but she also figures Elizabeth, as do, in different ways, Gloriana, Belphoebe, Fidelia, Una, Mercilla, Radigund, and Lucifera.[13]

That *Lucrece* is political is suggested both structurally and verbally. The Argument opens with a usurpation and closes, like the poem, with the overthrow of the monarchy. Shakespeare, therefore, besides fusing Lucrece's rape with the political story, provides a political frame for the story proper that creates an analogy between the two. Lucius Tarquinius is not only a tyrant who flouts Roman law; he has, like Shakespeare's Richard II, murdered a kinsman to achieve the crown (Arg.). The situation parallels that of the rape: in a lawless realm, Lucrece solicits Tarquin for justice (544, 626–644), the rape itself being conceived as a usurpation.[14]

The rape is further politically defined. Tarquin is a "usurper" (412), who seeks the "throne" and the "crown" (413, 216). The rape is an act of "treason" (361; see also 369). Even Lucrece's body parts evoke political entities: her heart is a "citizen" (465); it is also a "cabinet" of which she is "governess"[15] (442–43). Her face is a "map" (1712). Her breasts are "worlds" (408). She herself is alternately a "city" and a "land" (469, 439). And when she pleads with Tarquin, it is for the return of "majesty" (640), whose "exile" she expressly equates with rape. This figurative exile of majesty anticipates, both verbally and literally, the poem's conclusion: because of the king's "tyranny," "the Tarquins were all exiled and the state government changed from kings to consuls" (Arg.).

As already noted, the Lucrece story was identified with the Wars of the Roses, and in this connection our first view of Lucrece warrants close attention. Absent is the conventional Petrarchan hyperbole, or any description at all of Lucrece's features; what instead confronts us is a blazoned shield whose "heraldry" depicts two rivals—"beauty's red and virtue's white"—engaged in a "war" for supremacy (64–65, 71). That they are fighting for control of the crown is suggested by "queen," "sovereignty," and "seat," the last an Elizabethan synonym for "throne."[16] Spurred by mutual "ambition," the rivals have been battling for some time, as evidenced by the repeated exchanges of sovereignty between combatants having equal right of rule (67–70). What Lucrece's face inscribes is the Wars of the Roses, an allusion underscored by the reference to "This . . . war of . . . roses" (71). This war, in one guise or another, will become the poem's governing metaphor.

Integral to the political theme is the motif of rhetoric that permeates the work. The alliance between rhetoric and politics stretches from Plato and Aristotle down to modern times. Particularly in republican regimes, rhetoric was a vehicle for influencing the masses—and, as orators correspondingly recognized, for effecting revolutions. Tacitus, for instance, links the evolution of Roman eloquence to Rome's passage from republic to empire. As Davy Du Perron explains:

> The places where eloquence has always reigned and triumphed more have been in Republics and popular governments, for the reason that in those States, where deliberations depend on the multitude, the first particular that must be sought is that the people, who are, as they say, a many-headed animal, agree on a self-same intention. . . . [C]onsequently it is necessary to have recourse to a public and popular instrument which can move infinite persons at the same time and make them consent to a common resolution. A thing which must be attributed to eloquence . . . : for it is eloquence which manages whole assemblies of men . . . , makes itself mistress of their affections, shapes their wills as it suits these affections, and withdraws them from whatever it does not please to see them inclined to.

Montaigne further elaborates the connection between rhetoric and politics:

> It [rhetoric] is a tool invented to manipulate a mob and disorderly commoners, and is a tool used only in sick states, like medicine, in those where the vulgar, the ignorant, where all were in power, as in . . . Rome, and where things were in perpetual tempest, there orators thronged. . . . Eloquence flourished best in Rome when affairs were in their worst state and when the storm of civil wars agitated them. . . . From that it seems that the policies that depend on a monarchy need it less than the others: for the stupidity and facility that is found in the common people and which make them subject to be led and twisted by the sweet sound of that harmony without coming to weigh and know the truth of things by force of reason, this facility, I say, is not so easily found in a single man.[17]

This concept—revolution through rhetorical manipulation—is central to *Lucrece*, for it is rhetoric that is ultimately responsible for Rome's change from a monarchy to a republic.[18]

The coup d'état that will close the poem is set in motion by a contest between some Roman soldiers concerning whose wife is most chaste—a contest initiated during their post-prandial chit-chat when Collatine extols Lucrece's virtues. The competitors then post to Rome to test what everyone had "avouched"; and when only Lucrece is discovered virtuously engaged, the nobles yield Collatine "the victory" (Arg.).

The contest is conceived from the outset in political terms. The narrator, pondering Collatine's motive for unwisely "publishing" Lucrece's virtues, conjectures that the boast of her "sovereignty" ignited Tarquin's lust, or else envy that one of inferior rank should possess the "golden hap" (36–42)—a synonym for "crown."[19] The narrator also glances at Tarquin's ambition (at his "high-pitched thoughts" [41]). What ensues is a power struggle for Lucrece's possession—a power struggle prefigured in the "war" in Lucrece's face: there the source of the strife was "ambition," and the two combatants were so powerful—of such "sovereignty"—"That oft they interchange each other's seat" (68–70). "Seat" is a double entendre that renders the rape sexually and politically analogous. The rape, a figurative usurpation, replicates the poem's two political coups: the first when Lucius Tarquinius overthrows Servius Tullius and becomes king; the second when Brutus overthrows the monarchy and becomes consul. Tarquin will similarly usurp the seat of Collatine (289) and, like the red and white rivals in Lucrece's face, exchange "sovereignty" with the seat's possessor.

The sight of Lucrece precipitates an internal replication of this contest: a "disputation" (246) between reason and will for Tarquin's soul. Reason argues for justice (190–238)—for the suppression of "thoughts unjust" (189). Conquest, reason maintains, would be illusory since achieving "the crown" will incur eternal infamy (204–24). Will, however, triumphs (274–77); and with the defeat of reason (the monarchic element in man), the soul's "servile powers" (the passions and appetites, which comprise the Platonic analog of the masses in the human soul) gain ascendancy (295). It is at this point that Tarquin marches to Lucrece's bedroom.

The stages of the rape, narrated in terms at once sexual and political, replicate allegorically a sequence of political decline spanning monarchic collapse, mob rule, and civil war. Lust is synonymous with treasonous aspiration—with the "ambitious foul infirmity" that makes Tarquin covet "Lucrece' sovereignty" (150, 36); and ravishment is equated with seizing the "crown" (216), a double entendre that reinforces the analogy between usurpation and rape. The sight of Lucrece sleeping heightens monarchic desire, prompting thoughts of violently dispossessing the throne's occupant: Lucrece's breasts "in Tarquin new ambition bred, / Who, like a foul usurper, went about / From this fair throne to heave the owner out" (411–13). Swelling unchecked, the "servile powers" or passions eventually triumph. The results are anarchy and civil war:

> And they [the passions], like straggling slaves for pillage
>   fighting,
> Obdurate vassals fell exploits effecting,
> In bloody death and ravishment delighting,
> Nor children's tears nor mothers' groans respecting,
> Swell in their pride, the onset still expecting.
>   Anon his beating heart, alarum striking,
>   Gives the hot charge and bids them do their liking.
>   (428–34)

The political implications become explicit in Lucrece's plea. Lucrece equates Tarquin's lust with "misgoverning"—with the perversion of monarchy that shatters degree and incurs mob rule:

> "Thou art," quoth she, "a sea, a sovereign king;
> And lo, there falls into thy boundless flood
> Black lust, dishonor, shame, misgoverning,
> . . . .
> So shall these slaves be king, and thou their slave...."
>   (652–59)

She sues, accordingly, for "exiled majesty's repeal; / Let him return" (640–41).

The rape sounds the "doom" that will reverberate everlastingly (717–18): as Lucrece had prophesied, the collapse of degree renders the subjects the rulers, and the soul, ravaged by insurrection, is perpetually enslaved:

> She [his soul] says her subjects with foul insurrection
> Have battered down her consecrated wall,
> And by their mortal fault brought in subjection
> Her immortality, and made her thrall
> To living death and pain perpetual....
>   (722–26)

The sequence images in small the political events in Rome: a tyrannical king (Lucius Tarquinius) illegitimately "possessed himself of the kingdom" (Arg.), the Tarquins' tyranny resulting in abolition of the monarchy ("majesty's repeal") and the attendant rise of the "servile powers" or masses—a rise that will culminate in the mob rule of *Julius Caesar*.

Depicting the full history of the Trojan War, the Troy-piece is a visual allegory of the main action. Events are likewise initiated by the rape of another man's wife, which in turn sparks a cataclysmic war. The rape, however, is the war's secondary cause; its primary cause is the improvident rule of Troy's king, who violates justice and degree. As Lucrece observes:

> Had doting Priam checked his son's desire,
> Troy had been bright with fame and not with fire.
> (1490–91)

Like most of Shakespeare's flawed rulers, Priam is also vulnerable to appearances. Tarquin, like Sinon, is a "devil" (1513) who is outwardly a moral paragon: "fair [of] form" (1530), he appears humble, patient, just, and perfectly tempered (1505–14). Sinon is a variant of *Henry V*'s Scroop, who is similarly characterized and likewise identified with the devil. He also conspires with the enemy to betray a nation—to sell a "king to slaughter" and "his whole kingdom to desolation" (*H5* 2.2.170–73). Henry, however, is immune to appearances, maintaining the degree and discipline that win the war and seeing through the facade of the man who would have made of England another Troy.

Lucrece's death precipitates a new power struggle: one between father and husband for her possession, which parallels the initial contest for her "seat" between Tarquin and Collatine. It is during their "strife" (1791) that Brutus seizes leadership. Brutus, as critics have observed, is the work's most inscrutable character. How, then, are we to interpret his seemingly selfless act?

There are hints that Brutus's motives are less than altruistic. His dissemblance recalls that of Sinon and Tarquin. Even apart from its theological import, his pride (1809) links him to Sextus Tarquinius (see, e.g., 298, 432, and 438) and Lucius Tarquinius ("for his excessive pride surnamed Superbus" [Arg.]), both of whom, we may recall, are usurpers. Heightening the suggestion of political motive is the word "state" (1809). His use of "policy" (1815), with its Machiavellian overtones, further allies him with Tarquin, who equates "policy"—"A little harm done to a great good end" (528–29)—with the good accruing to Lucrece's compliance. Indeed, Brutus's disguise is straight out of Machiavelli's *Discourses:*

> And although Titus Livy assigns but one cause as the ground which induced him [Brutus] to practise this dissimulation, namely, that he might live in greater security . . . , none the less, in view of his con-

duct, one can well believe that he practised it also in order to escape observation and that he might get a better opportunity of downing the kings and liberating his country, whenever they gave him a chance.

Machiavelli is here teaching the political lesson "That it is a Very Good Notion at Times to pretend to be a Fool."[20] Further, the kiss Brutus bestows on the bloody knife is reminiscent of the kiss another Brutus will bestow on the doomed Caesar—a kiss that similarly heralds, in the name of justice, a regime's fall.

Also linking Brutus to Tarquin and Sinon is his assumption of their rhetorical mantle. It was Sinon, we will recall, whose "enchanting" words seduced the "credulous" Priam (1521–22); and Tarquin whose praise of Collatine "beguiled" the equally credulous Lucrece (1544) (we could also include Nestor, who "beguiled" the Greeks into storming Troy [1404–11]). All three characters, incidentally, are agents of destruction and of literal or metaphorical rape. Brutus's speech, like theirs, is designed to induce compliance through beguilement. As all four characters are obviously aware, persuasion hinges on the speaker's ability to beguile or enchant, a Ciceronian tenet that inherently entails duplicity.[21] As Brutus is also aware, another rhetorical axiom asserts that equally crucial to persuasion are the visual adornments that promote credibility; for the eye must be beguiled along with the ear. Such adornments, which fall under the rubric of delivery, include facial expression, mien, and gesture. That is why, Cicero claimed, delivery most affects the ignorant and the mob; "for . . . clever ideas frequently outfly the understanding of people who are not clever, whereas delivery, which gives the emotion of the mind expression, influences everybody."[22] Accordingly invoking sacred objects and ideals ("the Capitol that we adore," "heaven's fair sun," "our country rights," "this chaste blood"), Brutus caps his speech with the visual flourishes calculated to galvanize his audience into action ("This said, he struck his hand upon his breast, / And kissed the fatal knife, to end his vow" [1835–43]), transforming contempt (1811–13) into quasi-religious awe, and fractiousness into unity and resolve:

> [They], wondering at him, did his words allow.
> Then jointly to the ground their knees they bow,
>   And that deep vow which Brutus made before
>   He doth again repeat, and that they swore.
>
>   (1845–48)

But, as noted above, it is the people who effect revolutions, and rhetoric that must induce their revolt. Brutus, therefore, seeks out the populace, before whom he couples "bitter invective" (Arg.) with the greatest visual adornment of all: a display of Lucrece's bleeding body (1851). "[W]herewith the people were so moved that with one consent and a general acclamation the Tarquins were all exiled and the state government changed from kings to consuls" (Arg.). We are reminded of Antony's funeral oration in *Julius Caesar*, which similarly caps incendiary invective with a bleeding corpse. The result is, likewise, mass revolt. *Lucrece* anticipates that play: with the demise of the monarchy, the people will gradually amass the power that will evolve into mob rule. Brutus is Sinon reincarnate, who has sealed, in the narrator's punning phrase, Rome's "advisèd doom" (1849) in the same way Sinon sealed Troy's.

❋ ❋ ❋ ❋ ❋

The subtextual battle for the crown on which *Lucrece* centers hints more than a little at authorial concern with the unsettled succession. Even apart from the figurative Wars of the Roses informing Lucrece's depiction, the poem variously suggests an English milieu. "Of either's color was the other queen," the narrator states (66) regarding the commingled red and white in Lucrece's face. The line punningly invokes what Frances Yates terms "an all-pervasive commonplace of Elizabeth symbolism," the Queen as the double Tudor Rose in whom are united the white and red roses of Lancaster and York.[23] Nor is this literary use of the symbol, in which the red and white reside in the allegorical Queen's face, unique to *Lucrece*. In Spenser's *Shepheardes Calender*, for instance, Hobbinoll sings of Elisa's "angelick face," "The Redde rose medled with the White yfere, / In either cheeke depeincten lively chere"; and in Fulke Greville's *Caelica* (sonnet 82), a "virgin" sits "Under a throne . . . , / The red and white rose quartered in her face."

Additional motifs evoke Elizabeth. All of Shakespeare's sources stress Lucrece's chasteness. Shakespeare, however, transmutes chastity into quasi-divine virginity, Elizabeth's defining attribute; even though Lucrece is married, she is a "pure . . . shrine" (194) and a "picture of pure piety" (542).[24] Her breasts are "maiden worlds" (408). Further, she is identified with the moon: first when Tarquin draws the curtain "that hides the silver moon" (371) and again when she identifies herself with "The silver-shining queen" (786). The moon, of course, was Elizabeth's most popular symbol, and was copiously employed by contemporary writers in connection with her identification with Cynthia-Diana, goddess of chastity and of the moon.[25] The moon symbology logically encompassed the stars, which could represent Elizabeth's officials or attendants.[26] The "Ode to Cynthia," for instance, which the Earl of Cumberland sang to Elizabeth on May Day in 1600, describes Cynthia descending "With bright beames, and heauenly hew, / And lesser starres attended" to rule realms below; John Davies, in his poem *Orchestra* (1596), finds the perfect image of societal order in Elizabeth and her court, "she like 'the bright moon . . . in majesty', her court shining about her like 'a thousand stars.'"[27] In *Lucrece,* the moon's "twinkling handmaids" (787) suggest Elizabeth's maids of honor. "The silver moon" and "silver shining queen" (as well as the "silver white" in Lucrece's face [56]) may also allude to the Queen's penchant, in her later years, for silver and white attire.[28] In addition, the word "governess" (443) may allude to Elizabeth's title of Supreme Governor of the Church of England, which replaced "Supreme Head" by the supremacy bill of 1559. "Governess" occurs in only one other instance in Shakespeare's canon (*MND*, 2.1.103), notably in conjunction with the moon: "Therefore the moon, the governess of floods . . . ," Elizabeth subsequently being identified with the moon goddess in the same scene (2.1.155–64).

Compounding the significance of these elements is the poem's anachronistic institution of chivalry, which could not have failed to evoke Elizabeth. As is well known, the institution of chivalry was revived for Elizabeth's reign. In its reincarnation, Elizabeth becomes the virgin sovereign of her knights, "who not only show their fealty and devotion in the medieval sense but go on to find in her the heroine of their life's romance."[29] As Eric Mallin observes, "The chivalric premise lay behind virtually every late Tudor court formality," from progresses to conferrals of dignities, and adherence to it became a condition of courtier success.[30] Epitomizing the chivalric premise were the Order of the Garter, and the annual Accession Day Tilts performed in honor of the Queen's Accession. In 1595, George Peele recounts how Elizabeth's "loyal English knights in arms"

> Held justs in honour of her holiday,
> Ready to do their duties and devoir
> Against the mightiest enemy she hath,

> ....
> And with keen sword and battle-axe in hand
> To wound his crest, whatever foe he be
> That any way in her dishonour braves.[31]

To this may be compared Lucrece's request to the lords—whom she addresses as "knights"—to destroy her "foe" (1683). They must

> plight your honorable faiths to me,
> With swift pursuit to venge this wrong of mine;
> For 'tis a meritorious fair design
> To chase injustice with revengeful arms.
> Knights, by their oaths, should right poor ladies' harms.
> (1690–94)

"Bound in knighthood to her imposition," the lords immediately "promise aid" (1696–97). Not surprisingly, the chivalric ethos appears in none of Shakespeare's sources.[32]

If Lucrece evokes Elizabeth, Tarquin evokes Robert Devereux, second Earl of Essex. Throughout the poem, Tarquin is defined by warfare. He is "A martial man" (200), whose aggressive militarism becomes a metaphor for his rape of Lucrece: the rape is portrayed as a siege, led by a captain (298) and replete with battering rams, alarums, and charges. Lucrece is the besieged city (469)—a parallel in small of the besieged Ardea. It is noteworthy that Tarquin ends his threat to rape her "by brandishing his sword over her helpless body, a familiar gesture of military victory."[33]

Essex was likewise "a martial man"; considered England's premier warrior, his militarism was his most visible attribute.[34] Indeed, his enormous popularity derived in great measure from his martial image, an image he zealously cultivated both through his numerous military campaigns (by age thirty-four, he had fought in seven foreign expeditions and commanded four) and his penchant for jousting. George Chapman, dedicating his translation of the *Iliad* to him, equated him with Achilles, calling him "the Most Honored now living Instance of the Achilleian vertues eternized by divine Homere." As Mallin argues, while this bespeaks the requisite fawning over a potential patron, it also attests a cultural perception. That perception in a less flattering form was arguably shared by Shakespeare, whose Achilles in *Troilus* has been seen as figuring Essex.[35]

Aggressive militarism equally characterized his politics. Appointed to the Privy Council in 1593 at the age of twenty-six, Essex championed war with Spain, which he saw as a means to his own military glorification.[36] Although his struggle with the Cecils was primarily for control of patronage and policy, it was over war with Spain that the Council was chiefly at odds and that helped split it into two bitterly opposed factions: that of the peace proponents led by the Cecils, and that of the militants led by Essex.[37] That militarism climaxed in his treasonous revolt when, in an almost parodic reenactment of Tarquin's assault on Lucrece, he sought to storm the Queen's chambers and force her submission to his demands. He breathed, declared William Cecil, nothing but war, slaughter, and blood.[38]

Essex contemned the unlordly lineage of the Cecils. Their inferior birth compounded his resentment of their influence with the Queen, which he deemed, by virtue of his nobility, rightfully his. "Judge you," he told Sir Robert Sidney, " . . . whether it can be grief to a man descended as I am, to be trodden underfoot by such base upstarts."[39] In the poem the narrator, broaching Lucrece's "sovereignty," conjectures that

> Perchance that envy of so rich a thing,
> Braving compare, disdainfully did sting
>   His high-pitched thoughts, that meaner men should vaunt
>   That golden hap which their superiors want.
>   (39–42)

Essex could brook no rivals, military or political. On the Council, he sought to monopolize power and rule Elizabeth's court. Virtually the rest of his life was devoted to thwarting the policies, and the power, of the Cecils. The contest was not merely for supremacy; it was, to quote Wallace MacCaffrey, "for the mind and will of the sovereign"[40]—and, in the view of many, for sovereignty itself.

It was widely speculated that Essex was in fact aiming for the crown. Fueling this speculation was the popular adulation he cultivated, a practice ominously reminiscent of Shakespeare's Henry Bolingbroke. Essex had himself publicly established a connection with Bolingbroke by often patronizing and applauding a play, presumably Shakespeare's, on Richard II—a play he allegedly sponsored.[41] Following his revolt, the Council accused him of deliberately courting popularity in order to make himself king. The published indictment charged him with seeking to usurp the Crown and depose and kill the Queen;[42] and Elizabeth herself averred that had he reached the Court, "she was resolved to go out and face him and see which of the two should reign."[43] Indeed, it was rumored that he planned to use his Plantagenet blood as a pretext for snatching the Crown, a rumor prevalent enough that he had seen fit to assure King James of Scotland—Elizabeth's potential successor—of its untruth.[44] Tarquin's conquest is achieved militarily, but its motivation is political: spurred by envy and "foul" ambition, it seeks to displace a rival, achieve "sovereignty," and gain the "crown."

A kindred view of the Earl appears in a satire by Everard Guilpin printed in 1598, which derides Essex's ambition, duplicity, and courtship of the commons:

> For when great *Foelix* passing through the street,
> Vayleth his cap to each one he doth meet,
> And when no broome-man that will pray for him,
> Shall have lesse truage then his bonnets brim,
> Who would not thinke him perfect curtesie?
> Or the honny-suckle of humilitie?
> The deuill he is as soone: he is the deuill,
> Brightly accoustred to bemist his evill:
> Like a Swartrutters hose his puffe thoughts swell,
> With yeastie ambition: *Signior Machiauell*
> Taught him this mumming trick, with curtesie
> T'entrench himselfe in popularitie,
> And for a writhen face, and bodies moue,
> Be Barricadode in the peoples loue.[45]

And an anonymous poem apparently written after 1603 contains these lines: "Renowned Essex, as he past the streets, / Would vaile his bonett to an oyster wife, / And with a kind of humble congie greete / The vulgar sorte that did admire his life."[46] Both characterizations appear based on Shakespeare's description of Bolingbroke, who has been seen to figure Essex. Shakespeare's passage also glances at the monarchic ambition such courtship of the commons implies:

> Ourself and Bushy, Bagot here, and Green
> Observed his courtship to the common people,
> How he did seem to dive into their hearts
> With humble and familiar courtesy,
> What reverence he did throw away on slaves,
> Wooing poor craftsmen with the craft of smiles.
> . . . .

> A brace of draymen bid God speed him well
> And had the tribute of his supple knee,
> With "Thanks, my countrymen, my loving friends,"
> As were our England in reversion his,
> And he our subjects' next degree in hope.
>
> (*R2* 1.4.23–36)

That Shakespeare's contemporaries also discerned in these lines an allusion to Essex is suggested by Guilpin's and the anonymous poet's similar descriptions and apparent indebtedness to the passage; by the first Quarto's omission—indicating possible censorship—of Richard's deposition, a scene restored only after Elizabeth's death; and by contemporary analogies between Richard II and Elizabeth, the most famous being the one purportedly made by Elizabeth herself.[47] *The Rape of Lucrece* was written nearly concurrently with *Richard II*,[48] and its similarities are noteworthy: like Bolingbroke in breaching the kingdom and seizing the crown, Tarquin performs an encoded deposition.

That Essex was perceived as heir apparent, as destined to have a hand in the succession, or as sanctioning—or contemplating—a coup is further suggested by a treasonous book published in 1594. Titled *A Conference about the Next Succession to the Crowne of Ingland* and attributed to the Jesuit Robert Parsons, it examines various claimants to the throne and justifies Richard's deposition and Bolingbroke's accession. The book was dedicated to Essex because, as Parsons declares, "no man" is "fitter to receaue" a work on "the succession to the crowne of Ingland," "whether we respect your nobilitie, or calling, or fauour with your prince, or high liking of the people, & consequently no man like to haue a greater part or sway in deciding of this great affaire . . . then your honour, and those that will assist you." Parsons pointedly adds that he felt it prudent to expedite publication because "it is not convenient for your honour to be vnskillfull in a matter which concerneth your person & the whole realme."[49] It seems hardly coincidental that John Hayward's *The First Part of the Life and Raigne of King Henry IIII* (1599), similarly dealing with Richard's deposition and similarly censured as treasonous, was also dedicated to Essex, and in comparable terms: "Magnus siquidem es . . . futuri temporis expectatione" [Because you are great in regard to future expectations]. (The book was in fact used as evidence against him in both his trial following his failure in Ireland

and his trial following his 1601 revolt.) Thus, while the charges against Essex may have contained more propaganda than truth,[50] they bespoke a perception possibly shared by James himself.

Evidence suggests, moreover, that an assault on the Queen's chambers could be construed as tantamount to rape. The equation was bound up with Elizabeth's gender and particularly with her chastity, which she exploited in part to deflect the ever present threat of political rape from those who would quash her female authority. As Susan Frye argues, the threat of violence "had always been implicit in attempts to represent the queen's virtues to herself—from the device titled the Seate of Worthie Governance in her coronation entry, which insinuated that if Elizabeth did not conform to the city's ideas of virtue, she could expect to lose her 'seat,' to Leicester's desire [during the 1575 Kenilworth entertainments] to enact his queen's virtue as requiring his protection from the rapist Sir Bruse sans Pitie, to the assumption underlying *The Four Foster Children of Desire* that only Elizabeth's chaste beauty could disarm the threatening [phallic?] lances of the knights."[51]

These ideas, Frye contends, underlie book 3 of Spenser's *Faerie Queene*. Centering like *Lucrece* on the virtue of Chastity, book 3 depicts an allegorical power struggle between a queen and her courtiers. According to Frye, "Spenser's desire for a position of mastery was a projection of his response to the authority she posed as both a woman and his sovereign. He articulated that desire as a metaphoric assault on the queen herself through Amoret, as Belphoebe's twin.... In making Busirane the master of his own privy chamber, Spenser... exhibits the desires, frustrations, and fantasies that courtiers or would-be courtiers directed at Elizabeth." Frye concludes: "Erase the mediation of figurative language and one result is Essex's rebellion, a direct attempt to seize the queen and bend her to the rebels' will confused with a desire to displace her entirely."[52]

According to one of Essex's cohorts, the attack plan called for some men to secure the gate, some the hall, and some to accompany Essex so as to procure "passage to the privy chamber." That such an assault on the queen's inner rooms could be construed as a rape is suggested by Robert Cecil's alteration of a key verb in the testimony of two of the rebels, who stated that the men planned to "keep" various parts of Elizabeth's chambers; Cecil substituted "seize," "possess," and "master." "He concludes with an image of the physical consequences of such a 'passage to the privy chamber' that again leaves open whether he is describing the guards' bodies or the queen's body." Another rebel, arrested outside the privy chamber door, was indicted for treasonous intent. The deciding factors in his conviction were his potential proximity to the Queen's person and his admission that he meant to "force" Elizabeth to sign for Essex's release. "As the court's attorney put it in language ambiguous enough to suggest sexual meanings, 'Mark . . . he said they might "force" her majesty to do it: mark this word, "force." . . . "Go in unto her, and never leave her till she had done it."'"[53] This projected assault was prefigured in 1599 when Essex, unauthorized, left Ireland (where he had been sent to quell Tyrone's rebellion), returning to London with a contingent of two hundred soldiers. Entering the palace unannounced, "he rushed upstairs to the Presence Chamber, through it to the Privy Chamber and, finding that empty too, pushed his way into the queen's bedchamber," bursting in on her as she was dressing. Elizabeth stopped short of accusing him of treason.[54] The deed invites comparison with Tarquin's: armed with his militarily symbolic falchion, Tarquin deserts the besieged Ardea for Collatium; there he traverses several sequentially opening chambers en route to Lucrece's bedroom, where he commits "high treason" on "the silver moon" (369, 371). Interestingly, Busirane's three rooms also open sequentially, "like Elizabeth's presence chambers at Hampton Court, described in 1598 as 'adorned with tapestry . . . in some of which were woven history pieces,'"[55] a description that evokes both Collatium's topography and its Troy-piece. That *Lucrece* antedates Essex's actions by roughly five years need not negate its allegorical viability. As we know, fears of the Queen's overthrow and assassination were rife, and the work, I suggest, reflects the widespread conviction of the threat Essex posed to the Crown. Moreover, Essex had already deserted a military encampment, during the siege of Rouen in 1591, to which Tarquin's desertion of the besieged Ardea possibly alludes.[56]

Additionally suggestive of an English milieu is the Troy-piece. Largely owing to Geoffrey of Monmouth's account of England's apocryphal descent from Troy, England and Troy had long been equated. As the fifteenth-century *Liber Albus* records, London was founded in 4032 by Brut, Aeneas's grandson, who became Britain's first monarch. Brut built his city "in imitation of Great Troy," whereby it became known as New Troy or Troinovant; "whence it is that, even to this day, it possesses the liberties, rights and customs of

... ancient ... Troy." Tudor propaganda alleged the direct descent of Tudor monarchs from the line of British kings that extended from Brut, through King Arthur, to Cadwallader, and that had reappeared in the person of Henry VII.[57] Elizabeth in particular exploited this putative descent, as did the writers of the day. Thomas Watson, for instance, in a welcoming song written around 1591, hails her as the "beauteous Queene of second Troy"; George Peele, in his *Anglorum Feriae*, calls her "fair Queen of Brut's New Troy." Included in these paeans to the Queen's Trojan descent is Spenser's fulsomely protracted chronicle in *The Faerie Queene*; beginning in book 2, canto 10, it resumes and concludes in book 3, canto 3, as Merlin recounts the "famous Progenie" that Britomart will engender and that "Shall spring, out of the aunciient Troian blood" (3.3.22).[58]

Troy, accordingly, served as the great exemplar of London specifically and of England generally, and the fall of Troy loomed as a warning to all Englishmen.[59] Whether Shakespeare subscribed to the myth is immaterial; the Troy/England equation was such a cultural commonplace that his readers would almost certainly have made the connection.

Nor does Shakespeare confine that equation to *Lucrece;* it also informs *Troilus and Cressida* where, as Mallin argues, Troy represents England in the troubled last years of Elizabeth's reign. The play bears other resemblances to *Lucrece*: the Greeks are beset by faction, and the war—a contest between two opposed camps of courtiers for possession of a queen—is rooted in improvident rule. Alternately represented by Achilles and Hector, Essex is the play's pivotal encoded figure, whose "male-factored strategies" for subduing the queen's centrality provide the work's allegorical bulk.[60]

At the time *Lucrece* was written, England's political milieu notably resembled the poem's. As we have already observed, the Court was dominated by faction—by the Essex-Cecil rivalry for control not simply of policy but of the Queen herself. In addition, the unsettled succession, compounded by Elizabeth's age, heightened fears of a coup preceding her death, or a contest for the Crown after it. Either was likely to provoke civil war. In the poem, the contest between Collatine and Tarquin for Lucrece's "seat" preceding her rape, and between Collatine and Lucretius for her possession following her death, figures this situation, each of the latter claimants adducing reasons why he is her rightful heir (1800–1803). Like Elizabeth, however, the virginal Lucrece dies heirless, negating both rivals' claims of possession: "The one doth call her his, the other his, / Yet neither may possess the claim they lay" (1793–94). During their strife, Brutus opportunely seizes power, engendering revolution and toppling the monarchy. Brutus's tactic of seizing leadership during the men's contention recalls York's plan to seize the crown when "Humphrey with the peers be fall'n at jars" (*2H6* 1.1.251). Both exemplify the commonplace notion of the state's vulnerability during factional strife, which leaves the realm open to a coup from within and to invasion and takeover from without.

As already noted, one of the gravest threats to national security was considered to be the rhetorical incitement of the masses. In 1593, for instance, a statute was passed against those who would "corrupte and seduce her Majesties subjects, and . . . stirre them to Sedicion and Rebellion." In 1594, the indictment against Roderigo Lopez, the physician accused of plotting Elizabeth's death, included the charge that he conspired "to stir up a rebellion . . . within the realm." In 1599, Robert Cecil denounced the "libellous railers" who "move the common sort to sedition." And in 1601, John Hayward was charged with "cunningly insinuating that the same abuses being now in this realm that were in the days of Richard II, the like course might be taken for redress." His book, discussed above, on Henry IV had previously been pronounced "very dangerous to come amongst the common people," the Queen calling it "a seditious prelude to put into people's hearts boldness and faction."[61] That Shakespeare shared this concern appears in the events of *Lucrece* as well as in the Cade rebellion in *2 Henry VI* and in the savagery produced by the roiling of the populace in *Coriolanus*, and receives its most cogent expression in the anarchy and destruction following upon Antony's funeral oration in *Julius Caesar*.

That the Queen was ruled by favorites and accorded them undue power was a further concern that *Lucrece* appears to reflect. The charge went back to her relationship with Leicester, which had fostered predictions of England's ruin and analogies with Richard II.[62] Such analogies were later occasioned by Essex, appointed to the Privy Council at twenty-six by an aging queen captivated by his charm and beauty. His revolt was the logical outcome of the recalcitrance and insubordination that had marked his relationship with her and which she repeatedly and futilely sought to curb. But so powerful did she find his attractions "that he was able to pit his will against hers and reverse the role of sovereign and subject by compelling her to accept his refusal to obey her commands."[63] It is to this situation that Shakespeare appears to allude in *Henry V*, in his reference to the Earl's campaign in Ireland to quell Tyrone's revolt:

> Were now the General of our gracious Empress,
> As in good time he may, from Ireland coming,
> Bringing rebellion broachèd on his sword,
> How many would the peaceful city quit
> To welcome him!
>
> (5.0.30–34)

Generally interpreted as laudatory, the passage is, I submit, a veiled indictment of Elizabeth's relationship with Essex, punningly deriding the perversion of degree of a sovereign ruled by her favorite ("the General of our gracious Empress"). Moreover, when *Lucrece* was published, Elizabeth was roughly sixty years old. Essex was twenty-seven. Her attitude toward him had always been "half maternal while the earl's had been that of a petted child, confident that his charms would win whatever it was he desired."[64] These facts—a doting ruler, Essex's quasi-filial status, and his potentially treasonous recalcitrance and ambition—are collectively invoked in "doting" Priam's failure to curb his son's treasonous and illicit "desire" (1490). This failure, which leads to the burning of Troy, parallels the failure of Lucius Tarquinius to curb his son's similarly treasonous and illicit desire, which leads ultimately (in *Julius Caesar*) to the burning of Rome. When Troy falls, the moon/stars symbolism is again invoked: "little stars shot from their fixèd places / When their glass fell" (1525–26). The glass, as the poem elsewhere suggests, denotes the ruler. "Thou seem'st not what thou art, a god, a king," Lucrece earlier reproaches Tarquin; ". . . For princes are the glass, the school, the book, / Where subjects' eyes do learn, do read, do look" (601–16).[65] In the above lines ("little stars . . . fell"), Priam—and by extension, Elizabeth—is the fallen glass, while the stars, deserting their "fixèd places," image the shattered hierarchy such dotage has wrought.

It has been argued by Lily B. Campbell and others that Shakespeare could not have foreseen Essex's revolt. Yet circumstances suggest otherwise. Well before 1601, Essex had evinced traits that linked him in the national consciousness to Bolingbroke and that in any case boded ill if left unchecked. As early as 1584, he was associated with favorites who helped ruin three kings.[66] His insubordination was early apparent, as when he joined, unauthorized, the expedition against Spain (1589), deserted his troops in Rouen (1591), and, again unauthorized, knighted twenty-four followers before leaving France, an act potentially damaging to the state's balance of power.[67] As to the succession, he had already made overtures to James in 1589 and, alone among the great nobles, sought to woo him in the 1590s. By 1594, James was promising to reward him "in proper time and place" for his continued support.[68] Also ominous was his courtship of the people. As we have seen, the courtship of popularity was equated with the pursuit of political supremacy, such courtship being alone sufficient to establish a perception of Essex, years before his revolt, as a potential usurper. Indeed, William Cecil voiced something of such a perception in 1584.[69] That Essex was viewed either as destined to negotiate the succession or as outright countenancing deposition is also suggested by the books, noted above, by Parsons and Hayward and by Shakespeare's own *Richard II*. Even if one disputes Bolingbroke as an Essex figure, it is clear that at least some of Shakespeare's contemporaries viewed him as such. Indeed, we know that Essex seriously considered using the army to coerce the court,[70] that he had contemplated a coup while still in Ireland, and that he had not hesitated to exploit his popularity at the Scottish court for assistance in such a move.[71] Given England's volatile political climate, it scarcely needed a prophet to see that the Earl's ambition, insubordination, courtship of the people, and immense martial power boded disaster.

Why Shakespeare dedicated *Lucrece* to Southampton we can only guess. True, he was Shakespeare's patron. But he was also an ardent follower of Essex, and a prime contender for royal favor. The poem could thus be a warning to an impressionable youth, and future statesman, of the perils of following such a master, a warning Shakespeare possibly deemed a moral obligation. If so, it went unheeded: Southampton joined Essex in the revolt and was convicted by the same tribunal that sentenced Essex.

Returning to the *Republic*, we may now consider how *Lucrece* reflects the timocracy of Plato. The poem's opening finds Rome's monarchy intact and the masses in their prescribed place. But the philosopher king, along with the values he embodies, is gone, replaced by a ruling class devoted to the pursuit of war: as *Lucrece* begins, the king and his sons, with other members of Rome's nobility, including Collatine, are besieging Ardea. It is noteworthy that the rape of Lucrece, likewise depicted as a siege, originates at Ardea, the direct consequence of a contest devised by "the principal men of the army" (Arg.). The masses themselves appear little more than serfs: the king, "contrary to the Roman laws and customs," has "possessed himself of the kingdom" without "requiring or staying for the people's suffrages" (Arg.). Attesting to schism in the ruling order is the king's murder of his father-in-law for possession of the throne, an act additionally indicative of the timocrat's ambitious and materialistic bent and replicated in Tarquin's figurative theft of the crown from Collatine his kinsman.

The martial ethos is not confined to the Argument; it informs virtually every facet of the poem. It resurfaces in the "war" in Lucrece's face, in the battle between reason and will in Tarquin's soul, in the militarily-defined rape, in the Troy-piece, and—perhaps its ultimate expression—in the chivalric temper that stamps Rome's aristocracy. In wedding martial prowess to the pursuit of honor, the chivalric ethic epitomized the timocratic ideal. It is exampled in Tarquin, who ponders the "shame to knighthood and to shining arms" that rape will incur (197). It is exampled in the honor accruing to Collatine's feats of arms: as Lucrece listens, rapt, Tarquin

> stories to her ears her husband's fame,
> Won in the fields of fruitful Italy,
> And decks with praises Collatine's high name,
> Made glorious by his manly chivalry
> With bruisèd arms and wreaths of victory.
>
> (106–10)

And it is exampled in Lucrece's lordly coterie of knights who, pledging their "honorable faiths" to avenge her wrong (1690–91), are instrumental in bringing down the monarchy.

In *Lucrece*, we can perhaps discern a glance at the schism in England's own ruling order, a schism pivoting on the issue of war. As we have seen, the chivalric ethos characterized Elizabeth's reign, and it was an ethos of which Essex—England's greatest warrior who was similarly threatening to "possess himself of the kingdom"—was the consummate embodiment.

In *Lucrece*, then, Shakespeare operates within the story's tradition of political allegory, heightening the political implications through the commonplace Platonic analogy between soul and state. Usurpation, resulting from the perversion of reason, is equated with rape, incurring—in the individual as in the state—mob rule, anarchy, and desolation. Justice is thus the work's overarching theme, justice consisting in sovereignty by the monarchic element of reason, and injustice, by the state's "servile powers."

The rationale underlying the Wars of the Roses as the work's governing metaphor becomes still clearer when we recall that the political issues informing *Lucrece* parallel those informing the first tetralogy, which examines the cause of those wars: an incompetent king. The collapse of degree following upon the absence of any real head of state unleashes factional strife for control of the crown. The rival houses supplant each other on the throne and disorder rends the realm. Civil war inexorably follows.

That the allegorization of the Lucrece story intensified during periods of political turmoil goes far to explain the work's contemporary popularity. When Lucrece stabs herself, it is the corpse of England the reader beholds: her blood, "circl[ing] her body," compares her to a sacked "island" (1737–41). Her death immediately looses political factions embodied in husband and father, who vie for possession of that island; the strife in turn enables the demagogue to seize power, raze the monarchy, and instate popular rule. By the end of *Lucrece*, Shakespeare implies, the groundwork is laid for the second fall of Troy.

3
Coriolanus

As we saw in *Lucrece*, timocracy is predicated on the attainment of honor through martial endeavor. Owing, however, to the spirited element's appetitive bent, the timocrat also harbors a desire for wealth. The transition from timocracy to oligarchy occurs when that desire emerges supreme, rendering wealth the criterion for office and thus further eroding the sovereignty of reason on which the state's integrity depends.

As *Coriolanus* opens, we find Rome in a state of oligarchy, roughly fifteen years having elapsed since the Tarquins' expulsion. Rome is now a republic, its sovereign "head" supplanted by a multiplicity of heads in the form of a ruling elite.

Rome's oligarchical regime hews closely to the Platonic paradigm. As defined by Plato, oligarchy is a government based on property valuation, with sovereignty accruing to society's richest members. Sustained by usury and habituated to a life of luxury and sloth,[1] these rulers are indifferent to the plight of the people (*Rep.* 8.555, 556),[2] who grow poorer as their masters grow richer. This situation fosters social hatred and the defining attribute of the oligarchical regime: class conflict. The result is the sundering of the state into two disparate and embattled entities, "the one of poor, the other of rich men; and they are . . . always conspiring against one another" (*Rep.* 8.551; compare *Cor* 1.1.15–21, 81–82). The polity, in consequence, exists in a perpetual state of imminent revolution and civil war (*Rep.* 8.556–7)—the situation of Rome in *Coriolanus*. Resuming the political allegory begun in *Lucrece*, *Coriolanus* depicts England's next civil war in the making, prophetically charting the passing of power from the Crown to the commons. When the Tribunes try Marcius "in the name o' the people" for treasonously affecting "power tyrannical" (3.3.107, 70),[3] they prefigure both verbally and contextually Charles's trial "in the name of 'the people of England', on a charge of high treason for violation of 'the fundamental constitutions of this Kingdom.'"[4]

As is well known, James's political philosophy sprang from his theory of Divine Right and from that theory's corollary, the Roman law. Divine Right presumed the king's personal right, derived directly from God, to his throne.[5] Since kings wield divine power on earth, they are themselves tantamount to gods and invested with commensurate deific capacities that include absolute power over their subjects' property and lives.[6] Any obstacles to such power presented by the common law are nullified on the ground that the king's prerogative—as well as the king—is ordinarily above that law, which might therefore be dispensed with when the need arises.[7] As Charles McIlwain writes, "Of the reciprocal duties of *dominus* and *homo* so prominent in the mediaeval conception of English kingship there remains not a trace: it has been replaced entirely by the Roman conception of a king *legibus solutus*, placed at a distance so immeasurably above his *subditi* that he can in no way be bound by earthly law to the performance of any duties to them."[8]

The superfluousness of Parliament logically followed. Parliament, James maintained, is "nothing else but the head Court of the king and his vassals"; thus the king may "make daily statutes and ordinances . . . as hee thinkes meet," without its advice or consent.[9] This conviction, and the deific self-image from which it springs, are evoked in Marcius's perception of the commoners; they are

> woolen vassals, things created
> To buy and sell with groats, to show bare heads
> In congregations, to yawn, be still, and wonder
> When one but of my ordinance stood up
> To speak of peace or war.
>
> (3.2.10–14)

His attendant view of them as "Our musty superfluity" (1.1.227), together with his contempt for precedent (2.3.115–23), encapsulates James's convictions and is, as I will argue, at the heart of the play. It is in this context that *Coriolanus* will be considered.[10] James's policies pitted the Commons against the Crown, effectively splitting England into two antithetical entities. Exacerbating the schism were the disaffected nobility[11] and James's cavalier disregard of the Commons' grievances.[12] These policies gave rise to an opposition, which, unorganized at first, grew increasingly powerful and articulate under the aegis of the common lawyers. As Lord Thomas Ellesmere was to observe, "The popular state ever since the beginning of his Majesty's . . . government hath grown big and audacious, and in every session of parliament swelled more and more."[13]

"The influence of lawyers upon the new developments in the Commons can hardly be overestimated. . . . To the Common Law their deepest loyalty was engaged; [and] when James seemed to be undermining it, they were ready to join the Opposition," becoming not merely its abettors but its leaders. It was "with full consciousness of the new strength in the commons" that James in opening the second session of Parliament in 1605 "expressed open distaste [for] the new popular voice," and in particular for "some Tribunes of the people," by which he meant the common lawyers, those "tribunitial Orators" with "their 'Magna Carta' ideology."[14] *Coriolanus* concerns the rise of that opposition and its causes: the oppressive policies of a ruling elite epitomized by Marcius, who "asserts in its most extreme form the patrician claim to unlimited authority."[15]

The battleground of England's power struggle was thus Parliament, and the Commons prevailed largely because of the superior rhetorical strategies of the lawyers.[16] *Coriolanus* continues the theme, begun in *Lucrece*, of revolution through rhetorical manipulation. As we saw in *Lucrece*, political supremacy in a nonmonarchy is dependent on oratory, the vehicle of the power seeker for influencing the masses. Expanding upon that concept, *Coriolanus* depicts a power struggle waged through words, virtually the entire play consisting of rhetorical confrontations whose outcomes comprise its plot. Staged in the context of the current parliamentary debates,[17] the play reflects the "concern in England with the political consequences of rhetorical manipulation and with language as an instrument of political power," a concern prompted by the growing power of the House of Commons.[18] The play, however, is not *about* parliament; it is about England, whose ills the parliamentary subtext allegorically inscribes.

That parliament stood for the whole of England (or, alternatively, for the body politic) was a standard notion. As Sir Thomas Smith asserted in 1565, "the highest and most absolute power of the realm of

England consisteth in the parliament" because "every Englishman is intended to be there present . . . from the prince . . . to the lowest person in England. And the consent of parliament is taken to be every man's consent." Richard Hooker used similar language, declaring parliament "the body of the whole realm."[19] As the Commons warned James, the "overthrow of the . . . Privileges of our House" means the overthrow "of the Rights and Liberties of the whole Commons of your realm of England" and will affect "the whole body of this your kingdom."[20]

The governing metaphor of *Coriolanus* is, accordingly, the human body, to which Menenius's parable of the belly is central. Menenius's speech fuses three variants of that metaphor: the Platonic, the Christian, and the corporate. Two of these, the Platonic and the corporate, posit a hierarchy of members or faculties under a sovereign head, with unity contingent on that hierarchy's preservation.[21] All three concepts, however, accord in their basic premise: the necessity of each part, however lowly, to the good of the whole. As Corinthians states, "the eye cannot say vnto the hand, I haue no nede of thee: nor the head againe to the fete, I haue no nede of you. Yea, muche rather those membres of the bodie, which seme to be more feble, are necessarie."[22] In their dealings with James, the Commons revert to the body politic metaphor again and again. The realm, they remind James, consists of the king "and both houses, who . . . make but one politick body, whereof your highness is the head." The realm's stability depends on "each member under the head enjoying that right, and performing that duty, which for the honour of the head and happiness of the whole is requisite." The Commons' conclusion follows inexorably: "The wrong done us doth redound upon the whole land, and will be so construed."[23]

It is this situation—a state in which the commons are deemed superfluous by an absolutist, repressive regime—that Menenius's parable depicts. Ostensibly an exemplum of the ideal body politic, the structure Menenius posits is ruled not by a head, of which it is devoid, but by the body's "sink," the belly. The perversion of hierarchy inherent in such rule is implied not only by "sink," with its plethora of subversive connotations and its unorthodox locus of authority ("I' the midst o' the body" [1.1.97] rather than at the head),[24] but by its "cormorant" nature (1.1.120): Menenius's claim of the belly's selflessness—that it transmits sustenance to all members alike, retaining only the bran—is patently belied by a starving populace and a grain-hoarding, surfeiting, epicurean elite for whom the belly thus fittingly stands. These facts also serve to corroborate the charge that the belly is "idle and unactive" (1.1.97).[25] What is revealed, therefore, is a cannibalistic ethos, a body in which the sovereign organ of digestion devours the members it rules. As First Citizen aptly observes, "If the wars eat us not up, they will; and there's all the love they bear us" (1.1.82–84).

Menenius's parable further illustrates the patrician conviction of the commons' superfluousness—of their putative contribution of nothing to the state, in contrast to the all-contributing patricians:

> Touching the weal o' the common, you shall find
> No public benefit which you receive
> But it proceeds or comes from them to you
> And no way from yourselves.
>
> (1.1.150–53)[26]

This claim is likewise belied, by the "tradesmen" discharging their "functions" in their "shops" (4.6.8–9) and by Menenius's unwitting negation of his own premise: the body's members accuse the belly of disdaining

> Like labor with the rest, where th' other instruments
> Did see and hear, devise, instruct, walk, feel,
> And, mutually participate, did minister
> Unto the appetite and affection common
> Of the whole body.
>
> (1.1.99–103)

The nature of the belly, and of the rulers it represents, is underscored by the pun on "grave" (1.1.127). For this hierarchically perverse polity violates a key principle of the state's survival, the parts' necessity to the good of the whole, and must, as Marcius rightly foresees, destroy itself.[27]

The opening scene establishes the interrelationship among three things: the sundering of Rome absent a sovereign, unifying head; the ominous seditiousness and mutability of an oppressed but still leaderless populace; and the potential of oratory in channeling that seditiousness and thereby forging the political future of Rome. The masses, we will recall, are the Platonic analogue of the passions and thus a force for good or evil depending on how they are led. Ruled by the monarchic equivalent of reason, they are an ordered and constructive force conducing to the state's felicity; shorn of such leadership, they become a force of anarchy and destruction, swayed by any appeal to their passions as may be devised by the unscrupulous politician. Newly kingless and still unorganized, the populace of the opening scene are as yet morally neutral, nevertheless seeking to proceed with rectitude if they can only discern where it lies.

Instating the rhetorical motif is First Citizen's command to "hear me speak" (1.1.1–2), a line that will variously recur throughout the play. The scene transpires within the context of a debate that resonates with parliamentary rhetoric.[28] The citizens have "resolved" to die rather than starve. First Citizen, embodying the people's potential for evil, counsels killing Marcius in order to obtain "corn at our own price" (1.1.10–11). The people no sooner agree on this expedient, however, than they are diverted by "One word" from Second Citizen, who embodies the people's potential for good. This worthy reminds them of Marcius's service to Rome and charitably urges First Citizen not to malign him, since "What he cannot help in his nature" should not be accounted a vice. Their resolve to mutiny is rekindled by shouts from their cohorts, then re-defused by Menenius's "tale." Despite Marcius's entrance and invective, they remain sufficiently placated to heed the Senator's command to disperse, their vow of vengeance momentarily forgotten. Depicting the dangerous malleability of a mutinous but as yet unempowered populace, Scene 1 sets the stage for the power struggle to come. It also establishes a prototype of that struggle: the people are the recipients of two opposing arguments, one from their ranks counselling mutiny, the other from the patriciate counselling passivity. The patricians prevail because of their superior rhetorician, whose logic, "pretty tale," and flattery ("masters, my good friends, mine honest neighbors" [1.1.88, 59–60]) disarm his antagonists while affirming their belief that Menenius "hath always loved the people" (1.1.50).

The influence of rhetoric on moral potential is more amply demonstrated in Rome's war with the Volscians. Threatened and reviled (1.4.31–41), Marcius's troops twice desert him, first on the field of battle and then in the charge on Corioles. Their behavior prompts Marcius—and many critics—to tax them with cowardice, a charge belied, however, by their deeds under the civil and humane Cominius: manifesting a mean emblematic of moral virtue, they acquit themselves "Like Romans, neither foolish in [their] stands / Nor cowardly in retire" (1.6.2–3). The charge of cowardice is further belied by their subsequent behavior under Marcius himself, whose gracious and inspiring oration (1.6.66–75, 77–85) prompts their wholehearted and unstinting support.[29]

With the advent of the tribunate, the power struggle enters its next phase. The tribunate endows the commons with two crucial assets: leadership and—as the "tongues o' the common mouth" (3.1.23)—a voice and hence the power of speech. This voice will be increasingly pitted against the patriciate's in the battle for popular control, with victory accruing to the most rhetorically proficient side. Giving the commons a voice, therefore, is the first step to their empowerment, and to the anarchy such empowerment will ultimately bring. As Marcius punningly prophesies, "It will in time / Win upon power and throw forth greater themes / For insurrection's arguing" (1.1.219–21).

The contest intensifies with the Senate's award of the consulship to Marcius. The appointment requires the people's ratification which, owing to Marcius's valor in Corioles and his consequent popular adulation, is virtually assured. The Tribunes, however, know that if Marcius achieves power he will abolish theirs and that their political survival thus lies in turning the populace against him. They accordingly resolve to tell the people

> in what hatred
> He still hath held them; that to 's power he would
> Have made them mules, silenced their pleaders, and
> Dispropertied their freedoms, holding them
> In human action and capacity
> Of no more soul nor fitness for the world
> Than camels in their war. . . .
>
> (2.1.244–50)

This they propose to do when the occasion is most propitious—"At some time when his soaring insolence / Shall touch the people" (2.1.253–54)—causing them to forget his service to Rome. The patricians, meanwhile, expecting to make Marcius consul, have slated a ceremony at the Capitol to honor him, thereby to secure the backing of both commoners and patricians. To this meeting the Tribunes are accordingly summoned so that, as First Senator tells them, they may inform "the common body . . . what passes here" (2.2.53–54). The opening oration by Cominius, which compellingly details Marcius's lifelong valor, succeeds in eliciting from the Senate the conferral of consulship. When, however, Marcius learns that the conferral requires popular approval, which will mean donning the gown of humility and displaying his scars, he angrily advocates stripping the people of this ancient privilege. As the patricians prematurely toast Marcius's election, the Tribunes vow to warn the people of his "intent" (2.2.157).

In scene 3 the citizens stage another debate, this time on whether to ratify Marcius's appointment. First Citizen counsels approval. Second Citizen demurs. Third Citizen, invoking Marcius's heroism, argues that approval is morally obligatory since "Ingratitude is monstrous, and for the multitude to be ingrateful were to make a monster of the multitude" (2.3.9–11). As they resolve to accord him their votes, Marcius enters to solicit them in his gown of humility.

After he leaves, the citizens debate whether Marcius mocked them. Second Citizen's charge that "he flouted us downright" is countered by First Citizen's "No, 'tis his kind of speech" (2.3.160–61). The Tribunes settle the issue: declaring that Marcius is their implacable foe and that his election will doom their "liberties" and "charters" (2.3.181), they persuade the citizens not only to revoke their approval but to take the case to the populace-at-large. As the Tribunes are aware, success hinges on rhetorical proficiency, which the childlike citizens sorely lack. The Tribunes, therefore, rehearse the citizens in the most effective way to present their case:

> *tell* those friends
> They have chose a consul that will from them take
> Their liberties....
>
> *Say* you chose him
> More after our commandment than as guided
> By your own true affections....
>
> *Say* we read lectures to you,
> How youngly he began to serve his country....
>
> *Say* you ne'er had done 't—
> Harp on that still—but by our putting on.
> (2.3.213–52; emphasis added)

The situation parallels Menenius's rehearsing of the rhetorically inept Marcius (2.3.50–61) as he prepares to ask the citizens for their votes.

Act 3 heralds a shift in the balance of power that springs directly from the commons' new "voice." Led by the Tribunes, the people have evolved into an organized, articulate opposition, amassing enough strength to begin curbing the patriciate's authority. Indicative of this shift is their revocation of Marcius's election and, more symbolically, the Tribunes' barring of Marcius's passage because "The people are incensed against him" (3.1.34). The people, that is, have begun taking the law into their own hands—in allegorical terms, have seized the law-making initiative that will culminate in the transfer of power from Crown to commons. The Tribunes' action prompts an altercation, during which Marcius reiterates his contempt for the people (3.1.69): he would starve them, strip them of their lawfully-established representatives, and accord them the status of pariahs, unmingled with the "honored" nobility (3.1.75). Branding him "a traitorous innovator" and "A foe to th' public weal" (3.1.178–79), the Tribunes again convey his sentiments to the people, with whose resulting backing they sentence him to death. The sentence sparks the first physical skirmish between the two sides, further indicative of the escalating power of the people and a harbinger of the civil strife to come. Another debate ensues: the Tribunes argue why Marcius deserves death; Menenius, why he should be spared. Menenius ultimately prevails, but only after he agrees to bring Marcius to "Where he shall answer, by a lawful form, / In peace, to his utmost peril" (3.1.335–36). The balance of power is now roughly equal; the Tribunes have backed down. But the patricians must now answer to the Tribunes, who designate Menenius "the people's officer" (3.1.340) and command him to bring Marcius to the marketplace for trial. Should he fail to do so, the death sentence will stand. This scene parallels 1.1: both scenes depict rhetorical confrontations ending in the sparing of Marcius following Menenius's intercession. This time, however, Menenius faces an organized citizenry, and while he again prevails, it is just barely. In 1.1, moreover, insurrection is quashed with a tale; in 3.1, it erupts in violence, bringing Rome to the brink of civil war.

In the next scene, the patricians prepare to salvage their faltering authority by means of Marcius's amends to the populace. The scene is the counterpart of 2.3; as the Tribunes had rehearsed the plebeians in revoking Marcius's election, so the patricians rehearse Marcius in recanting what he has "spoke" (3.2.39). Cominius advises answering the people's accusations "mildly" (3.2.141); Menenius, "fair speech"; and Volumnia, servility and Machiavellian dissimulation:

> *say to them,*
> Thou art their soldier, and being bred in broils
> Hast not the soft way which, thou dost confess,
> Were fit for thee to use, as they to claim,
> In asking their good loves; but thou wilt frame
> Thyself, forsooth, hereafter theirs, so far
> As thou hast power and person.
> (3.2.80–88; emphasis added)

She additionally schools him in delivery, the use of visual adornments to enhance credibility by engaging the eye along with the ear—the rhetorical device, we will recall, Cicero claimed most influenced the ignorant and the mob:[30]

> Go to them, with this bonnet in thy hand,
> And thus far having stretched it—here be with them—
> Thy knee bussing the stones—for in such business
> Action is eloquence, and the eyes of th' ignorant
> More learnèd than the ears. . . .
> (3.2.75–79)

"This but done," Menenius assures him, ". . . their hearts were yours" (3.2.88–89).

The Tribunes, bent on retaining their initiative, are honing their own rhetorical strategy in preparation for Marcius's trial. Sicinius instructs the Aedile to assemble the people;

> *And when they hear me say* "It shall be so
> I' the right and strength o' the commons," be it either
> For death, for fine, or banishment, then let them,
> *If I say* "Fine," cry "Fine!", if "Death," cry "Death!",
> Insisting on the old prerogative
> And power i' the truth o' the cause.
> (3.3.14–19; emphasis added)

They then plan to incense Marcius, since "once chafed" he will speak "What's in his heart" (3.3.28–30).

The trial takes the form of another debate between the representatives of both sides for control of the people. It commences with Marcius's command, "hear me speak!" (3.3.44). Predictably, the charge of treason moves Marcius to rage, affording the Tribunes their opportunity to incense the people against him:

> Mark you this, people?
> ....
> What you have seen him do and heard him speak,
> Beating your officers, cursing yourselves,
> Opposing laws with strokes, and here defying
> Those whose great power must try him—even this,
> ....
> Deserves th' extremest death.
>
> (3.3.80–89)[31]

As the people clamor for his death, the Tribunes pronounce sentence, commuting death to exile, however, in view of his service to Rome. For the first time, the intercession of Menenius fails to sway the citizens, and with Marcius's banishment "in the name o' the people" (3.3.107), political ascendancy shifts to the commons.

Although the power struggle now moves to Antium, Shakespeare makes clear that the Volscian state is simply a mirror image of the Roman one, thus rendering them thematically interchangeable. Central are their parallel regimes: both are republics governed by a patriciate whose impotence takes identical form: when Second Lord urges trial by process for Marcius (5.6.131–32), he is overruled, as was Menenius, by the people, whose edict prevails. The two commonalities thus attest equivalent power. Their fickleness also assumes similar form: as the Romans variously extol, censure, lionize, and ultimately condemn Marcius, so do the Volscians. The three Roman citizens who, learning of Rome's imminent sacking, immediately repent their decision to banish him (4.6.146–65) are paralleled by the three Volscian servingmen who, learning that the man they sought to banish was Marcius, immediately laud him (4.5.7–53, 154–67). Both states possess a martial Goliath each, moreover, imaging the other in envy, wrath, pride, and renown. The inhabitants are similarly interchangeable: as Aufidius punningly informs the Volscians, Marcius has betrayed "your city Rome" (5.6.97). Finally, both states are characterized by schism, which encompasses not only their oligarchical polities but—in the case of Antium—the divided leadership of the army, which will prompt the same struggle for supremacy transpiring in Rome. The two states thus are thematically congruent, and Marcius's death at the hands of the Volscians is tantamount to his death at the hands of the Romans.

In Antium, however, the combatants have altered: now that the commons are firmly ascendant, the remaining battle will be fought not by classes but by individuals, to whose supremacy an increasingly powerful populace continues to hold the key.

Perceiving Marcius's usefulness to his drive to conquer Rome, as well as the chance to destroy the sole obstacle to his success, Aufidius makes Marcius his "partner" (5.6.38) in the war against Rome. Their mutual envy and desire for martial supremacy render strife certain, and Marcius's acquiescence in the partnership becomes particularly ironic in light of his earlier warning: "when two authorities are up, / Neither supreme, how soon confusion / May enter twixt the gap of both and take / The one by th' other" (3.1.112–15). The inevitable power struggle quickly follows, actuated by Aufidius's bitter resentment of his troops' adulation of Marcius and by his own corresponding decline to the status of "follower, not partner" (5.6.38). As his Lieutenant declares,

> Your soldiers use him as the grace 'fore meat,
> Their talk at table, and their thanks at end;
> And you are darkened in this action, sir,
> Even by your own.
>
> (4.7.3–6)

It had been wiser, the Lieutenant aptly observes, not to have "Joined in commission with him, but either" to "Have borne the action of yourself or else / To him had left it solely" (4.7.14–16). The result of the partnership is a sundered command replicating that of the state: Aufidius "is cut i' the middle" (4.5.206–7).[32]

The rhetorical stakes broaden with the arrivals of the three embassies, each of which presents an argument as to why Marcius should spare Rome. Cominius, invoking friendship and "the drops . . . we have bled together" (23–24, 5.1.10–11), prevails not at all. Menenius, stressing fatherly love and calling Marcius "son" (5.2.71–72), touches him more closely and causes him, despite his professed immovability, to yield slightly (5.3.16–17). To Volumnia, however, Marcius capitulates completely, not simply because of her more cogent argument but because she enlists those very strategies of visual persuasion she had urged upon him—strategies necessary, as she ironically had apprised him, because "the eyes of th' ignorant" are "More learnèd than the ears" (3.2.78–79). She arrives, therefore, accompanied by his wife and child, disarming him even before she speaks (5.3.22–29). Her visual stratagems become progressively more potent: she first bows, then kneels, climaxing her great oration with a command to Marcius to behold his wordless son, who "kneels and holds up hands for fellowship" (5.3.175).[33]

The events leading to Marcius's death in Antium replicate almost exactly those leading to his banishment from Rome, Aufidius having supplanted the Tribunes as Marcius's rival for popular support. Aufidius knows that Marcius will have to justify to the people his surrender of Rome. He also knows—as had the Tribunes before him—that they must "proceed as we do find the people" (5.6.15), who consider Marcius a hero and whose allegiance will accrue to the most compelling speaker. Third Conspirator therefore advises Aufidius to kill Marcius "Ere he express himself or move the people / With what he would say" (5.6.54–55), and then to regale them with his own fabricated version of events (5.6.57–58). Like the Tribunes, however, Aufidius plans to trap Marcius into causing his own downfall by inciting him to rage and orchestrating the crowd's response. In public view, accordingly, he calls Marcius a traitor, capping his catalog of charges with the taunt calculated to drive Marcius to fury: "thou boy of tears" (5.6.105). The taunt elicits the anticipated response:

> "Boy"? False hound!
> If you have writ your annals true, 'tis there,
> That, like an eagle in a dovecote, I
> Fluttered your Volscians in Corioles.
> Alone I did it. "Boy"!
>
> (5.6.118–22)

Aufidius turns to the crowd:

> Why, noble lords,
> Will you be put in mind of his blind fortune,
> Which was your shame, by this unholy braggart,
> 'Fore your own eyes and ears?
>
> (5.6.122–25)

As the Lords counsel restraint (Second Lord, echoing Menenius, urges proceeding by trial), the people deliver their unanimous reply: "Tear him to pieces!—Do it presently!" (5.6.126; compare the Tribunes' parallel charge, parallel speech, and parallel orchestration of the people, as well as the people's parallel response at 3.3.68–89). The mandate enables Aufidius to override the Lords' counsel and to slay his arch rival with impunity. As he prepares to justify the murder to the patricians, he prefaces his speech with the words that began the play: "hear me speak" (5.6.138).

By the play's end the patricians have been reduced to impotence and blood vengeance has supplanted law. The killing thus heralds not only popular supremacy but mob rule. Gone are the simple, childlike citizens of the early scenes, whose sole condition for giving Marcius their votes was "to ask it kindly" (2.3.75); led by the demagogic Tribunes, the "infantlike" "many-headed multitude" (2.1.37, 2.3.16–17) has matured into a full-grown Hydra, of which their cry "Tear him to pieces!" (5.6.126) is emblematic.[34] That same cry occurs in *Julius Caesar* as the mob slaughters the poet Cinna because of his name. Paralleling their evolution into a monster is the growth of Marcius "from man to dragon" (5.4.13; see also 4.1.30). The dual monstrosity microcosmically images the realm, "The beast / With many heads" (4.1.1–2), which was a common metaphor for the kingless state; as the Speaker informed Parliament in 1567:

> [A]s the bodie yf it should wante a head were a greate monster, soe is it lykewise yf it have many headdes . . . ; although in the body be diveres memberes which be made of fleshe, bones, sinowes and joyntes, yet the one heade therof governeth wisely the same, which yf it should wante wee should be worse then wild beastes without a head and so worthelie caled a mo[n]sterous beaste. Againe, yf the bodie should be governed by many heades, then the same would soone come to distructione by reasone of the contraversie amonge them, who wold never agree but be destroyed without any forren invasion. Therfore God saieth it is needfull that the people have a kinge . . . ; and soe therfor the beste governmente is to be ruled by one kinge, and not many.[35]

Invoking the same metaphor, Elyot terms the democracy of ancient Athens "a monster with many heads" (*Governor*, 6). The concept derives from Plato, whose "multitudinous, many-headed monster" (*Rep.* 9.588) represents the appetitive element in man and was so named because of the myriad lawless, competing whims of the affections (compare Henry V's expulsion of "Hydra-headed willfulness"

(*H5* 1.1.36). The corresponding displacement of the king by the masses (the Platonic analogue of the passions and appetites, and likened by Plato to a mighty "beast" [*Rep.* 6.493]), produces a "multi-headed" state (compare "the many-headed multitude" of *Cor* 2.3.16–17). Thus, even if one disputes the interchangeability of Antium and Rome, it is clear that the escalating power of the people in Rome must eventuate in the mob supremacy characterizing Antium.

It is commonly argued that Marcius is the moral antithesis of the plebeians, who are allegedly brutal, inconstant, and base. "The contrast between Coriolanus and the citizens of Rome is antipodal," Eugene Waith representatively asserts. "Whatever he most basically is they are not."[36] In fact, the two antagonists are morally identical; two extremes devoid of a mediating "head," they attest precisely the same defects and are thus equally unfit to rule.

Each is taxed with being "absolute" (3.1.93, 3.2.41)—in political terms, with aspiring to unlimited authority. Each thus seeks to topple the other's duly elected representatives: as the Tribunes would revoke Marcius's election to the consulship, so Marcius would "throw their power i' the dust" (3.1.173). Menenius succinctly points the moral: "On both sides more respect" (3.1.184). The people's capacity for savagery is more than matched by that of Marcius, the "thing of blood" (2.2.109) who would slaughter his famished countrymen (1.1.196–99) and who "Run[s] reeking o'er the lives of men as if / 'Twere a perpetual spoil" (2.2.119–20). Marcius is merely the most obvious example of the brutality that characterizes the patricians, who are blithely starving their countrymen to death. More central, however, are the antagonists' parallel inconstancy and malleability, for it is these traits that lead directly to Marcius's fall. Marcius considers constancy a supreme virtue, that which distinguishes him (and his class) from the commons. "I'll fight with none but thee," he informs Aufidius: "for I do hate thee / Worse than a promise-breaker" (1.8.1–2). It is the people's inconstancy, accordingly, that most excites his contempt; as he tells the citizens,

> He that depends
> Upon your favors swims with fins of lead
> And hews down oaks with rushes. Hang ye! Trust ye?
> With every minute you do change a mind
> And call him noble that was now your hate,
> Him vile that was your garland.
>
> (1.1.178–83).

The significance of this speech lies in its irony: Marcius is unwittingly describing himself.

Marcius's changes of mind are multitudinous. Having sworn never to appear in the marketplace or don the gown of humility to achieve the consulship (2.1.230–33), he forthwith does both. Finding the ritual intolerable, he decides to abandon the pretense and the pursuit of office, then instantly, and inexplicably, reverses himself: "I am half through; / The one part suffered, the other will I do" (2.3.123–24). Following his subsequent alienation of the people and his vow to remain "thus to them" even were he to face "Death on the wheel" (3.2.2), he capitulates under pressure from his mother. Volumnia had counselled dissemblance, the use of flattery to regain the people's backing. Torn between pleasing his mother and performing an intolerable task, he reverses himself no less than three times: "I cannot do it" (3.2.40), "I will do 't" (3.2.103), "I will not do 't" (3.2.122), "Look, I am going" (3.2.136). The scene concludes with his vow to return consul, "Or never trust to what my tongue can do / I' the way of flattery further" (3.2.137–39). The vow renders patently ironic Menenius's claim that Marcius "would not flatter Neptune for his trident" (3.1.262) as well as Marcius's own words to the plebeians: "He that will give good words to thee will flatter / Beneath abhorring" (1.1.166–67). His latest vow is broken in turn: the Tribunes' goading prompts a barrage of invective even as Menenius cries, "Is this the promise that you made your mother?" (3.3.93). Banished from Rome, he promises family and friends that they will "Hear from [him]" always (4.1.52), yet Menenius reports that they "hear nothing from him" (4.6.20). In Antium he joins forces with the man he had sworn to kill (1.2.34–36). This initiates his most reprehensible reversal of all: his betrayal of Rome. Breaking faith with Aufidius, he betrays Antium in turn: having vowed to ignore further suppliants from Rome (5.3.17–21) and proclaiming his immovability yet again ("I'll never / Be such a gosling to obey instinct, but stand / As if a man were author of himself" [5.3.34–36]), he forthwith capitulates to his mother, thus cementing his doom. He is as changeable as the populace he abhors, a parallel he punningly and unwittingly affirms in his self-righteous assertion to the patricians:

> For
> The mutable, rank-scented meiny, let them
> Regard me as I do not flatter, and
> Therein behold themselves.
> (3.1.68–71)

We are reminded of Caesar, whose claim of immovability likewise stems from a conviction of superiority to the "fools" he contemns, yet who dies precisely because, capitulating to Decius's flattery, he reverses his decision to remain at home. Marcius is also as childlike, as volatile, and as rhetorically malleable as the populace: his mother controls him through alternate praise and rebuke, and in Antium as in Rome, he is brought down by a single word (in Rome, "traitor" [3.1.165]; in Antium, "boy" [5.6.105]).

Nor is inconstancy confined to Marcius: it characterizes the patricians generally. Pressed by the Tribunes, Menenius, in language recalling that of Marcius's volte-faces, reverses his refusal to solicit Marcius's mercy for Rome ("No, I'll not go" [5.1.1]; "I'll undertake 't" [5.1.49]). To the Tribunes he is imperious or submissive, as expedience dictates: initially they are "ridiculous subjects," "the herdsmen of the beastly plebeians," and "a brace of unmeriting, proud, violent, testy . . . fools" (2.1.84, 94, 43–45); subsequently they are "worthy tribunes," "good Sicinius," and "your country's friend" (3.1.271, 195, 222). More lethal is the inconstancy of Volumnia. Having schooled her son to despise the people (3.2.8–14), she demands his abject humility towards them; having molded him into a killing machine, she exhorts him to spare Rome. Only Virgilia is unshakable: no amount of cajoling—not even Valeria's promise to tell her news of her absent husband—can break her resolve to remain at home "till my lord return from the wars" (1.3.76).

That Marcius figures James I seems likely; the resemblances between the two figures (some of which we have already noted) are copious and often pronounced. Marcius's "rougher accents" (3.3.59) evoke James's Scottish accent. Like Marcius, James was self-righteous and politically inflexible, and lost his temper upon little provocation; his tantrums in court and Parliament were notorious. Also notorious was his contempt for the masses. He loathed crowds, "chafed at the petty tyranny of public ceremonies,"[37] and was averse to showing himself to the people, to whom he remained largely inaccessible.[38] "[T]he Accesses of the People made him so impatient," wrote Arthur Wilson, "that he often dispersed them with Frowns, that we may not say with Curses."[39] The Venetian ambassador concurred; as opposed to the late Queen, he observed in 1607, "this King manifests no taste for [the people] but rather contempt and dislike," being "more inclined to live retired . . . than openly." "The result is he is despised and almost hated."[40] We may compare Marcius's contempt for the plebeians, the curses he heaps upon them, his hatred of public appearances and ceremonies, and his being "talked of more than seen" (4.1.31). This last comment additionally evokes James's incessant absences from London, "year in and year out, for weeks and months on end," to pursue his hunting.[41] "His avoidance of court business . . . was notorious," states Alvin Kernan, "and the court whispered that he spent all his time at one of his hunting lodges, where he drank, enjoyed his favorites, . . . and listened to . . . gossip." As the Venetian Ambassador observed, his Majesty "leaves all government to his Council and will think of nothing but the chase." "And so one may truly say that he is Sovereign in name and in appearance rather than in substance and effect."[42] Marcius's response to the mutinous citizens (he calls them "dissentious rogues" and advocates hanging and quartering [1.1.163, 189, 196–99]) recalls the response to a group of Midlands protesters in 1607: resolved to "manfully dye" rather than "be pined to death for want" (compare the citizen's resolve "rather to die than to famish" [1.1.4–5]), many were imprisoned and subsequently hanged and quartered.[43] James nevertheless fancied himself "a louing father" to his subjects, "caring for them more then for himselfe"[44] (compare Menenius's rebuke of the citizens for slandering "The helms o' the state, who care for you like fathers" and who selflessly furnish their sustenance while ending up with "the bran" [1.1.75, 145]). Like the policies of the patricians, moreover, those of James "brought abuses which the Commons were not slow to point out," and—as with the commoners in the play—"redress of grievances became their constant theme."[45]

Towards the play's end, Marcius wields absolute power. Ensconced in his chair of state, he dispenses doom like some deity, deeming himself unanswerable even to the Lords: he makes a treaty with Rome without consulting them, incurring their irrevocable alienation. We are reminded of James's conviction of the king's absolute, deific power over his subjects—the "power of raising, and casting downe: of life, and of death"[46]—; of his conviction of Parliament's superfluousness; of his contempt for precedent (compare Marcius's contempt for "custom," 2.3.117–21, 180–81); of his attempts to override the results of the Goodwin-Fortescu election (compare Marcius's refusal to recognize the election of the Tribunes); of his unpopular peace treaty with Spain (1604); and of his unstinting efforts to effect union with Scotland, without parliamentary approval and despite profound national antipathy to the move. The charge that Marcius is "a traitorous innovator," affecting "power tyrannical" and "one sole throne, without assistance" (3.1.178, 3.3.70, 4.6.34), could not have failed to evoke James, at whom a like charge was in fact obliquely levelled: in a 1604 speech in Parliament, the Speaker, alluding to James's efforts to quash the Commons' power, warns:

> [P]rinces, by the perfection of their examples, and by the virtue of their just commands, become to God acceptable, to the world renowned, to their people beloved, . . . and in the end with glory immortalized: but if their commands be unjust, unmerciful, cruel, devouring, lawless, unreasonable, and imprudent, he loseth the glorious title of a good king, and becometh eternized with the deathless fame of an hellish tyrant.[47]

Coriolanus, then, continues the political degeneration initiated in *Lucrece*. It charts the passing of power from the patriciate to the people during a sequence of decline spanning oligarchy, democracy, and mob rule. The power struggle is integral to the play's structure: when the play opens, the patricians are supreme, the populace impotent; at the play's midpoint, the balance of power is approximately equal; and at the play's conclusion, the people are supreme, the patricians impotent. Reinforcing the interdependence of theme and structure are three parallel scenes each presenting a rhetorical confrontation between patricians and plebeians over Marcius's fate. In 1.1, the plebeians' resolve to kill Marcius is easily defused by Menenius's tale. In 3.1, resolve erupts into violence. Menenius, urging proceeding by trial, again prevails but barely, and is now answerable to the commons. In 5.6, mob sentiment triumphs over the counsel of Second Lord, who also urges proceeding by trial; as the people cry "Tear him to pieces," Marcius is slaughtered like a beast. The people's savagery is thus commensurate with their degree of empowerment, a Platonic phenomenon that reaches its height in *Julius Caesar*.

In *Coriolanus*, one seeks in vain for "The kingly-crownèd head" (1.1.114) and the harmonious, ordered polity envisaged by First Citizen. One sees instead a sundered and embattled state and the triumph of lawlessness and mob supremacy. The irony is inescapable: Marcius reincarnates the oppressive and tyrannical Tarquins he fought to destroy; banished and destroyed in turn, he reemerges in the person of Aufidius. That Aufidius is a re-embodiment of Marcius is suggested not only by their like characteristics but by Aufidius's prophecy of "renewal" in Marcius's fall (5.6.48). This pattern, begun in *Lucrece* with Brutus's displacement of Tarquin, similarly informs *Julius Caesar* as one tyrant metamorphoses into another in the ceaseless struggle for political dominion.[48]

We are reminded of Ulysses' speech on degree in *Troilus*; it describes the anarchy that "rend[s]" the state absent the "med'cinable" sway of a king:

> Then everything includes itself in power,
> Power into will, will into appetite;
> And appetite, an universal wolf,
> So doubly seconded with will and power,
> Must make perforce an universal prey
> And last eat up himself.
>
> (*Tro* 1.3.91–124)

What Ulysses describes is the belly ethos of *Coriolanus*.

4

Julius Caesar

AT THE END OF *CORIOLANUS*, POPULAR SUPREMACY HOLDS SWAY. The attendant triumph of lawlessness and mob rule, both heralded by Marcius's slaughter, marks the passage of democracy into tyranny—the focus of *Julius Caesar*. *Caesar* depicts the next stage of the political decline set forth by Plato: with the triumph of the poor over their patrician oppressors, the class warfare characterizing oligarchy has ceased, along with oligarchy and its successor, democracy, which was born with the advent of the tribunate. Democracy has in turn given way to tyranny, and to the concomitant concentration of power in one man: the people's champion.

To understand fully this phase of Rome's decline, we must turn to Cassius's only soliloquy in the play:

> Well, Brutus, thou art noble. Yet I see
> Thy honorable mettle may be wrought
> From that it is disposed. Therefore it is meet
> That noble minds keep ever with their likes;
> For who so firm that cannot be seduced?
> Caesar doth bear me hard, but he loves Brutus.
> If I were Brutus now, and he were Cassius,
> He should not humor me.
>
> (1.2.308–15)

Scholars have attributed at least part of this speech to a passage in Plutarch, in which Cassius's friends urge Brutus to beware "Caesars sweete intisements, and . . . tyrannicall favors: the which they sayd Caesar gave him, not to honor his vertue, but to weaken his constant minde, framing it to the bent of his bowe."[1] Plutarch's version, however, lacks the curious reference to inverse alchemy—to the sullying of the mind's "mettle" through association with baser elements—that marks Cassius's speech. "Mettle," as Bevington's gloss notes, is a variant of "metal." "As *honorable mettle* [or noble metal], gold cannot be transmuted into base substances, and yet Cassius proposes to do just that with Brutus" (1026 n, 1030 n; brackets Bevington's). This concept of contamination, added by Shakespeare to his source, becomes one of the play's governing metaphors. I shall argue that the notion expressed in this metaphor derives from the *Republic* and that the downfall of both Caesar and Brutus is the consequence of their contamination—a contamination that also explains Rome's tyrannic regime.

Shakespeare never lets us forget that the Caesar of his play is a changed Caesar, a profoundly declined Caesar, little resembling "the noblest man / That ever lived" (3.1.258–59). He does this through allusions to Caesar's former conquests, impaired judgment, physical infirmities, lately acquired superstitiousness, and previous disdain for the fantasies, dreams, and ceremonies that now govern his life.[2] The cause of this decline—first in Caesar and then in Brutus—is the real subject of the play, and it is grounded on the concept of inverse alchemy Cassius describes.

Plato devotes an extended portion of the *Republic* to discussion of the corruption of the philosophic nature, which he prefaces with a description of the metals that theoretically comprise the human soul. The masses or Workers are framed of brass and iron, the Auxiliaries of silver, and the Guardians of gold (3.415). Because the masses are unavoidably corrupt, the philosopher must keep to his own environment since all seeds when deprived of "proper nutriment or climate or soil, in proportion to their vigour," will be tainted. The noblest natures are most prone to such injury; thus the philosopher, in "alien soil, becomes the most noxious of all weeds" and the author "of the greatest evil to States and individuals" (6.491–92, 495).

Elaborating this concept, Socrates states:

> [T]he diviner metal is within them [the Guardians], and they . . . ought not to pollute the divine by any such earthly admixture; for that commoner metal has been the source of many unholy deeds, but their own is undefiled. . . . And this will be their salvation, and they will be the saviours of the State. But should . . . [pollution

occur], they will become . . . enemies and tyrants instead of allies of the other citizens; . . . plotting and being plotted against, . . . [living in] greater terror of internal than of external enemies, and the hour of ruin, both to themselves and to . . . the State, will be at hand. (3.416–17)

Some preliminary parallels between the *Republic* and *Caesar* immediately emerge. At the play's outset, the plebeians' "basest mettle" is remarked (1.1.61). Caesar's constant association with the masses is suggested both by his alienation from the patriciate and by the enveloping throng of citizens that marks all of his public appearances.[3] Indeed "plotting [to become king] and being plotted against," he is threatened wholly by internal enemies, and his hour of ruin—and Rome's—is at hand.

Proclaiming the masses the greatest vitiators of the philosophic nature, Socrates explains—in a passage exhibiting thematic as well as scenic and stylistic affinities with the play—how corruption occurs:

> When they meet together, . . . at an assembly, . . . or in any other popular resort, and there is a great uproar, and they praise some things which are being said or done, and blame other things, equally exaggerating both, shouting and clapping their hands, and the echo of the rocks and the place in which they are assembled redoubles the sound of the praise or blame—at such a time will . . . any private training enable him [the philosopher] to stand firm against the overwhelming flood of popular opinion? or will he be carried away by the stream? Will he not have the notions of good and evil which the public in general have—he will do as they do, and as they are, such will he be? (6.492)

To this we may compare the following passage:

> Why, there was a crown offered him; and being offered him, he put it by with the back of his hand, thus, and then the people fell a-shouting. . . . He put it the third time by, and still as he refused it the rabblement hooted and clapped their chapped hands. . . . If the tag-rag people did not clap him and hiss him, according as he pleased and displeased them, . . . I am no true man. (1.2.221–61)[4]

His friends and fellow-citizens will also wish to exploit him, Socrates continues; "Falling at his feet, they will . . . honour and flatter him, because they want to get into their hands" the power he will possess. This will fill him with "boundless aspirations," and he will "elevate himself in the fulness of vain pomp and senseless pride" (6.494). Although Socrates here describes the young philosopher, Caesar's ascent hews closely to the sequence Socrates describes: surrounded by flatterers, which include the mass adulators through whom he has risen to power, Caesar has become pompous and vainglorious, aspiring illegitimately to kingship[5] and impiously equating himself with the gods (3.1.75).

Such tainting, as Socrates observes, leads to the one who is corrupted assuming the nature of his corrupter—to his becoming "[such] as they are" (6.492). Caesar claims throughout to transcend "ordinary men," citing his immunity to the flattery and base fawning "which melteth fools." Further, he grounds this claim on what he conceives to be the inviolability of his exalted nature:

> These couchings and these lowly courtesies
> Might fire the blood of ordinary men,
> And turn preordinance and first decree
> Into the law of children. Be not fond
> To think that Caesar bears such rebel blood
> That will be thawed from the true quality
> With that which melteth fools. . . .
>
> (3.1.37–43)[6]

The irony, of course, is that Caesar had indeed been "thawed," from his determination to remain at home, by Decius's flattering interpretation of Calphurnia's dream, moreover twice reversing his decision—and it is this inconstancy that leads directly to his death.[7] Notwithstanding his assertions to the contrary, therefore, he is as fickle and as credulous as the "fools" he contemns, his judgment similarly predicated on appearances.[8] It is thus one of the play's great ironies that "the noblest man that ever lived" descends to the brute level of the mob, a fact underscored by the beast imagery that pervades the play: the people are "sheep," Caesar is a "lion" and a "wolf," and the conspirators are "apes" and "hounds."[9]

These images recall Socrates' description of the tyrant, that man in whom "the basest elements of human nature have set up an absolute despotism . . . over the higher."[10] As Socrates explains, tyranny follows democracy when the insatiable desire for freedom leads to anarchy, the populace finally taking command of the state. The citizens "chafe impatiently at the least touch of authority and at length . . . cease to care even for the laws . . . ; they will have no one over them." They then procure "some champion whom they set over them and nurse into greatness." Eventually, the protector becomes a wolf: "having a mob entirely at his disposal, he is not restrained from shedding the blood of kinsmen," killing some and banishing others. The rich begin to hate him; "And if they are unable to expel him, . . . they conspire to assassinate him" (8.562–66).

Again, the parallels between Plato's text and Shakespeare's are striking. The play opens on a Caesar who is the darling of the mob, who has just slain not a foreign enemy but a Roman and kinsman,[11] who has banished another fellow Roman, and who is hated by a patriciate that conspires to kill him. Cassius terms him a tyrant and a wolf (1.3.104–5), linking—as does Plato—the two concepts. Further, unlike the initially subjugated plebeians of *Coriolanus*, this populace is insolently contemptuous of the law: although it is "a laboring day," they have discarded their prescribed working attire and, literally and figuratively, their "rule" (1.1.4, 7), taking an unauthorized holiday to witness Caesar's triumph.[12] This divestment of the garb emblematic of their ordained place in society emphasizes their hierarchical breach. Their contempt for authority, further underscored by their reported hatred of kingship (1.2.244–66), culminates in their destruction of Rome.[13] Also suggesting the Platonic provenance of the scene are the representative cobbler and carpenter, who have no corollary in Plutarch. The following exchange occurs between Socrates and Glaucon:

> Suppose a carpenter to be doing the business of a cobbler, or a cobbler of a carpenter; and suppose them to exchange their implements or their duties . . . ; do you think that any great harm would result to the State?
> Not much.
> But when the cobbler or any other man whom nature designed to be a trader . . . attempts to force his way into the class of warriors . . . , for which he is unfitted, and either to take the implements or the duties of the other; . . . then I think you will agree . . . that this . . . meddling of one with another is the ruin of the State.

Conversely,

> the division of labour which require[s] the carpenter and the shoemaker and the rest of the citizens to be doing each his own business, and not another's, [is] a shadow of justice. (4.434, 443)

The real tyrant, Socrates emphasizes,

> is the real slave, and is obliged to practise the greatest . . . servility, and to be the flatterer of the vilest of mankind. He . . . is full of convulsions, and distractions, even as the State which he resembles. (9.579)

Caesar's servile flattery of "the common herd" (1.2.264) cements the parallel:

> When he came to himself again, he said if he had done or said anything amiss, he desired their worships to think it was his infirmity. Three or four wenches . . . cried, "Alas, good soul!" and forgave him with all their hearts. (1.2.268–73)[14]

The "distractions" Socrates mentions are manifested in Caesar's unreason; the "convulsions," in Caesar's epileptic fits. Both are replicated in the civil turmoil that besets Rome.[15] Indeed, references to sickness—of the characters, of the state, and of the cosmos—pervade the play. The very earth "Shakes like a thing unfirm" (1.3.4), the cosmos mirroring the corrupted "faculties" and altered nature of Rome's head:

> But if you would consider the true cause
> . . . .
> Why birds and beasts from quality and kind,
> Why old men, fools, and children calculate,
> Why all these things change from their ordinance,
> Their natures, and preformèd faculties,
> To monstrous quality—why, you shall find
> That heaven hath infused them with these spirits
> To make them instruments of fear and warning
> Unto some monstrous state.
>
> (1.3.62–71)

Caesar, as Cassius observes, is "Most like this dreadful night" (1.3.73). The concept recalls Socrates' equation of justice with health and well-being, and injustice with deformity and disease, justice consisting in the "natural order and government" of the soul's faculties, and injustice in a perversion of the natural order (4.444). "Natural" is the key word: each element maintains the place and function appropriate to its nature. Any deviation from this principle fosters the growth of a monster (9.588–89).[16]

All these infirmities reflect the flawed judgment of the ruling faculty; for, as Socrates emphasizes (9.588–89), the ambitious man is devoid of reason, being governed largely by will (9.588–89).[17] This concept also conceivably underlies the lion image that defines Caesar (1.3.75, 106; 2.2.46): as Socrates explains, pride occurs when the lion and serpent elements in the soul disproportionately gain strength (9.590). Socrates equates the lion with the faculty of will (just as he equates the appetites with the serpent or "many-headed monster"; hence the analogous "many-headed multitude" of *Coriolanus*). The irrational man "feast[s] the multitudinous monster and strengthen[s] the lion," thus becoming slave to both (9.588–89). It is perhaps significant that Caesar, apprising Decius of his immediately-to-be-reversed decision to remain at home, explains, "The cause is in my will" (2.2.71).[18] Hence the irony of Brutus's comment: "I have not known when his affections swayed / More than his reason" (2.1.20–21).

In addition to mirroring the ruler's ills, the state also mirrors his political temperament; and Caesar's tyranny is paralleled by that of the populace. For it is not Caesar who rules; it is the mob, the state thus replicating that soul "in which the basest elements of human nature have set up an absolute . . . 'tyranny' over the higher, the very negation of that principle of justice whereby each element, by doing its proper work, contributes to the well-being of the whole."[19] Indeed, it may not be an overstatement to assert that the mob is the play's real protagonist, for they control not only Caesar and the other patricians but virtually the entire course of events. Their subjugation of Caesar is manifested in his previously noted servility and in his repeated refusal of the crown though "he would fain have had it" (1.2.239–40). Lest the audience doubt Caesar's subjugation, it is underscored by his symbolic gesture of surrender: offering the crowd his throat to cut. The conspirators are no less ruled by the mob; they enlist Brutus solely because they fear popular reprisal. As Casca observes, in another reference to alchemy,

> O, he sits high in all the people's hearts;
> And that which would appear offense in us,
> His countenance, like richest alchemy,
> Will change to virtue and to worthiness.
>
> (1.3.157–60)

The point is reiterated by Brutus himself:

> Let's be sacrificers, but not butchers, Caius.
> ....
> Which so appearing to the common eyes,
> We shall be called purgers, not murderers.
>
> (2.1.167–81)

Later, Cassius exhorts Brutus not to let Antony address the crowd because "the people may be moved" (3.1.236); Brutus will allow Antony to do so, but only if he agrees to speak well of Caesar, cast no blame on the conspirators, and make clear that he speaks by the conspirators' permission,[20] all of which, Brutus contends, will "advantage" them in the eyes of the people (3.1.244). Similarly, Metellus urges their recruitment of Cicero because his silver hair and reputed "judgment" will "purchase" the people's "good opinion" (2.1.144–49).[21] Antony equally defers to the mob. Clearly recognizing that they control the fate of the counterconspiracy, he humbly addresses them as "friends" and "masters," manipulating them through calculated appeals to their supremacy: "You will compel me then to read the will?" And when he asks, "Shall I descend? And will you give me leave?" Third Plebeian accords him the requisite permission: "You shall have leave" (3.2.158, 161, 164). Indeed, we remain cognizant of the mob's preeminence even when they are offstage, both through repeated references to their actions and through the shouting that twice disrupts the dialogue.

Antony's oration also appears to derive from the *Republic*. The supreme politician, Antony is the consummate version of such figures as *Lucrece*'s Brutus and *Coriolanus*'s Tribunes and Aufidius—he who studies "the tempers and desires of a mighty . . . beast" and learns

> how to approach and handle him, also at what times and from what causes he is dangerous or the reverse, . . . and by what sounds . . . he is soothed or infuriated; and . . . when, by continually attending upon him, he has become perfect in all this, he . . . makes of it a system or art, . . . [calling] this honourable and that dishonourable, or good or evil, or just or unjust, all in accordance with the tastes and tempers of the great brute. (6.493)

The passage seems the basis not only of Antony's psychology but also of the motifs he invokes. Thus Socrates' "good . . . evil" becomes "The evil that men do lives after them; / The good is oft interrèd with their bones"; Socrates' "just . . . unjust" becomes "O masters! If I were disposed to stir / Your hearts and minds to mutiny and rage, / I should do Brutus wrong, and Cassius wrong, . . . / I will not do them wrong"; and "honourable . . . dishonourable" becomes the oration's celebrated refrain, "And Brutus is an honorable man." These elements find no basis in Plutarch, who presents a brief and antithetical account: Antony moves the people to rage by displaying Caesar's bloody garments and terming "the malefactors, cruell and cursed murtherers."[22]

Shakespeare's Caesar—partially deaf, figuratively blind, sustained by mass adulation, and ruled by a populace he should theoretically command—markedly resembles the captain in Socrates' parable of the ship of state. This captain "is taller and stronger than any of the crew, but he is a little deaf and has a similar infirmity in sight, and his knowledge of navigation is not much better." The sailors quarrel about the steering, each believing "he has a right to steer, though he has never learned the [pilot's art] . . . , and they are ready to cut in pieces any one who says the contrary. They throng about the captain, . . . praying him to commit the helm to them." At length "they mutiny and take possession of the ship," having first "chained up the noble captain's senses with . . . some narcotic drug" (6.488). The resemblance is the more striking in that no mention of Caesar's deafness appears in any of Shakespeare's known sources.[23]

Shakespeare, then, as James Hanford puts it,

> by making the corruption of society result from a substitution of will or appetite for reason, touches on the principle by which Plato explains not only the growth of democracy but the consequent development of democracy into tyranny as well. . . . The tyrant is the embodiment in a single person of the lawlessness of the community. The brute appetites in him have gained full sway; "he has purged away temperance and brought in madness to the full," [winning] mastery of the state by championing the lawless indulgence of the populace.[24]

As the *Republic* informs Shakespeare's characterization of Caesar, so it informs his characterization of Brutus. Brutus is not merely Caesar's parallel; Brutus figuratively *becomes* Caesar through a like process of reverse alchemy that morally debases and destroys him. To quote Gary Miles, "this implicit convergence of personalities and roles" is underscored by "the apparition that is simultaneously the ghost of Caesar and Brutus' own 'evil spirit'" (4.3.284)[25] and by the shout, "Let him be Caesar." It is perhaps further underscored by the fact that the term "Caesar" had by Shakespeare's time become generic for an autocrat or absolute monarch.[26]

We may recall Socrates' statement that the philosopher will be thronged by "friends and fellow-citizens" who, wishing to use him for their own purposes, "honour and flatter him," filling him with senseless pride. They will, moreover, "do and say anything to prevent him from yielding to his better nature and to render his teacher [i.e., philosophy] powerless, using to this end private intrigues." "[T]he very qualities," accordingly, "which make a man a philosopher may ... divert him from philosophy, no less than riches and ... the other so-called goods of life." Thus the noblest minds "become pre-eminently bad" (6.494–95, 491). Brutus, we may recall, not only possesses a noble nature but is also a philosopher;[27] and it is precisely his contamination by friends and fellow-citizens—who similarly recruit him for their own purposes and who honor and flatter him in order to win him—that destroys him.[28] His downfall parallels Caesar's; these "friends" and "countrymen," as Brutus in fact terms the conspirators, are the moral correlative of the mob, a fact denoted not only by the beast imagery and participation in murder common to both (the killing of Caesar morally parallels the killing of Cinna), but by their implicit identification with the appetites: all except Brutus "Did that they did in envy of great Caesar" (5.5.70). Brutus's association with them therefore incurs the same debasement that befell Caesar through his like association with the mob. Those "very qualities," moreover, that make him a philosopher—his virtue and his idealistic devotion to honor—divert him from philosophy; thus "the noblest Roman of them all" slays Caesar for what he conceives to be the common good.

Initiating the process of debasement are Cassius's flattering advances: he remarks Brutus's "hidden worthiness," invokes Brutus's noble ancestry, and forges letters glancing at "the great opinion / That Rome holds of his name" (1.2.59, 318–19). Brutus's initial response is emblematic of the as-yet-unsullied state of his soul:

> Into what dangers would you lead me, Cassius,
> That you would have me seek into myself
> For that which is not in me?
>
> (1.2.63–65)[29]

By the conclusion of their encounter, however, the flattery has begun to work; and it is Cassius's recognition of Brutus's imminent defilement through association with the likes of himself (i.e., Cassius) that prompts his soliloquy.[30] The term "humor" at 1.2.315 refers to "wrought" earlier in the speech, implying Cassius's refashioning, so to speak, of Brutus's "honorable mettle."[31] Two metaphors, therefore, are at work in this passage: one of alchemy, the other of metalworking, which Shakespeare interrelates and fuses. Plato similarly links the two metaphors: thus Socrates explains how "the greatest of all Sophists," the populace, fashions the philosopher after its own heart (6.492). Brutus's corruption, however, is not total until receipt of the letters; as Cassius observes, "Three parts of him / Is ours already, and the man entire / Upon the next encounter yields him ours" (1.3.154–56).

As in the *Republic*, corruption is signaled by internal chaos, as the soul's hierarchy collapses:

> Since Cassius first did whet me against Caesar,
> I have not slept.
> ....
> The genius and the mortal instruments
> Are then in council; and the state of man,
> Like to a little kingdom, suffers then
> The nature of an insurrection.
>
> (2.1.61–69)

Brutus's condition has begun to parallel Caesar's; the lower faculties are in contention with reason, vitiating the soul's integrity and replicating the growing anarchy of the Roman state. This replication is punningly emphasized in Caius Ligarius's greeting to Brutus shortly before the assassination: "Soul of Rome!" (2.1.322).[32]

Brutus's ensuing descent into tyranny is denoted by his despotic rule of a realm that is the microcosmic parallel of Caesar's. Acclaimed figurative king of the conspirators—a role underscored by Fourth Plebeian's punning assertion that "Caesar's better parts / Shall be crowned in Brutus" (3.2.51.52)—he overrides or rejects each one of their proposals: that they bind themselves with an oath, that they sound Cicero, and that they dispatch Antony along with Caesar. Later, he vetoes Cassius's objection to letting Antony speak at Caesar's funeral,[33] and just as disastrously overrules Cassius's abler judgment on military procedure, pompously alleging "better" reasons (4.3.202). Ultimately, he becomes as arrogant and imperious as Caesar. The fact is attested by his contemptuous dismissal of Cassius: "Away, slight man!" (4.3.38) (the phrase will recur almost verbatim in Antony's assessment of Lepidus as "a slight, unmeritable man" [4.1.12] as Antony's tyranny in turn supplants Brutus's). His hubris and self-aggrandizement likewise recall Caesar's: he cites the "too great a mind" that precludes his captivity (5.1.116), assures Octavius that he could not die more honorably than by Brutus's sword (5.1.59–61), and self-righteously exempts himself from Cassius's threats:

> For I am armed so strong in honesty
> That they pass by me as the idle wind,
> Which I respect not.
>
> (4.3.68–70)

As with Caesar, corruption effects a "monstrous" alteration. "It will not let you eat, nor talk, nor sleep," Portia observes;

> And could it work so much upon your shape
> As it hath much prevailed on your condition,
> I should not know you Brutus.
>
> (2.1.253–56)

As Socrates concludes:

> Thus . . . is brought about . . . that ruin . . . of the natures best adapted to the best of all pursuits; they are natures which we maintain to be rare at any time; this being the class out of which come the men who are the authors of the greatest evil to States and individuals. (6.495)

Shakespeare, then, adds to his Platonic paradigm of constitutional decline Plato's theory of the composition of the soul in order to explain fully the passage of democracy into tyranny. Initially engendered by abolishment of the monarchy, Caesar's Rome, with its mob supremacy, is a final consequence of kingless rule. Caesar is the embodiment of this decline: debased by his association with the masses, he has sunk from a prince to a tyrant, enslaved by the very elements he champions. Brutus's decline is the microcosmic parallel of Caesar's and results from a like defilement. An idealistic philosopher, Brutus exemplifies the rare and noble nature vitiated through contamination by society's basest elements. Precisely because of that nobility, he destroys Rome. The ultimate irony of the play is, then, Platonic; and again, as in Plato, the leader images the "soul" of the state he theoretically commands.

Why Shakespeare composed *Caesar* is suggested by a number of parallels between the play's political milieu and England's. At the time, a continuing concern remained in the person of the Earl of Essex, "whose arrogant pride, assurance of high place, hold over Elizabeth's affections, and complete command of popular favour made him a standing danger to the state."[34] It is this danger, I shall argue, that the play reflects.

As we saw in chapter 2, a perception that Essex was seeking the crown dated back to the early 1590s. By 1599, when *Caesar* was written, the concern over Essex had markedly increased, several things having conspired to exacerbate the threat he posed well beyond that reflected in *Lucrece*. While the Privy Council continued to be dominated by the two factions respectively led by Essex and the Cecils, Essex's feud with the Cecilians for control of royal policy had escalated into open conflict.[35] His degenerating influence with the Queen, his jealousy of the power wielded by the Cecils, and his conviction that they were poisoning her against him drove him to increasingly rash behavior, including his actions during the famous ear-boxing incident with Elizabeth in 1598,[36] which stopped just short of regicide when he abortively reached for his sword; and his ignominious and unauthorized return from Ireland in 1599, a prelude to his subsequent revolt. Adding to the perception of Essex as a threat was his courtship of the masses, always associated with potential usurpation; and the appearance of John Hayward's allegedly treasonous book, *The First Part of the Life and Raigne of King Henry IIII*, which centered on the fall of Richard II and Bolingbroke's role in effecting it. Like the earlier treasonous book of Robert Parsons, this one was also dedicated to Essex, already identified in the national consciousness with Bolingbroke,[37] in words with unsettling implications: "For you are great indeed, both in present judgment and in expectation of future time"—language appropriate for an heir apparent to the throne. Indeed, at his trial, Robert Cecil adduced as proof of Essex's seditious intentions "the book written on Henry IV, making this time like that of Richard II, to be reframed by him as by Henry IV."[38] Hayward's book appeared in March 1599—one month before Essex left as Lord Deputy for Ireland to quash the rebellion led by the Earl of Tyrone, after having persuaded the Queen and the Council—by denigrating other candidates while pressing his own singular qualifications—to grant him the post.[39]

It was not surprising, therefore, that his departure—"at the height of a popularity that no subject had enjoyed in Tudor times" and with "the greatest army that had left English shores during the reign"—occasioned serious alarm.[40] What he wanted, his adversaries suspected, "was simply command of an army, 'to engage the swordmen to him. Yea, so eager was he about the business that divers feared he was hatching some dangerous design'"[41]—a sentiment shared by the queen herself and buttressed by the concurrent boast of some of his followers that he had a better claim to the crown than any of his competitors by reason of his Plantagenet blood.[42] A letter to John Harington from a friend at Court going as an officer to Ireland encapsulates the concern: the Earl, it asserts, "goeth not forth to serve the Queen's realm, but to humour his own revenge. . . . Essex hath enemies; he hath friends too. . . . I sore fear what may happen."[43] During the ensuing months, "the civil peace of the realm hung in the balance, at the mercy of the uncertain impulses"—and the monumental army—"of the tormented nobleman at Dublin."[44]

These fears were quickly justified: Essex, defying the Queen's orders, made his irresponsible crony Southampton Master of the Horse, knighted thirty-eight henchmen in two months (which, like those he had created in France, were tantamount to a body of personal retainers and thus potentially damaging to the balance of power in the state),[45] and secretly negotiated with Tyrone who promised that, if Essex heeded his advice, "he would make him the greatest man that ever was in England."[46] Capping these events were his unauthorized desertion, in September, of his post, followed by his hasty return to Court to justify himself, where he burst unannounced into Elizabeth's bedchamber.[47] A charge of treason came the following summer; among the allegations was the charge that he had conspired with Tyrone to "let him [Tyrone] rule under the Pope in Ireland, until the Earl was fully confirmed to the Crown and reconciled to the Pope," when "by the Pope's command" Tyrone would submit to Essex under the pope.[48] Although no doubt largely propagandistic, these charges seem less than fantastical given that Essex had in fact considered appropriating two or three thousand of his troops, landing in Wales where he had a large following, and then storming the Court and purging it of the Cecilians, a plan he abandoned only because his cohorts Southampton and Blount opposed it as imprudent and because taking over an army would require their aid.[49]

Whether Shakespeare had wind of this plan is less material than the widespread belief, even before Essex departed for Ireland, that he was harboring just such treasonous intents—a belief Shakespeare arguably shared. Written virtually concurrently with *Caesar*, *Henry V*, in an allusion to the Earl's as yet unconcluded Irish campaign, contains the following lines:

> Were now the General of our gracious Empress,
> As in good time he may, from Ireland coming,
> Bringing rebellion broachèd on his sword,
> How many would the peaceful city quit
> To welcome him!
>
> (5.0.30–34)

In addition to its veiled censure of the Queen's governance by her favorite ("the General of our gracious Empress"), the passage both suggests Shakespeare's perception of the threat Essex posed and prophetically augurs the Earl's 1601 revolt as well as the popular backing it theoretically would inspire:[50] feted by an adoring populace who forsake the pale of peace to embrace him, Essex brings "rebellion" on the sword that defines him, "broached" denoting not "spitted" (the standard interpretation) but "set on foot, started, introduced."[51]

It is these concerns and this perception that *Caesar* appears to address. Like England, Rome is dominated by two rival, mutually hostile factions harboring antithetical political ideologies.[52] The leader of one faction is bitterly envious of the leader of the other, whose overthrow he secretly contrives through rebellious conspiracy. Essex, in the summer of 1599, was similarly attracting rebellious conspiracy,[53] drawing, like Cassius, the disreputable, the politically mediocre, and the politically alienated, including the disgruntled noblemen and office seekers the Queen had failed to satisfy through patronage. Like the play's conspirators, Essex sought to rally the local populace behind his revolt (although this occurred in 1601, after the writing of *Caesar*, the move had long been anticipated given his pursuit of popularity; consider, for example, Shakespeare's above-noted prognostication of it in *Henry V*). Also like Cassius, he believed in the use of violence for the defense of honor and for the pursuit of "legitimate" political ends[54] (compare 1.3.108–11 and Cassius's justification of assassination on grounds of the nobleness of the enterprise), and "could not live as anything but the first of men"[55] (compare Cassius's pathological jealousy of Caesar and his resentment at being an "underling" [1.2.141]), a trait that ultimately incurred the Queen's mistrust (compare Caesar's distrust of Cassius, 1.2.192–95). Elizabeth he contemned as an old woman frustrating his greatness, an inferior female whose mind was "as crooked as her carcass"[56] (compare Cassius's depiction of Caesar as feeble-tempered, sickly, and vile [1.2.100–29, 1.3.111], a false deity who keeps the superior Cassius in a position of humiliating and degrading subservience). Caesar's characterization of Cassius is equally applicable to Essex:

> Such men as he be never at heart's ease
> Whiles they behold a greater than themselves,
> And therefore are they very dangerous.
> (1.2.208–10)[57]

But Essex is also figured in Caesar—in his quest for supremacy, in his martial triumphs, in his heroic stature, in his courtship of and veneration by the rabble, in the fear and dislike he inspires in members of his own class, and in the potential for mob rule that inheres in such a figure. Flavius's depiction of Caesar as the idol of the "vulgar," who seeks to "soar above the view of men / And keep us all in servile fearfulness" (1.1.70–75), equally describes Essex. Indeed, more than one Elizabethan linked Essex with Caesar, Sir Robert Naunton, for instance, comparing Essex's followers and advisors during his revolt to the followers of Caesar.[58]

There are also resemblances between Caesar and Elizabeth. While the aging and declined Caesar need not necessarily figure the Queen,[59] the following details—almost all of them Shakespeare's additions to his source—seem calculated to press the connection:

(1) Caesar's heirlessness. Plutarch contains two separate accounts of the Lupercalia (*Antonius*, 12–13, *Caesar*, 62). While both report Antony's participation, including his offer of a crown to Caesar, neither mentions Calpurnia's barrenness, Caesar's concern about it, or even her presence at the event. The issue of childlessness (which Caesar terms a "sterile curse" [1.2.9]) receives added emphasis by reason of its prominence: it is the first topic Caesar broaches on entering the play. Caesar, as David Daniell notes, needs an heir; lacking a legitimate son, he is—like Elizabeth—dynastically vulnerable.[60]

In Plutarch, Caesar adopts as his son his great-nephew Octavius and names him his heir. Shakespeare, however, omits this fact; in the play, the people, not Octavius, are termed Caesar's heirs (3.2.147). (Plutarch nowhere refers to the people as Caesar's heirs, instead reporting that Octavius was charged with distributing items "bequeathed" by Caesar "unto the people of Rome" in his capacity as Caesar's "lawefull heire by will" [*Antonius,* 15–16].) Shakespeare's additions possibly allude to Elizabeth's own "cursed sterility" and to her insistence, when pressed to marry, that she was wed to England and her subjects were her children.

(2) Caesar's vulnerability to flattery, epitomized by his succumbing to Decius's interpretation of Calpurnia's dream (see also Decius's remark at 2.1.203–9). None of these details—the dream, the interpretation, or the remark—appear in Plutarch (cf. Plutarch's reference to Caesar's "great wisdome"). Elizabeth's vanity and her proneness to (and cultivation of) flattery were well known and widely deplored.

(3) Caesar's implied profession of immortality (when he equates himself with the gods [3.1.75; see also 1.2.60]) and his related, repeated refusals to heed warnings of impending death. Both evoke Elizabeth's steadfast refusal to address the succession despite her increasingly imminent demise and despite warnings that her inaction would sentence England upon her death to the "bloody sword."[61] In this regard, Elizabeth's deafness metaphorically parallels Caesar's. Caesar's deific self-image also contains parallels with that generated by the cult of the Virgin Queen, the fervent adulation of whom aroused not only enthusiasm but hostility and charges of idolatry.[62]

(4) Caesar's pronouncements of changelessness. Closely related to Caesar's professed immortality, these pronouncements—contained in another of Shakespeare's additions, the North Star speech (3.1.59–74)—evoke Elizabeth's motto, *semper eadem* (always the same), similarly belied by the old Queen's frequent indecision and mind changes in matters of state.[63] The motto informed Elizabeth's identification with the moon ("That ever in one change doth grow / Yet still the same: and she is so," as the Elizabethan John Dowland put it) as well as her persona as the eternal Petrarchan beloved, who was attended—even in her sixty-ninth year, according to John Davies— by the "fresh youth and beauty" of "Time's young hours." Hence her portraits, until almost her death, as a beauty immutably young.[64]

Further evoking England's contemporary political scene is the crown that Caesar covets and that will shortly cost him his life.

By the play's end, nothing has changed. The power struggle proceeds apace, as one tyrant metamorphoses into another in the ongoing battle for supremacy. This fact is impressed on us from the outset, as Caesar arrives "in triumph over Pompey's blood" (1.1.51); Caesar is in turn vanquished and displaced by Brutus, who is displaced by Antony, who is displaced by Octavius. That the triumvirs reincarnate the conspirators is underscored by the parallel scenes 2.1 and 4.1, in which each group debates what political foes to kill and Lepidus supplants Brutus as the vehicle to mute culpability. Brutus also re-embodies the ancestor whose name he bears and whose antimonarchic role he tacitly assumes as he prepares to destroy the man who "would be crowned" (2.1.12). Thus did Lucius Junius Brutus "from the streets of Rome / The Tarquin drive, when he was called a king" (2.1.53–54). More ironic still, Caesarism has been resuscitated: "another Caesar" (5.1.55) controls Rome,[65] a figure at once Caesar's spiritual successor and incarnation.[66] The spirit of Caesarism will play itself out in the final stage of tyranny that marks *Antony and Cleopatra* as the new victors battle each other for dominion, and sovereignty ultimately accrues to the sole man left alive.

5

Antony and Cleopatra

Antony and Cleopatra portrays Rome in the final stage of tyranny. Enervated by the strife attending five centuries of kingless rule, Rome remains racked by faction and civil war as its rulers continue the battle for dominion.

Tyranny, we will recall, evolves from the inordinate desire for freedom that begets democracy. It is born when the people, contemning law, contrive to throw off the reins of authority, a situation culminating in mob rule. Eventually the people's champion becomes a "wolf"; backed by a beguiled mob, he embarks on a campaign of purgation, first of the people's putative enemies and then of those who are threats to his power. Thus he becomes "himself the overthrower of many, standing up in the chariot of State with the reins in his hand, no longer protector, but tyrant absolute" (*Rep.* 8.566). Concomitantly, the power struggle shifts from classes to individuals, each seeking to capture or retain control of the state; in the plays, these combatants include Pompey against Caesar, Caesar against the conspirators, the conspirators against Antony and Octavius, and the triumvirs against each other.[1] It is this final phase of tyranny that *Antony and Cleopatra* concerns. Dispatching rivals with impunity, the rulers have become laws unto themselves; as Octavius instructs Thidias concerning Cleopatra, "Try thy cunning, Thidias. / Make thine own edict for thy pains, which we / Will answer as a law" (3.12.31–33). The Senate, correspondingly, has vanished, replaced by "The senators alone of this great world" (2.6.9), the triumvirs themselves,[2] whose power nevertheless remains grounded in the loyalty of the fickle masses.

Replicating in small this political ethos are the play's love relationships. In both spheres, the political and the amatory, allegiances are founded on expedience. All of the relationships in the play are accordingly defined by the rhetoric of disordered love, whose attributes of faithlessness, licentiousness, and betrayal are subsumed under the governing metaphor of whorishness. The shifting alliances of the rulers ethically replicate those of the fickle masses, the "slippery people" (1.2.192) whose "love" is predicated not on merit but on self-interest. Hence the burgeoning strength of the lately-loathed Pompey, who, "Rich in his father's honor, creeps apace / Into the hearts of such as have not thrived / Upon the present state" (1.3.50–52). Lured by his "name and power" (1.2.196) rather than by any intrinsic virtue, the disaffected forsake Caesar for Pompey, rendering him Rome's newest "beloved"; as Antony puts it, "the hated, grown to strength, / Are newly grown to love" (1.3.48–49). A sequence of double entendres encapsulates the whorishness of such "love":

> This common body,
> Like to a vagabond flag upon the stream,
> Goes to and back, lackeying the varying tide
> To rot itself with motion.
> (1.4.44–47)

A synonym for *populace*, a "common body" is also a trull, and the "varying tide" her succession of paramours. The act of copulation is denoted by "to and back."[3] Such love is the consequence of "headlessness," the absence of the monarchic element of reason that brings into order the self-serving affections constituting the Platonic analogue of the masses.

The defection from one paramour to another thus pervades every level of society: it characterizes not only the populace but the rulers who break oaths and treaties, and their subordinates who, "whatever their personal preferences, depend on pillage and spoil to pay their legions, and must therefore gravitate to the stronger side; while tributary kings seek the best bargain from whichever conquering emperor or queen they can."[4]

With their myriad infidelities, the protagonists epitomize this ethos. Like the society they image, they are "headless": Antony has made "his will / Lord of his reason" (3.13.3–4), vitiating the hierarchy on which the soul's integrity rests. Both lovers, concomitantly, subordinate justice to desire, a prime manifestation of tyranny. The corruption of reason is reflected in their arbitrary and despotic rule, exampled in Cleopatra's beating of the messenger for apprising her of Antony's marriage to Octavia; by Antony's parallel beating of Thidias for serving Caesar and, in that capacity, for usurping Antony's right to kiss Cleopatra's hand; and by his veto of every suggestion that would have saved him at Actium.[5] "[U]nlike even the revolutionary tribunes in *Coriolanus*," notes Paul Cantor, the lovers "appeal [neither] to law [n]or custom in making . . . their decisions."[6]

The love/tyranny nexus that defines both protagonists similarly defines the realm they rule, reflecting the Platonic axiom that the State ethically images its ruler. As tyranny evolves from the excess of freedom characterizing democracy, so the tyrant evolves from the dissoluteness characterizing the democratic man (*Rep.* 9.571–573), lawlessness and injustice defining State and individual alike. The tyrant emerges when the master passion of eros achieves lordship over the soul's "idle and spendthrift" appetites (*Rep.* 9.573), effecting total surrender to sensual desire. As Nicholas White explains, "Among the various appetites of the lowest part of the soul, 'lust' (*erōs*) is depicted by Plato as having a special nature that makes it capable of holding the position of, first, leader . . . of the other appetites, and later [owing to its unremittingly obsessive nature] as dictator or tyrant among them."[7] "The overwhelming and unquenchable appetites that possess the tyrant motivate his actions," finally leading him "to seek the political power that enables him to satisfy his appetites without hindrance by the law."[8] "The rule of lust or *erōs*, which prevails in the soul of the dictatorial man, is [thus] tantamount to a condition of complete and perfect injustice"[9]—the analog of the regime in the dictatorial State. Hence total freedom passes into total slavery: thrall to his insatiable lusts, the tyrannical man becomes incapable of acting voluntarily (*Rep.* 9.577).

Plato's portrait of the tyrant is one of complete sensual debauchery. Driven by the desire for pleasure, he lives "amid clouds of incense and perfumes and garlands and wines, and all the pleasures of a dissolute life." He is drunken and lustful, passing his time in "feasts and carousals and revellings and courtezans" (*Rep.* 9.573). Sensuality leads to emasculation: his soul grows "dainty," and "he lives in his hole like a woman." The public tyrant is the most miserable of all: "compelled to pass his life . . . fighting and combating with other men," he "grows worse from having power," becoming ever "more jealous, more faithless, more unjust, [and] more friendless" (*Rep.*

9.579–80). Thus tyranny, like both oligarchy and democracy, is driven "by the principle of desire, but a desire which is both for gain and for enjoyment, a desire which belongs to a single individual, to whom the rest of the State is sacrificed. Tyranny . . . is the worst of constitutions, and the tyrant, who uses his strength to satisfy his lust and his greed, is the worst of men."[10] All of these attributes, ultimately including volitional paralysis, define Antony.

Opposing the irrational tyrant to the rational king, Plato's paradigm of tyranny became a Renaissance commonplace. Thus Sir Thomas Elyot defines a king as one whose soul has "intiere & ful auctorite over the sensis"; a tyrant, as one "whose soule rulith not but excludinge from hir, Knowledge and Raison, suffreth hir selfe to be gouerned bi the sensis."[11] Shakespeare's *Henry V* invokes the same concept:

> We are no tyrant, but a Christian king,
> Unto whose grace our passion is as subject
> As is our wretches fettered in our prisons.
>
> (*H5* 1.2.241–43)

The king places public good above private; the tyrant, a slave to his desires, places private good uppermost.

If Antony is the embodiment of Plato's tyrannic man, Cleopatra is the personification of Eros.[12] Shakespeare suggests the connection by repeatedly conflating her with Antony's attendant, Eros, whereby, through the device of apposition, the two characters become one and the same. Examples of such conflation include the following: "she, Eros, has / Packed cards with Caesar" (4.14.18–19); "Eros!—I come, my queen.—Eros!—Stay for me" (4.14.50); "No, my chuck. Eros . . ." (4.4.2); and "My queen and Eros" (4.14.97).

Notwithstanding a sizable consensus to the contrary, therefore, the play concerns neither the triumph nor the ennobling power of love but the perverse love, rooted in vitiated reason, that dooms the state. "Antony is no private man" notes Thomas Stroup; "he is a pillar of the world. The personal and private affairs of public men cannot remain personal and private. . . . Thus the actions of a man, especially a public man, affect all men; and the play is consciously designed to illustrate the point."[13] Indeed, the political implications of the affair are repeatedly stressed: Philo laments the decline of "The triple pillar of the world" (1.1.12), Caesar decries the increased burden Antony's dalliance places on his partners (1.4.16–25), and

Antony himself concedes that Rome's welfare mandates his complete renunciation of Cleopatra (1.2.135).

Reflecting the self-serving desire informing Plato's tyrannic paradigm, both plots—the political and the amatory—center on a quest for power that is rooted in self-gratification uninformed by the legitimate concerns of rulership. In this respect, the two plots are not only parallel; each determines the course of the other. Antony seeks power for the homage and omnipotence it confers: the deference of kings (3.13.91–93), ransoming lives with "jests" (3.13.183–84), and "play[ing]" with "half the bulk o' the world . . . as I pleased, / Making and marring fortunes" (3.11.63–64), all of which render him "the greatest prince o' the world" (4.15.56). To this concept of greatness, ethical considerations are irrelevant; princeship is a self-serving and egotistical game (note the words "play" and "jests"); it consists not in the administration of justice, the ruler's prime function, but in unrivaled conquest, untrammeled whim, and in garnering, in the words of Eros, "the worship of the whole world" (4.14.86). What most grieves Antony is the loss of this preeminence to Octavius: "All come to this? The hearts / That spanieled me at heels, to whom I gave / Their wishes, do . . . melt their sweets / On blossoming Caesar" (4.12.20–23). It is this threat to his "greatness," no less than his sensual infatuation, that shapes his relationship with Cleopatra. For it is not Cleopatra of whom he is jealous; it is Caesar.

This jealousy is apparent at the men's first meeting, in their preliminary jockeying for supremacy (Antony declines to sit first since it will compromise his "superiority") and in his concern that his brother is undermining his authority with Caesar (2.2.54). Caesar's threat to his preeminence likewise underlies Antony's meeting with the Soothsayer. "[W]hose fortunes shall rise higher, / Caesar's or mine?" Antony asks (2.3.16–17). When the Soothsayer replies "Caesar's," adding that Caesar will "overpower" Antony and diminish his "lustre," Antony determines to return to Cleopatra: "He hath spoken true. The very dice obey him. . . . I will to Egypt" (2.3.34–39). Similarly, what grieves him after Actium is not his loss of the battle or even of his kingdoms but that he must now defer to Caesar; must "To the young man send humble treaties, . . . / And palter in the shifts of lowness" (3.11.61–62). When he speaks of Cleopatra, it is to tax her with sullying his glory by conspiring with Caesar (4.12). To "blemish Caesar's triumph," he even plans to kill her:

> The witch shall die.
> To the young Roman boy she hath sold me, and I fall
> Under this plot. She dies for 't.
>
> (4.12.47–49)

His whipping of Thidias is likewise motivated by jealousy of Caesar. What riles him is that Thidias is a subordinate of Caesar's and thus a reminder of his own faltering power. He chides Cleopatra, therefore, for letting such a fellow kiss her hand and for flattering Caesar by flirting with his underling (3.13.125–27, 159–60). "[B]e thou sorry," he instructs Thidias,

> To follow Caesar in his triumph, since
> Thou hast been whipped for following him.
> . . . .
> Get thee back to Caesar.
> Tell him thy entertainment. Look thou say
> He makes me angry with him; for he seems
> Proud and disdainful, harping on what I am,
> Not what he knew I was.
>
> (3.13.138–46)

That the beating stems from jealousy of Caesar rather than of Cleopatra is affirmed by his subsequent command to Cleopatra to kiss the hand of his own subordinate Scarus as a reward for Scarus's valor against Caesar at Actium.

Nor does Antony die for love of Cleopatra. Unable to stem the decline of his stature resulting from Caesar's increasing appropriation of his power, he proposes to defeat Caesar by the ultimate weapon: suicide. When, therefore, he commands Eros to kill him, it is to "strik[e] not me, 'tis Caesar thou defeat'st" (4.14.68). When Eros demurs, Antony drives the point home:

> Wouldst thou be windowed in great Rome and see
> Thy master thus with pleached arms, bending down
> His corrigible neck, his face subdued
> To penetrative shame, whilst the wheeled seat
> Of fortunate Caesar, drawn before him, branded
> His baseness that ensued? . . .
> Come, then, for with a wound I must be cured.
>
> (4.14.72–78)

His final thoughts are of Caesar, specifically the victory over Caesar that his death has achieved: "Not Caesar's valor hath o'erthrown Antony, / But Antony's hath triumphed on itself" (4.15.15–16).

More reprehensible from the standpoint of princeship, Antony contrives a war for the sole purpose of "stain[ing]" Caesar (3.4.26–27), notwithstanding the lives he will sacrifice in the process. Before the battle of Actium, moreover, he ignores Enobarbus's heavily corroborated counsel to fight Caesar by land, ignoring as well the counsel of the common soldier who sees more clearly than his leader the folly of engaging Caesar at sea; indifferent to the welfare of his men, Antony will fight Caesar at sea simply because Caesar has dared him to do so (3.7.30). The war is itself prompted by Caesar's disparagement of Antony's stature. Caesar, reports Antony,

> Spoke scantly of me; when perforce he could not
> But pay me terms of honor, cold and sickly
> He vented them, most narrow measure lent me;
> When the best hint was given him, he not took 't,
> Or did it from his teeth.
>
> (3.4.6–10)

Caesar defeats Antony precisely because he possesses those traits Antony lacks. When he responds to Antony's challenge, it is not to salve his honor, but because of Antony's injury to Octavia and the genuine threat to his power posed by Antony's aggression (3.6.82–84). Further, unlike Antony, Caesar is impervious to trivial insult—to words signifying "little" or "nothing" (2.2.36). In contrast to Antony who fights Caesar at sea simply because Caesar dared him to do so and who contrives a war in retaliation for Caesar's disparagement, Caesar declines both of Antony's challenges, refusing to let Antony's insults goad him into rashness:

> He calls me boy, and chides as he had power
> To beat me out of Egypt. My messenger
> He hath whipped with rods, dares me to personal combat,
> Caesar to Antony. Let the old ruffian know
> I have many other ways to die, meantime
> Laugh at his challenge.
>
> (4.1.1–6)

Yet with Antony Caesar has much in common, including a concept of greatness founded on appearances and on the dominion to which he single-mindedly aspires. What concerns him is the judgment of history, whose accolades he seeks to ensure by the demagogic tactic of manipulating the public eye and ear. To quote David Kaula, "The public image Caesar consistently tries to present is that of the just, conscientious ruler. Already in his opening words he is showing Lepidus how fair-minded he can be about Antony":[14] "You may see," he tells Lepidus, adducing a catalog of Antony's wrongs to support his claim, that "It is not Caesar's natural vice to hate / Our great competitor" (1.4.1–3). "[Y]ou shall see," he tells his subordinates, inviting them to his tent, "How hardly I was drawn into this war, / How calm and gentle I proceeded still / In all my writings. Go with me and see" (5.1.73–76). Aware that his power hinges on popular support, he enlists the same tactic of rhetorical manipulation Antony had used so effectively ten years earlier (a tactic Antony ironically now censures): he reads his will in public, presumably because, like his adoptive father's, it contains bequests beneficial to the people.

It is this superficial concept of greatness which motivates the play's final power struggle: that between Caesar and Cleopatra. Caesar views Cleopatra as his ultimate trophy. Hence the necessity of taking her alive: parading the captive legend before the public eye will furnish the ultimate testament to his greatness (5.1.65–66), for it will enable "the world [to] see / His nobleness well acted," which her death will preclude (5.2.43–45).[15]

Frustrating this plan, however, is Cleopatra's equally exalted and egotistical concept of greatness, to which her self-image, likewise predicated on conquest, is similarly tied. For Cleopatra, however, conquest entails sexual mastery, specifically mastery of the kings of the earth: Julius Caesar, "great Pompey" (1.5.32), and Antony (the list also potentially includes Octavius), all of whom enhance (and advance) her "majesty." Her supreme reward to the messenger bringing desirable news is giving him her hand to kiss, "a hand that kings / Have lipped" (2.5.29–30). To Caesar she was "A morsel for a monarch" (1.5.32). Her suicide is the ultimate testament to her "greatness," for it is an act "fitting for a princess / Descended of so many royal kings" (5.2.326–27).

Predictably, she employs messengers not in affairs of state but to solidify her sexual power: to convey love letters (1.5.79–81), to spy on Antony (1.3.2–5), to track Octavia (2.5.113–16, 3.3.7–36), and to beguile Caesar (3.13.73–78). As with Antony, rulership is literally a "sport," consisting in billiards, fortune-telling, and fishing, and in drinking mandragora to induce oblivion. For the common weal she cares not a jot; "Melt Egypt into Nile," she cries upon hearing of Antony's marriage to Octavia (2.5.79; see also 2.5.95–97), echoing Antony's parallel sentiments concerning Rome (1.1.35–36).

But her hold over the kings of the earth is not an end in itself; it is "inseparable from the power struggle for control of Egypt and the world, within which it originates and with which it always remains entangled."[16] Indeed, defeating Caesar would give her potential control of the Roman Empire. That such control is either contemplated or in progress is suggested by her expanding rulership over Antony's domains (3.6.8–11); by the proclaimed kingship of her sons and the assignment to them of "Great Media, Parthia, and Armenia . . . Syria, Cilicia, and Phoenicia" (3.6.14–16); by Antony's prophecy, already partially realized, that "All the East . . . shall call her mistress" (1.5.48–49); and by her request for "conquered Egypt" for her son (5.2.19). Following Antony's defeat, Cleopatra asks one thing of Caesar: Egypt's crown for her heirs (3.12.17–18). "[W]hatever real political power remains to her," therefore, "depends upon her hold over Antony." Witness her vow to behead Herod upon learning of Antony's marriage to Octavia, her sole female rival: "That Herod's head / I'll have; but how, when Antony is gone, / Through whom I might command it" (3.3.4–6).[17] It is Caesar's threat to her power and image, no less than her threat to Caesar's, that prompts their final contest.

That it is antipathy to Caesar rather than love of Antony that motivates her final actions is variously conveyed. Although Antony is dying, she denies, in quick succession, all three of his last requests. The reason for her refusal of his first request—that she come down so he can kiss her—is explicit: she recalls his prediction, following her flight at Actium, of Octavia's certain vengeance and Caesar's equally certain exhibition of her to the lowly plebeians, both of which will increase her rivals' luster and diminish hers:

> Dear my lord, pardon—I dare not,
> Lest I be taken. Not th' imperious show
> Of the full-fortuned Caesar ever shall
> Be brooched with me. If knife, drugs, serpents, have
> Edge, sting, or operation, I am safe.
> Your wife Octavia . . . shall acquire no honor
> Demuring upon me.
>
> (4.15.23–30)

She invokes, it should be noted, the dagger and serpents she will indeed use against herself when Caesar arrives to take her. Antony's next requests—that she give him some wine and let him "speak a little"—she also denies. "No," she interrupts him, "let me speak," then garrulously proceeds to denounce the "huswife Fortune" (4.15.44–46). "Hast thou no care of me?" (4.15.62) she cries as Antony expires, whereupon, declaring that "We have no friend" (4.15.95), she resolves to die.

But not before determining Caesar's intentions. Were it grief at Antony's death that prompts her resolve, she would have dispatched herself forthwith. Nor need she have waited for the loquacious bearer of figs; she already has a whole arsenal of death—"knife, drugs, serpents"—at her disposal. What most distresses her about Antony's demise is that there remains not a single potentate to advance her power; all have perished in the battle for dominion, including Antony, her last bulwark against Caesar. Hence the necessity of learning Caesar's plans concerning her. After Actium, she had seen the proverbial handwriting on the wall; since her political power depended on sexual mastery of the kings of the earth, she must seduce Caesar into letting her retain Egypt. She had therefore dispatched a messenger confessing his "greatness," submitting herself to his "might"—and requesting the crown of the Ptolemies for her heirs (3.12.16–18). Later she requests Egypt for her son (5.2.19). As Caesar's net tightens, she heightens her campaign of obsequiousness and flattery: "Say to great Caesar," she instructs the hapless Thidias,

> I kiss his conquering hand. Tell him I am prompt
> To lay my crown at 's feet, and there to kneel
> Till from his all-obeying breath I hear
> The doom of Egypt.
>
> (3.13.74–78)

The ruse buys time but not knowledge of Caesar's plans. She therefore sends a messenger to inquire into Caesar's "intents" so that, as she explains, playing on two levels of meaning, "she preparedly may frame herself / To th' way she's forced to" (5.1.54–56).

Caesar returns his own seductive message: he will treat her honorably and kindly (5.1.57–60). But Caesar is also buying time until he can seize her. Apart from contriving to tempt her with creature comforts and flattery, he returns no specific reply to her request lest "by some mortal stroke / She do defeat us" (5.1.64–65). For good measure, he sends his spy Proculeius to reassure her—and then to report back to him her response.

The entrance of Caesar's soldiers prompts her first attempt at suicide—with the dagger she had threatened to use should Caesar try to capture her. Another suicide resolve follows her disarming by Proculeius. Her reason—defeat of her rivals and preservation of her image—is explicit. "Know, sir," she tells Proculeius,

> that I
> Will not wait pinioned at your master's court,
> Nor once be chastised with the sober eye
> Of dull Octavia. Shall they hoist me up
> And show me to the shouting varletry
> Of censuring Rome? Rather a ditch in Egypt. . . .
>
> (5.2.51–56)

Dolabella arrives. To him she extols Antony's virtues—and then, cunningly determining that his compassion is sincere, queries him outright regarding Caesar's plans. Caesar will, Dolabella asserts, lead her in triumph.

Caesar himself enters, and the two arch-deceivers confront each other for the first time. Each seeks to outwit the other: Cleopatra through professed deference to Caesar's "greatness"; Caesar through equal deference to Cleopatra and with reassurance of honorable intent. But Cleopatra sees through Caesar's deceit: "He words me, girls, he words me" (5.2.191). The deceit is confirmed with the arrival of Dolabella, who gives her the information she seeks: within three days Caesar will seize her and her children. Again, the prospect of sullied "greatness"—of being reduced to a trull by the commoners she detests—appalls her:

> Now, Iras, what think'st thou?
> Thou an Egyptian puppet shall be shown
> In Rome as well as I. Mechanic slaves
> With greasy aprons, rules, and hammers shall
> Uplift us to the view. In their thick breaths,
> Rank of gross diet, shall we be enclouded
> And forced to drink their vapor. . . . Saucy lictors
> Will catch at us like strumpets, and scald rhymers
> Ballad us out o' tune. The quick comedians
> Extemporally will stage us and present

>   Our Alexandrian revels; Antony
>   Shall be brought drunken forth, and I shall see
>   Some squeaking Cleopatra boy my greatness
>   I' the posture of a whore.
>
>   (5.2.207–21)

Not a word about the fate of Egypt, or of her children, whom Caesar had threatened to kill should she take her life. What concerns her is vanquishing Caesar; and with Iras's reply that she will scratch out her own eyes before submitting to such disgrace, Cleopatra gleefully concurs: "Why, that's the way / To fool their preparation and to conquer / Their most absurd intents" (5.2.224–26). Suicide, she concludes, will keep her exalted image timelessly intact, for it "shackles accidents and bolts up change" (5.2.6). Hence her command to her attendants to "Show" her "like a queen" (note the irony of "like" and "show" and of the queen/quean pun). As she contemplates the basket of figs, she thinks upon Antony, not, however, in terms of reunion but of thwarting Caesar: "I see him rouse himself / To praise my noble act. I hear him mock / The luck of Caesar" (5.2.284–86). As she applies the asp to her breast, she never mentions her beloved; only her regret that the worm can't speak so that she might hear it "call great Caesar ass / Unpolicied!" (5.2.305–8). Lest the romantically inclined still impute her suicide to love, her motive is conceded by Caesar himself: "She leveled at our purposes and, being royal, / Took her own way" (5.2.336–37). The parallels with Antony are noteworthy: both lovers commit suicide to defeat Caesar, and the last thoughts of both are of having vanquished Caesar.

Nor does Cleopatra's lust for mastery end with Caesar's defeat; she seeks to control Antony even in death, attempting to expedite her demise in order to prevent Iras from reaching, and kissing, him first. The attempt, prefaced by her statement that "This proves me base" (5.2.300), ironically negates the ostensible nobility of her immediately preceding relegation of her earthly "elements" to "baser life" as she prepares to meet Antony. Further undercutting that nobility are her skewed crown (5.2.318), symbolic of the "quean" beneath the royal trappings; and the deadly kiss she bestows on Iras.

Her kiss kills because it is venomous; the ultimate testament to the kind of love she embodies, it is the culmination of her continuing identification with serpents, an identification rendered explicit in Antony's reference to her as "my serpent of old Nile" (1.5.26).[18]

The asp she suckles and which she terms her "baby" (5.2.309) is, metaphorically speaking, exactly that: the progeny of Eros and her adulterous "husband" (5.2.287), born of a woman with "aspic" in her "lips" (5.2.293)—a sense punningly reinforced by Lepidus's earlier comment to Antony: "*Your* serpent of Egypt is bred *now* of *your* mud by the operation of *your* sun" (2.7.26–27, emphasis added). We should relatedly note the poison constituting her metaphorical diet (1.5.27–28), the "poisoned hours" Antony has passed with her (2.2.96), and the poisoned shirt of Nessus she figuratively lays upon him (4.12.43).[19]

Amplifying the play's central metaphor of whorishness is the motif of marriage. There is Antony's adulterous union with Octavia, which additionally exemplifies the ephemeral marriage of policy characterizing amatory and political alliances alike. The uniting of the triumvirs against Pompey, for instance, is capped with an allusion to the marriage service: "That which combined us was most great," Lepidus reminds his subtextual "partners" or spouses, "and let not / A leaner action rend us" (2.2.23, 19–20).[20] The marriage motif likewise informs Caesar's reference to Antony as "my mate in empire" (5.1.43), whom he quickly forsakes; and the "jointing" of Fulvia and Lucius (1.2.96), who cease hostilities to unite against Caesar. Enobarbus's gloss on the triumvirs' union applies to almost every alliance in the play: "[I]f you borrow one another's love for the instant, you may, when you hear no more words of Pompey, return it again" (2.2.109–11).

The rulers' relationships with their subordinates are also framed in the rhetoric of marriage. Antony treats his men like handmaids—men he has, in Enobarbus's apt phrase, transformed to women (4.2.37). On the eve of Actium, he asks them to "[W]ait on me tonight" and to "make . . . much of me" (4.2.21–22). Again the words of the wedding service are invoked: he is not, he assures them, turning them away "but, like a master / Married to your good service, stay[s] till death" (4.2.31–32). This vow he forthwith breaks during the Battle of Actium, when he adulterously forsakes them to follow Cleopatra. The lovelessness of this "marriage" is again conveyed as the dying Antony futilely implores "him that loves me" to kill him. As his men opportunistically desert to Caesar, the phallic subtext underscores their adultery: "This sword," declares Dercetus, withdrawing the weapon from Antony's body, "but shown to Caesar, with this tidings, / Shall enter me with him" (4.14.116–17).[21] The marriage motif culminates in Cleopatra's projected union with her "husband" who, she envisions, will be as false in love in heaven as he was on earth (5.2.301–3).[22]

Only Enobarbus loves truly. Having had his counsel continually ignored, he defects out of desperation, not policy, and even then his love for Antony never flags. Emblematizing the nature of this love is the imagery surrounding his death, the counterpart of the deaths of the protagonists: "illuminated by the moon, the 'sovereign mistress of true melancholy' (4.9.15), [the scene] has the atmosphere of a lover dying for the sake of his beloved, even to the point of Enobarbus expiring with the name of Antony on his lips."[23] Like the bereaved lover of literary tradition, Enobarbus also dies of a broken heart. The scene is Shakespeare's invention.

In the play, then, suicide functions not as an act of love but as the ultimate weapon in the battle for control of the world. The point is underscored repeatedly, through the rhetoric of power struggle and conquest surrounding the lovers' deaths: Cleopatra dies to "conquer" Caesar's "intents" (5.2.225–26); Antony dies to "defeat" Caesar (4.14.68) and to ensure that "none but Antony" will "conquer Antony" (4.15.17–18); and Caesar asserts that suicide by Cleopatra will "defeat" him (5.1.65).

Although we can only conjecture why Shakespeare wrote *Antony and Cleopatra*, the play hints strongly at topical concerns. Few in Shakespeare's audience, least of all the king himself, would have failed to identify Octavius with James, an identification James zealously promoted from the outset. His coronation medal proclaimed him Caesar Augustus of Britain; his coronation banners, "Augustus Novus." Throughout his reign, poets and divines eulogized "our Augustus," analogizing, for instance, James's efforts to unite England, Scotland, and Wales to Caesar's reunification of the Empire, and James's treaty with Spain to Caesar's *pax Romana*.[24] Caesar's imperial ambitions and despotism further evoke James, in particular James's unsanctioned assumption by proclamation of the title of King of Great Britain, his quest for absolute power, and his belief that the king is the fount of, and above, the law.

But it is not only Caesar who figures James; it is also—and especially—Antony and Cleopatra, who embody the infamous licentiousness and decadence of James and his court. The lovers' neglect of rulership for "sport" (1.1.49) recalls James's neglect of statecraft for hunting, "year in and year out, for weeks and months on end," at his various country abodes.[25] James's chronic truancy caused many difficulties, including the frequent necessity of conducting government by correspondence—as it is in the play—and of leaving state management to his ministers and council[26] (compare Ventidius's uncertainty regarding what strategy to pursue "when him we serve's away" [3.1.15]). The emasculated Egyptian court, peopled by eunuchs and "pretty dimpled boys" (2.2.212), evokes James's homoerotic dalliances and suspected pederasty; his court as "a place of '. . . bawds, mimics and catimites [sic],' where debauchery was in fashion and practiced openly";[27] and the effeminacy characterizing the court itself: as one courtier put it, "the love the king shewed [his favorites] was as amorously convayed, as if he . . . thought them ladies; which I have seene Sommerset [Carr] and Buckingham labour to resemble in the effeminatenesse of their dressings; though in w[horish] lookes and wanton gestures, they exceeded any part of woman kind my conversation did ever cope withall"[28] (compare Enobarbus's statement that Antony transforms his men to women [4.2.37], Canidius's that "we are women's men" [3.7.71], and Antony's donning of Cleopatra's attire). Meanwhile, riot and excess reigned supreme; gambling orgies and epicurean feasts supplemented such pastimes as telling fortunes and concocting love potions and aphrodisiacs, which figured prominently in the court's amorous games[29] (compare 1.2.1–80). Amid all this were "A doting king playing with himself and his minions in public, young men of good families prostituting themselves to get ahead, [and] the peers and great ones of the realm falling down drunk, rioting, gambling, and whoring their substance away. Sneak thieves stole fortunes, petty knaves and upscale sluts traded in treason and poison, while virtue was made a laughingstock."[30]

The danger of such debauchery was not merely the sullying of king and court (Marlowe's *Edward II* and Shakespeare's *Richard II* suggest, among other things, the perils of sodomy in statecraft) but the ruin of the State. "Passion," as James Emerson Phillips writes, "and particularly sexual passion, was considered to have a devastating effect on the governing abilities of the ruler."[31] In addition, as already noted, a Platonic (and a Renaissance) axiom asserted that the State ethically imaged its ruler, a corrupt ruler fostering a corrupt State. As John Webster explains in *The Duchess of Malfi,*

> a Princes Court
> Is like a common Fountaine, whence should flow
> Pure silver-droppes in generall; But if't chance
> Some curs'd example poyson't neere the head,
> Death, and diseases through the whole land spread.
>
> (1.1.12–16)[32]

The play alludes to this concept again and again: in the sensual indolence of the people surrounding Cleopatra; in Canidius's conviction that their leader's unmanning has spread to his men (3.7.70–71);[33] in Antony's comment that his troops' cowardice reflects his own (3.11.7–8; see also 3.10.28–29); and in his anguished realization following Enobarbus's defection that his deeds have "Corrupted honest men" (4.5–17).

With its unity and defenses vitiated through the upheaval that morally diseased rule engenders, the State is vulnerable to overthrow from within and without. In *Lucrece,* faction enables Brutus to topple the monarchy; in *Caesar*, it leads to the burning of Rome. In *Coriolanus,* Antium, capitalizing on Rome's civil turmoil, prepares to attack Rome "in the heat of their division" (4.3.17); in *Antony and Cleopatra,* Pompey, capitalizing on the triumvirs' rift, plots to seize control of the Empire, itself rent by the faction and strife emblematic of its divided and embattled helm.

Whether Samuel Daniel's *Tragedy of Cleopatra* is topically slanted is uncertain (it predates Shakespeare's play by perhaps ten years). Its "moral," however, parallels Shakespeare's, Daniel articulating explicitly what Shakespeare implies. Addressing Egypt, the Chorus wonders why "those meanes that made thee great" could not prevent "confus'd Disorder" from supplanting law (1196–1200).[34] The fault, the Chorus decides, lies with

> the[m] that have the sterne in guiding,
> tis their fault that should prevent it. . . .
> We imitate the greater powres,
> The Princes manners fashion ours.

And:

> The wanton luxurie of Court,
> Did forme the people of like sort.
>
> (1210–15, 1228–29)

Specifically, Egypt's fall stems from Cleopatra's "disordred lust" (226). "Ryot" having wasted the country's strength, Caesar gained "easie entrance"; "And thus is Egypt servile rendred / to the insolent destroyer" (1239–45). "And so," concludes the Argument, "hereby came the race of the *Ptolomies* to be wholy extinct, and the flourishing rich kingdome of Egypt utterly overthrowne and subdued." The lesson for England is obvious.[35]

The concept of tyranny informing the play, then, closely adheres to that articulated by Plato. Encompassing every level of society, disordered love characterizes all of the play's alliances, with the protagonists its supreme exemplars. Reinforcing the theme of disordered love is the motif of whorishness. Lawless and licentious, consumed in "feasts . . . and revellings and courtezans," Antony is Plato's quintessential tyrannic man. Like such a man, he passes his life "combating with other men," growing "more jealous, more faithless, more unjust, [and] more friendless": ultimately, everyone deserts him, including his troops and the devoted Enobarbus. The faithlessness characterizing his marital alliances also defines his relations with his men, whom he adulterously forsakes on the field of battle. As with Plato's tyrant, debauchery eventuates in emasculation and in the enslavement manifested in volitional paralysis: in his final moments, the once-peerless warrior lies utterly helpless and must be ignominiously hoisted aloft by a group of women. Disordered love likewise drives the rivalry of the principals: all pursue power for self-gratification and all sacrifice the State to personal gain, ends wholly inconsistent with felicitous rule. Thus the law of lust or eros, which governs the soul of the tyrannical man, similarly governs the dictatorial state, whorishness being the defining attribute of both. In the State as in the soul, the result is complete injustice. It is perhaps not coincidental that almost all the traits characterizing the tyrannical man in this play also characterized James.

Not one ruler in the play is fit to govern, including Caesar, who, while more politically astute than the others, is as morally void. Indeed, his professed justice and compassion are belied throughout: in his above-noted lawlessness (3.12.31–33), in his contempt for the masses (1.4.44–47), in his pawning of Octavia, in his deposing of Lepidus, in his hanging of Alexas, and in his deception, or attempted deception, of every politically significant character in the play.[36] Caesar and Antony are merely two extremes of the same moral spectrum; if Antony embodies passion without reason, Caesar embodies reason without passion, lacking in consequence the pity, mercy, and humaneness on which justice depends.[37] His quest for power is as self-serving as that of the others, and as divorced from the legitimate aims of rule. This conception of Octavius is not unique to Shakespeare; it accords with views contained in Elizabethan histories of Rome. As Robert Kalmey points out, Octavius is considered an "ideal prince *only after* he is crowned Emperor in Rome after the defeat of Antony; *before* this precise occasion, the same Elizabethan histories of Rome characterize Octavius as a vicious tyrant who foments bloody civil war and a reign of terror solely for his personal gain." Thus, as a triumvir, "Octavius is revealed ... as a pernicious demagogue" and "an ambitious and overreaching tyrant."[38]

The end of the play heralds a new millennium, in which the world "Shall bear the olive freely" (4.6.6–7). But peace is imminent through no virtue of the victor, who possesses the world by conquest and not by right;[39] it is imminent owing to the destruction of every rival for supremacy; the consequent cessation of five centuries of civil strife; and the emergence of the lone survivor as "Sole sir o' the world" (5.2.119), whose trophy is the war-torn, spiritual wasteland that is Rome.

We are reminded of the account of Tacitus, which at least some contemporary playgoers probably would have recalled:

> The violent deaths of Brutus and Cassius left no Republican forces in the field. Defeat came to Sextus Pompeius in Sicily, Lepidus was dropped, Antony killed. So even the Caesarian party had no leader left except the 'Caesar' himself, Octavian. . . . Indeed, he attracted everybody's goodwill by the enjoyable gift of peace. Then he gradually . . . absorbed the functions of the senate, the officials, and even the law. Opposition did not exist. War or judicial murder had disposed of all men of spirit.[40]

6

Titus Andronicus

CRITICS HAVE LONG REMARKED THE BEWILDERING POLITICAL LANDscape of *Titus Andronicus*. Although the play is ostensibly set in the fourth century A.D., its government finds no basis in Roman history. As Jonathan Bate queries, "[I]s the state a commonwealth or a monarchy, is succession based on election or heredity?"[1] The ambiguity springs from the play's constitutional hodgepodge: Saturninus claims the crown on grounds of primogeniture, while the younger Bassianus, repudiating primogeniture for desert, argues for election; and both brothers urge the use of arms to enforce their claim. Titus, meanwhile, elected emperor "by common voice" (1.1.21), declines the office on grounds of age and names Saturninus instead, who is accorded the requisite popular ratification. The opening scene thus posits four conflicting modes of succession: primogeniture, election, nomination, and force of arms. As T. J. B. Spencer famously remarked, "It is not so much that any particular set of political institutions is assumed in *Titus*, but rather that it includes *all* the political institutions that Rome ever had."[2]

Compounding the problem are the play's theological mélange, which includes pagan, Roman Catholic, and Reformation elements —blood sacrifice and a ruined monastery, among others—and the charges of artistic incompetence the play continues to provoke. T. S. Eliot, for instance, deploring the "wantonness" and "irrelevance" of its crimes, pronounced it "one of the stupidest and most uninspired plays ever written."[3] Yet *Titus* was immensely popular on the Elizabethan stage, doing more than perhaps any other play to establish Shakespeare's dramatic reputation.[4] The question, given its seeming flaws, is why.

An answer is suggested by Bate:

> The most urgent question facing England in the 1590s was the succession to the unmarried and childless Elizabeth, and in particular the preservation of the Protestant nation against the possibility of another counter-Reformation. . . . Arguments about the basis on which the succession should be decided—heredity, election, desert—were widespread, as was fear of tyranny and foreign invasion. All this suggests that the issue of succession and the mixed nature of Roman government explored in the first act of the play would have had strong contemporary overtones. The descent into imperial tyranny could well have looked like a warning as to what might happen once Astraea, the virgin Queen, had left the earth.[5]

Titus, I will argue, ponders the implications of the Elizabethan succession crisis within the context of Platonic constitutional theory: encapsulating a political decline analogous to that encompassed by the other four works, the play moves from monarchy to democracy to tyranny, a decline deriving from the monarchic collapse incurred by lack of a successor. *Titus*, however, envisages the most horrific consequences of all: the decline culminates in rulership by a foreign foe, in the destruction and dynastic extinction of the rightful successors, in the descent of the realm into barbarism, and in the utter devastation of the state.

The Unsettled Succession

Between 1589 and 1595, when *Titus Andronicus* is commonly supposed to have been written, two interrelated crises dominated the national consciousness: the unsettled succession and the enmity between England and Spain. The dangers of an unsettled succession were many: a power struggle between contenders was likely, which could bring schism, civil upheaval, and war. There were the attendant dangers of sedition, from sources both at home and abroad; of insurrection; and of a political assassination or coup. Above all loomed the threat of another Armada, which could doom the Protestant succession and lead to England's subjugation by Spain. Exacerbating this danger were the Jesuits, who championed England's forcible conversion by Spain as well as the possibility that a Spanish landing would be supported by a sizable number of English Catholics.[6]

At the heart of the succession crisis was the uncertainty about what the determining principle of succession should be. Politically, writes Howard Nenner, James VI was the most likely successor,

> but as a constitutional matter it was far from certain whether he had the only right, or even the best right, to follow Elizabeth to the throne. There was simply no contemporary agreement as to whether the crown ought to pass automatically at the death of Elizabeth to the next in the hereditary line; whether the next in the hereditary line might be passed over because of a 'legal' incapacity to rule; whether the next monarch ought to be determined in parliament; or whether the queen should be exhorted in the waning days of her life to nominate and determine her own successor....
> ... The experience of history, even when limited to English precedents, offered little promise of resolution, because it afforded justification for every hypothesis that had been advanced. It seemed that the prince could succeed to his right by heredity, by election, by nomination of his predecessor, or by conquest. These were the four broad categories of possibility, and on the basis of one or more of them a new king would claim his throne.[7]

Heredity was considered the most desirable alternative, because it promised the greatest political stability. The successor was known in advance, thus foreclosing dispute; and it afforded unbroken governmental transition, precluding the judicial and civil disruption an interregnum virtually assured. Heredity, nevertheless, contained drawbacks. What if the next in blood was Catholic—like Elizabeth's once-potential successor, Mary Stuart—which, given Mary's liaison with Philip of Spain, would result in a Catholic successor and possible subjection to Spain?

Election, too, posed problems. Particularly in the case of Elizabeth, who refused to address the issue of succession, some sort of posthumous election seemed likely. This would result in an interregnum and in the upheaval attending the cessation of Parliament's authority on the sovereign's death. Election, moreover, was subject to the dangers of ambition, contention, and sedition since there were no historically established rules or procedures guaranteeing acceptance of the elected contender by the rejected claimants. Thus in elective kingdoms, the Elizabethan historian Sir Thomas Craig had observed, "all things lie open to rapine and pillaging," since "men stick at nothing when they aim at sovereignty and a crown."[8]

As for nomination, Mary's demise made likely the reversion of England's crown to her son James. James, however, was an alien and was therefore barred from succeeding by English common law. As discussed below, he was also prevented by Henry VIII's will.

Absent an agreement "on the critically important question of how the right to succeed Elizabeth was to be determined—whether by some principle of heredity, by Henry VIII's will, by an eleventh-hour designation by the queen, or by an equally belated act of parliament—there would be the dangerous possibility of the queen's dying without a known and certain successor, and of a determination having to be made by force of arms." Such was, in fact, anticipated: as Elizabeth lay dying, the navy stood poised against foreign invasion, "while every county, and especially London, was alerted to the possibility of civil unrest."[9]

Henry VIII's Will

Henry VIII—like many Elizabethans—believed that the dynastic uncertainties attending monarchic succession had been the fountainhead of England's civil wars. It was largely to preclude such uncertainties that Henry, in 1546, composed his last will, in which he laid down the principles calculated to assure the succession of his line. Anticipating the possible heirlessness of his issue, Henry relegated the succession to the Suffolk descendants of the younger of his sisters, Mary, thereby disqualifying the Stuart line of her elder sister Margaret. Thus the will at once invalidated any Stuart claim to the crown and the law of primogeniture on which that claim was likely to be based. These principles came to comprise what William Carroll calls "the very bedrock of monarchical right." Paradoxically, however, they only succeeded in muddying the waters, "[t]he history of claims of sovereign power and right in the century and a half between Henry VIII and Charles I" being fraught with controversy and confusion over the will's terms.[10]

To Stuart polemicists—which included most English Catholics, who had placed their hopes for a Catholic successor in the Queen of Scots—the law of primogeniture was paramount; Suffolk polemicists, conversely, "put their faith in Henry VIII and used the will as their standard in the succession battle."[11] The Suffolk and Stuart cases were accordingly well known,[12] Robert Parsons, for instance, invoking Henry VIII's will to prove invalid James's claim to the throne.[13]

These issues, I will argue, underlie *Titus Andronicus*. The play explores the implications of a Stuart or analogous successor, implications that include a Catholic foreigner on the English throne, the establishment of an alien ruling dynasty, and England's subjection to Scotland and Spain.

The Queen of Scots

In the last decades of Elizabeth's reign, England's political crisis intensified in the face of what appeared to be an international Catholic conspiracy against Elizabeth and the Protestant Succession. To quote Florence Sandler,

> The focus of the conspiracy, both in her life and death, was the Catholic Queen of Scots. From the time of her arrival in England in 1568 and her virtual imprisonment by Elizabeth's orders, Mary's claim to succeed to the English throne became increasingly a religious question, and a *cause célèbre* for the Counter Reformation in its drive against Protestantism. Her more impatient followers were not content to let the Protestant Queen live out her reign. The Rebellion of the Northern Earls, with a plan to put the Queen of Scots upon the throne, proved to be only the first of a series of popish plots for insurrection or assassination, and it provoked the papal bull, *Regnans in Excelsis* (1570), excommunicating Elizabeth and absolving her subjects from their allegiance in order to pave the way for Mary's accession.[14]

Mary's execution in 1587 merely rechanneled the threat she posed. Owing to James's apostasy, Mary, shortly before her death, had willed the crown and committed the Catholic cause to Philip of Spain. Lending a semblance of legitimacy to this transfer of right was Philip's distant descent from Edward III, theoretically enabling him to assert a claim to the crown (which he actually intended for his daughter Isabella) and buttressing his claim to suzerainty over England asserted more than twenty years before—a claim sanctioned by Popes Paul IV, Pius IV, and Gregory XIII. Philip, it was rightly suspected, would seek to enforce this claim by use of arms and would look to Elizabeth's Catholic subjects for support. It was suspected, too, in light of the failed Armada, that Spain was conspiring to subvert Scotland in order to gain military access to England, the suspected collusion exacerbating the already deep antipathy of England towards Scotland.[15]

Nor did the possibility of a Stuart succession cease with Mary's demise; it would become concentrated in James, whose pursuit of the crown long antedated his mother's death. Although James insisted, on grounds of heredity, that his right to the crown was indefeasible, his professed Protestantism, which had made him the most appealing contender, nevertheless remained suspect or unassured. In 1589, he had aroused suspicion by his lenient treatment of two Roman Catholic earls who, the English government discovered, had been in contact with Spain. In 1592, these same earls were implicated in the matter of the "Spanish Blanks," a secret plan for Spain's invasion of England. James, it was suspected, not only knew of the plan but was considering converting to Catholicism and enlisting Spanish aid himself in order to press his claim to the English crown.[16] Thanks to James's double-dealing, Rome had always harbored hopes of his conversion, or of a Catholic era under his reign.[17] Thus, notwithstanding Mary's demise, her claim "remained as [the] burning issue" up to Elizabeth's death.[18]

The other factor militating against James was his Scots birth. To a majority of English, Scotland was a foreign nation, violent, treacherous, and barbaric, a view buttressed by such contemporary English historians as Holinshed and William of Newberry; hence their aversion to union with this northern neighbor.[19] As opposed, however, to Suffolk polemicists, who relied on the common law to bar a Stuart from succeeding, Stuart polemicists relied on the argument, advanced by such lawyers as Plowden, that the crown is a perpetual corporation, and therefore the issue of foreign birth did not apply. Plowden further maintained that the crown not only rendered a foreign claimant English, but a king's foreign wife as well.[20]

These issues gave rise to a spate of plays pondering the implications of a foreigner on the English throne. Two such plays, Marie Axton persuasively argues, are George Peele's *Edward I* and Robert Greene's *Friar Bacon and Friar Bungay*; both address the specter of a Spanish Infanta at England's helm, and "the question of the crown's power to transform Edward I's Spanish wife into an English Queen."[21] Thomas Kyd's *Spanish Tragedy* concerns the validity of Spain's claim to the English throne. Another play exploring the issue of foreign rule is the anonymous *Locrine*. The work concerns "Brute's eldest son who, after becoming supreme ruler of the British Isles, defeats a Scythian invasion only to fall in love with the invaders' foreign queen," with disastrous political consequences.[22] The resemblances to *Titus* are noteworthy. *Titus* additionally raises the issue of the Crown's capacity for naturalization: alluding to the concept of crown-as-corporation, Tamora, proclaimed Empress of Rome upon wedding Saturninus, declares herself "incorporate in Rome, / A Roman now adopted happily" (1.1.463–64).

It is against this background that *Titus Andronicus* will be studied. The play opens on a "headless Rome" (1.1.186), a metaphor at once emblematic of Rome's kinglessness and a prefiguration of the decapitations and other dismemberments that will image the rapine of the larger body politic. In progress is a turbulent interregnum following upon the recent death of Rome's king:[23] an unsettled succession has engendered a bitter factional, and fraternal, contest for the crown along with the threat of civil war as each brother exhorts his followers to back him with arms (1.1.2–4, 17). The situation has obvious affinities with both England's succession crisis and the controversy surrounding Henry VIII's will: Saturninus, the elder son of the late emperor/king, who bases his claim to the crown on primogeniture, evokes the Stuart (and Catholic) polemicists, who championed the descendants of the elder sister of Henry VIII; Bassianus, the younger son, who pleads for election on the ground that he is more deserving, evokes the Suffolk (and Protestant) polemicists, who repudiated primogeniture in favor of the "worthier" descendants of the younger sister. At least one scholar infers that Shakespeare would have favored primogeniture,[24] yet the consequences of Titus's choice of Saturninus—consequences that include tyranny, rape, murder, and the ruin of the state—strongly suggest otherwise.

The Roman Catholicism with which Titus is thus identified is augmented by the allusions and rituals surrounding the Andronici. It is generally assumed that "Pius," Titus's surname (1.1.23), alludes to Virgil's Pius Aeneas in conjunction with the play's Troy motif. But the name also evokes Pius V, whose infamous bull—excommunicating Elizabeth, absolving her subjects from their allegiance, and encouraging her deposition and assassination—was the most significant event of Elizabeth's reign; from that "cursed bull," according to the Calendar of State Papers, "sprung all the rebellions, treasons, and devilish practices since attempted" against England.[25] To quote A. O. Meyer, "No event in English history, not even the Gunpowder Plot, produced so deep and enduring an effect on England's attitude to the catholic church. . . . Englishmen never forgot their queen's excommunication," and the bull influenced the government's Catholic policy for the rest of her reign.[26]

There is also the reference to Lucius's "popish tricks and ceremonies" (5.1.76). One of these "ceremonies" (the word could not have failed to evoke the popish "idle ceremonies" that the Reformers denounced and that were a staple target of Protestant fulminations) is the ritual sacrifice of Alarbus (indeed initiated by Lucius), which contains marked affinities with the Mass. Condemned as blasphemous in Article 31 of the Church of England's Thirty-Nine Articles of Religion, the Mass was viewed by Protestants as a blood or propitiary sacrifice, idolatrous and cannibalistic. Thus Thomas Becon, in a characteristic polemical epithet, labels Catholics "bloody sacrificers." As Becon explains, all bloody sacrifices ceased with Christ; Catholics, however, take upon them "to sacrifice the Son of God, and to make him meat." "Christ spake spiritually of eating with faith," asserts John Jewel, but Catholics "under[stand] grossly of eating with the teeth; as though they should swallow down his flesh into their bodies, as other meats."[27] Like this "sacrifice" of Christ, that of Alarbus is necessary to benefit the living and the dead: "That so the shadows be not unappeased, / Nor we disturbed with prodigies on earth." Titus's unburied sons, whose souls still hover on the banks of Styx, can then "rest" "[i]n peace" and quiet (1.1.100–1, 88, 150–56). To these elements may be compared those of the Mass, which, like Titus's words over the tomb of his slain sons (1.1.90–95, 150–56), was a prayer for the dead: "Take, O holy Trinity, this oblation [i.e., the bread and wine putatively constituting the body of Christ], which I, unworthy sinner, offer . . . for the salvation of the living, and for the rest or quietness of all the faithful that are dead."[28] Also like the Mass, the sacrifice of Alarbus is propitiary: it is performed to "appease" the "shadows" (1.1.100) and the ghosts of Titus's sons. "Many significations have the papists invented for . . . [the Eucharistic] cake," writes Becon; among them "a sacrifice propitiary for the sins of the people that be living in this world" and "a satisfactory sacrifice for the souls that lie miserably puling in the hot fire of purgatory, to deliver them from the bitter pains and grievous torments that they there suffer."[29] Analogous are Titus's "unburied" sons who, pending a sacrifice, remain stranded "on the dreadful shore of Styx" (1.1.88), their suffering and locale corresponding to the suffering in the Catholic "underworld" of Purgatory. In both cases, this interim of torment is preliminary to the soul's transfer to its final abode; in the classical realm, Hades; in the Catholic, heaven. Also noteworthy is Titus's statement that the sacrifice is "religiously" necessary (1.1.124), and Lucius's assurance that "we have performed / Our Roman rites" (1.1.142–43). What the ritual thus suggests is a parody of the Roman Catholic Mass, a ritual that even the barbarous Tamora condemns as "cruel, irreligious piety" (1.1.130). This equating of heathen and Catholic ritual also evokes a precept of Protestant polemics: that in its ceremony, idolatry, and superstition, Roman Catholicism was a form of paganism.[30]

The device of blood sacrifice to satirize the Mass was not unique to Shakespeare. Spenser's Geryoneo, who figures both Philip of Spain and the Spanish Inquisition, erects in his "Church" (*FQ* 5.11.19) an idolatrous altar; here he offers "in sinfull sacrifice / The flesh of men," "powring forth their bloud in brutishe wize" (5.10.28), along with which the victims are tortured and "burnt in flame" (5.11.19; compare the burning of the dismembered and disemboweled Alarbus [1.1.127–29, 143–44]).

A further parody of the Mass resides in the "feast" Titus prepares for Tamora, which centers on the alleged cannibalism attaching to the Catholic doctrine of transubstantiation. The centerpiece of this "banquet" is a pie, its crust comprised not of flour and water but of the blood (or "liquor" [5.2.199]) and pulverized bones of Tamora's sons. The crust encloses the sons' heads. This pastry corresponds to the "cake," as the Eucharistic wafer was synonymously termed; the "liquor" or blood corresponds to the wine. Further, as Bate suggests, Titus's earlier command to Lavinia to "Receive the blood" as he slits his victims' throats (5.2.197) recalls, and parodies, the language of the holy Eucharist.[31] Also, papal decree had designated the Church of Rome as "mother." The name "Holy Mother Church" reflected the Catholic belief in the Virgin Mary as maternal intercessor between the sinner and Christ, a concept Protestants, who rejected mediation, condemned. *The Faerie Queene* contains one of the more famous parodies of the concept: following the dismemberment of the monster Errour, who figures the Roman Church as unholy mother, her brood "devours her body and blood in a lurid travesty of transubstantiation and the Mass."[32] Similarly, Tamora's consumption of the pie—"Eating the flesh that she herself hath bred" (5.3.62)—becomes a literal parody of eating the Son, by the whorish and "unhallowed dam" (5.2.190) who, I will argue, figures papal Rome and its Church.

In sum, then, the succession crisis on which the play opens, Titus's insistence on primogeniture to resolve it, and the allusions and ceremonies that define the Andronici strongly hint at the dynasty's association with Roman Catholicism and Stuart polemics—an association furthered by the subtextual papistry of the contender to whom Titus awards the crown.

Saturninus's Catholicism is variously implied. He invokes "priest and holy water" (1.1.324), the latter another example of popish ceremony. His administration of "justice" contains popish overtones: he promises to remit the execution of Titus's two sons, falsely charged with the murder of Bassianus, if one of the Andronici sends him a severed hand: "And that shall be the ransom for their fault" (3.1.156). The promise, including the language surrounding it ("pardon," "ransom," "redeem," "grace," "merited," "purchased," "bought"), hints at the Theology of Indulgences, "the remission of temporal [as opposed to eternal] punishment for sin, in response to certain prayers or good works" by means of a "treasury of merits" which Church authority dispenses,[33] a practice condemned by Protestants on the ground that only Christ's merits could save the sinner; while the commercial language ("purchased," "bought") additionally suggests the blasphemous practice of selling pardons. Protestants, moreover, utterly denied the efficacy of works in the remission of sin. Gallows humor follows Saturninus's offer as the Andronici vie for the privilege of chopping off a hand, a parodic "good work" that will "purchase" the remission of Titus's sons' "punishment" for their "sin." Reflecting the absurdity of the salvational efficacy of works as well as the true nature of papal "justice," Saturninus's promise is predictably a hoax, the emperor gleefully returning Titus's hand with the severed heads of his sons.

Titus, instructing the Clown on how to obtain "justice" at the emperor's hands, tells him to convey to Saturninus a "supplication," which refers to Titus's written "oration" (4.3.105, 95) while playing on the religious nuances of the word. The Clown must act "like an humble suppliant"; "And when you come to him, at the first approach you must kneel, then kiss his foot, then deliver up your pigeons, and then look for your reward" (4.3.113, 105–8; see also

1.1.473–74, 481). A further satire on the salvational efficacy of works (the Clown's "reward" for his gift is hanging), this depiction of the emperor evokes a staple of Protestant polemics. The Geneva Bible glosses Rev. 14.15—". . . worship [of] the image of the beast"—as, being required to "Receive the ordinances & decrees of the seat of Rome, & to kisse the vilens fote." This ritual became one of the prime significations of the Pope's blasphemous and idolatrous pride; as John Jewel declares,

> [I]t is not for nought that St Gregory saith: . . . "The king of pride is even at hand." In the pope's own book of the ceremonies of Rome, it is written thus: . . . "The emperor elect, . . . when he cometh to the foot of the pope's throne, he kneeleth down. . . [; and] when he cometh unto the pope's feet, he kisseth them devoutly." . . . Likewise . . . "The empress being crowned immediately kisseth the pope's foot." . . . Thus may the pope call himself "Lord of lords, King of kings." . . . [T]he pope suffereth the faithful to worship him, and to fall down before him, and to kiss his feet; which things the angel of God would not suffer St John the evangelist to do unto him.[34]

Edwin Sandys likewise denounces the "beastly pride" of the pope, who "compelleth princes to cast themselves down before him, and to kiss his filthy feet."[35] The concept goes back at least as far as Luther's *Passional Christi und Antichristi* (1521), in which a picture of Christ washing the feet of his disciples is countered by one of the Pope "allowing his feet to be kissed by secular rulers. The caption cites the Canon Law on the kissing of the Pope's feet, and explains: 'The Pope takes it upon himself to imitate certain tyrants and heathen princes, who offered their feet to be kissed by the people.'"[36]

Like that of "Pius," Tamora's name appears to be Shakespeare's invention (she is "Attava" in *The History of Titus Andronicus*, an anonymous prose tale generally believed to be either a copy or a close derivative of Shakespeare's nonextant original source). J. C. Maxwell conjectures that "Tamora may recall Tomyris, queen of the Massagetae, . . . who revenged her son's death on the Persian king Cyrus"; Bate, that her name fuses *amor* (her sexual love) with its object, the Moor.[37] I wish to posit a further, complementary possibility: that "Tamora" conflates *amor* (or, spelled backwards, *roma*) and *Mary*, linking her to both Rome and the Queen of Scots. To the Protestant, Rome was the great spiritual harlot, the Whore of Babylon depicted in Revelation. As Thomas Rogers declared, "If ye spell

Roma backward . . . ye shall find it to be Amor: love in this prodigious [i.e., perverted] kind," a sentiment he punctuates with some verse: "At Rome the harlot has a better life / Than she that is a Roman's wife."[38] When vocalized, "Tamora Queen of Goths" could, to Shakespeare's topically sensitive audience, easily evoke "Mary Queen of Scots." The Scots/Goths equation is augmented by the almost identical names of the inhabitants' countries (Scotland/Gotland) and by Shakespeare's frequent elision of *s* and *g*, which would have rendered "Goth" and "Scot" vocally similar or identical, e.g., "barbarou*s* Goths" (1.1.28), "traitorou*s* Goths" (4.1.95), and "Lasciviou*s* Goth" (2.3.110). The last is applied expressly to Tamora (lasciviousness was, according to Mary's detractors, a salient attribute of the Scots queen).

Particularly to Protestants, Tamora would have evoked Mary in additional ways: in her whorishness and adultery, in her murderer-paramour, in her displacement of and collusion in the destruction of the rightful female heir to the throne, and in her league with another barbarous foreigner for the rack of the nation holding her captive. She is also (like Mary) the queen of a northern, putatively uncivilized realm additionally resembling Scotland in its warrior culture and in the epithets, stereotypically applied to Scotland, that define the Goths: "barbarous" (1.1.28), "traitorous" (4.1.95), and "warlike" (2.1.61, 4.4.110, 5.2.113).

Tamora is a variant of Spenser's Duessa, a personification of the Roman church in general and of the Queen of Scots in particular.[39] Specifically, she figures the threat that Mary both alive and dead posed throughout Elizabeth's reign. Protestants commonly viewed the Scottish queen as a latter-day embodiment of that "stinking strumpet," the Whore of Babylon,[40] "or, as she was called in the English Parliament, a 'professed member of Antichrist.'"[41] The moral opposition between Lavinia and Tamora, sister-in-law rivals for the throne, carries overtones of Protestant apocalyptic discourse as derived from John Bale's *Image of Both Churches* (1548) and elaborated in John Foxe's *Acts and Monuments.* Central was its antithesis between the True, Protestant Church and the False, Roman one, or, alternatively, between Jerusalem and Babylon, or between their personifications, the Bride and the Whore. Initially epitomizing this antithesis was the struggle between the two royal sisters for the seat of power: "Catholic Mary, allied with Spain and Rome, with the blood of the saints upon her skirts; Protestant Elizabeth held in captivity during her sister's reign." This concept, at the heart of the new Protestant historiography and a mainstay of Protestant polemics, was deployed particularly during Elizabeth's last two decades, in the face of the heightened papal onslaught against the Protestant Succession.[42] The Queen of Scots became another manifestation of the Whore, being so portrayed, for instance, by Spenser in the figure of Duessa. Spenser employs the concept of the Two Churches in his Legend of Holiness, in which Una, the Bride, personifies the true, Protestant Church, and Duessa, the harlot, the false Roman one. Conversely, "As Protestant Queen and Governor of the Church, Elizabeth might . . . be seen as the apocalyptic Bride, representing in her virginity the return of the True Church ('A pure virgin, spotted as yet with no idolatry', as John Jewel, following Augustine, described the Primitive Church)."[43]

The opposition between Una and Duessa warrants comparison with Lavinia and Tamora. Lavinia, a synecdoche for England (and possibly a figuration of Elizabeth), is the virginal bride, the legitimate betrothed of Protestantism, figured in Bassianus; Tamora, a figuration of the Babylonian Whore, embodies what Sandler terms "the papalist complex of apostasy and sexual perversion which had obfuscated the True Protestant Faith and the doctrine of Chaste Marriage"[44] here represented by Lavinia and Bassianus. Further suggesting this nexus are the Christlike sanctity and purity with which Bassianus is imbued. He lies in the pit like "a slaughtered lamb" (2.3.223). In contrast to Aaron and Tamora, who are associated with darkness throughout (even down to Aaron's blackness, symbolic of the evil he embodies), Bassianus is light-giving even in death: he wears "A precious ring that lightens all this hole" (2.3.227), double entendres additionally denoting his virginity. The attribute of virginity is reinforced by his likeness to Pyramus "When he by night lay bathed in maiden blood" (2.3.232), indicative of Bassianus's figurative rape by Tamora's agents. Further Christlike overtones reside in the elder tree (2.3.272)—the species, according to legend, on which Judas hanged himself—that marks Bassianus's grave.[45]

Aaron

As the enmity between England and Spain escalated into war, the conflict became, for both sides, tantamount to a religious crusade.

The effect in England was the heightened politicization of apocalyptic thought. The defeat of the Armada in particular perpetuated the conviction that England was God's elect nation and Spain the epitome of evil. "Commentators made the point that bloodthirstiness and lust were notoriously the marks of Antichrist and the Babylonian Whore," while "The Puritan minister Thomas Rogers showed that Spain was the greatest protector of the Roman 'brothel house.'"[46]

Is this "illicit" alliance, and the bloodthirstiness and lust of its partners, figured in the play? Tamora, we are told, is "with the lion deeply . . . in league" (4.1.100). The lion is Aaron, another barbarous foreigner, who holds Tamora "in amorous chains" (2.1.15), dominates the partnership, and (aside from Titus) devises most of the play's atrocities: the killing of Bassianus and of Titus's sons, the axing of Titus's hand, and the rape of Lavinia.[47] In the prose tale, in contrast, the Queen is the main perpetrator of the crimes, the Moor serving as her "main Engine to bring about her Devilish Designs."[48] Also absent from the story are Aaron's political ambitions, his catalogue of atrocities (5.1.63–65, 104–42), and his repeated demonization: in the play, he is "the incarnate devil" (5.1.40), "fiendlike" (5.1.45), and "misbelieving" (5.3.143), all traits (and epithets) applied to the papal Antichrist. While it can be argued that these features are indebted to Christopher Marlowe's Barabas, Aaron's composite character clearly is not. Nor is the bulk of it indebted to the prose tale.

One of the more striking departures from the nameless Moor of the prose tale is Aaron's politicization. His interest in Tamora is not venereal but political: through her he will "mount aloft," wear "pearl and gold," and effect the wreck of the Emperor and Rome (2.3.30–39, 2.1.12–24). He also has dynastic aspirations: hence his scheme to exchange his child for the fair one of a Moorish countryman, the white child to "be receivèd for the Emperor's heir, / And substituted in the place of mine" (4.2.160–61). (Aaron's child, we are reminded, is "of royal blood" and Aaron's "firstborn son and heir" [5.1.49, 4.2.93; see also 5.1.28–30], a variation of the primogeniture motif—also Shakespeare's addition—that suffuses the play.) This offspring is harbored in "a ruinous monastery" (5.1.21), a reminder of the dissolution of the monasteries, which was one of the most significant consequences of England's break with Rome. The terms applied to the child—"tadpole" and "loathsome . . . toad"

(4.2.86, 68)—evoke the "loathly frogs and toades" emitted by Spenser's Errour (*FQ* 1.1.20), which allude to the "uncleane spirits like frogges" emitted from the mouth of the Babylonian Whore's Beast (i.e., papal Rome) in Rev. 16.13.[49] As John King points out, amphibians were traditionally associated with heresy, Bale, for instance, identifying frogs with Roman Catholic practices.[50] Aaron's scheme to replace his "slavish weeds" with attire of "pearl and gold" (2.1.18–19) further recalls the Babylonian Whore of Revelation, who is bedecked "with golde and . . . pearles" (Rev. 17.4). Thus Spenser's Duessa, who figures the Whore of Babylon or Roman Church, wears "scarlot red, / Purfled with gold and pearle" while Britomart, who figures Elizabeth/England, despises gold and pearl (*FQ* 1.2.13, 3.4.18).

Shakespeare has also heightened Aaron's crimes. Aaron's catalogue of atrocities—murders, rapes, massacres, and the mutilation of corpses, to name but a few—contains parallels with the atrocities of the Spanish Inquisition and, in 1576, of the Spanish Fury in the Netherlands, in which women were raped, corpses mutilated, and thousands of citizens maniacally murdered—atrocities of which all Englishmen were aware.[51] By the 1580s, accordingly, Spanish aggression had become the overriding English concern and force the dominant theme. "Especially in the wake of the [Armada]," writes Richard Mallette, "commentators concentrate on the military power of 'the Romish beast and his company,' who 'prepare themselues with mighty forces, threatening great terrour vnto this land . . .'"; and "[a]nticipation of Spanish hostility, not to mention actual examples of it, is of the greatest urgency in the last two decades of the Elizabethan reign.[52] This dual threat of invasion and rapine imbued English apocalyptic thought with an added dimension: the virginal Bride could also be seen as England, whom the forces of Antichrist perpetually sought to ravish.

As earlier noted, invasion and rape had long been metaphorically equated. Shakespeare, for instance, depicts Tarquin's rape of Lucrece as a military invasion, and, in *Henry V*, Scotland's forays into England as attempted rapes;[53] while William Harrison uses the metaphor of England as a violated body, "a common receptacle for strangers," to describe the island's invasion by foreign cultures.[54] The device figured widely in religious propaganda: Protestant polemicists freely utilized the metaphor of the raped nation to allegorize Spain's military depredations. George Gascoigne's *Spoyle of Antwerp* (1576), for instance, featured a woodcut depicting Antwerp as a gravely distressed female raped by the Spanish, and a 1585 entertainment showed the Spanish assaulting the female figure of Leiden on stage.[55] In England, the rape metaphor encompassed not only the nation but the Church, "That spotless Dame whose ravishment was sought / By tyrant's rage that bloody ruin brought."[56]

Given the nexus between Protestant apocalyptic thought and the military might of the papal Antichrist, it thus becomes possible to see Aaron as a personification of Spain (or Philip), who, in collusion with the Babylonian Whore (Tamora/Mary), engineers the rape/dismemberment of the spotless Bride (Lavinia/England) and the murder of her Christlike spouse and "true-betrothèd love" (1.1.407) (Bassianus/the True, Protestant Church). Adding weight to this interpretation are Tamora's "ministers," Rape and Murder, the aptly-named offspring of the Babylonian Whore; and Lavinia's repeated identification with martyrdom (3.1.81, 3.1.107, 3.2.36), which would have recalled one of the most widely read books in England, Foxe's *Book of Martyrs*, as his *Acts and Monuments* was alternatively called—a compendium of Protestants martyred at the hands of Antichrist, in which mutilation was the keynote.[57] In view of the historical link between Moors and Spain, it seems likely that Aaron's Moorishness would have further identified him with Spain. It is perhaps noteworthy that another Moor—Shakespeare's Othello—dispatches himself with his "sword of Spain" (*Oth* 5.2.262). The English identification and even conflation of Moors with Jews, deriving from the related histories of the two in Spain, may also account for Aaron's Jewish name.[58]

In contrast to his role in the prose tale, Aaron is the "Chief architect and plotter" of the play's villainies (5.3.122; see also 5.1.98). Counselling "policy and stratagem" (2.1.104), he tells Tamora's sons that their only "hope" of possessing Lavinia is to take her "by force," a "speedier course than lingering languishment" (2.1.118, 110). Prior to this counsel, the thought of rape has occurred to neither brother, each of whom intends to woo Lavinia for his love. Their resulting quarrel—during which Demetrius claims Lavinia by right of primogeniture—is about to turn deadly when Aaron intercedes with his advice.

Aaron's push to replace "languishment" with "force" can thus be seen as an allusion to the Catholic insurgents under the aegis of Spain who, loath to "languish" in wait for Elizabeth's death and risk a Protestant successor, saw force as the sole assurance of restoring

Catholicism to England. Force, as Aaron reminds the brothers, is the "speedier course"; and "This way, or not at all, stand you in hope" (2.1.110, 119). His plan to rear his son as a warrior and commander—a detail absent in the prose tale—further identifies Aaron with military force.

Again the play bears comparison with book 5 of *The Faerie Queene*. A discourse on "the danger to England from Spanish aggression," book 5 centers on the "forged guile, / And open force" (7.7) of the papal Antichrist.[59] Particularly pertinent is Spenser's Souldan, a barbarous pagan on the order of Aaron, who figures Philip/Spain. This fiendishly impious "miscreant" (see especially *FQ* 5.8.28) "seekes by traytrous traines" to "subuert [the] Crowne" of the virgin queen Mercilla (who figures Elizabeth) and to "spill" her "sacred selfe" (5.8.18–19). By means of treachery and guile, Geryoneo (another embodiment of Philip/Spain) progresses from a foothold in Protestant Belgium to total possession (5.10.7–14); he then imposes "the yoke of inquisition," sacks the realm, and reduces the country to "seruile bond" (5.10.27). Like Lavinia, Belge is deprived "of her rightful sovereignty by a predatory invader," therein embodying "the most sinister peril the English fear for their own monarch and nation."[60] Duessa, who figures the Queen of Scots, likewise seeks "to depryue / Mercilla of her crowne, by her aspyred, . . . And tryumph in their blood, whom she to death did dryue" (5.9.41).

Lavinia's mutilation is the microcosmic parallel of Rome's. Her dismemberment is replicated in "headless Rome" (1.1.186), in Rome's "severed" polity (5.3.68), and in the "broken limbs" of the body politic (5.3.72). Described as the infliction of a "wound" (3.1.90–91), her rape images the figurative one of Rome, "the civil wound" inflicted by "the fatal engine" of the alien invaders (5.3.86–87). The potentially deadly fraternal rivalry for possession of Lavinia precisely replicates that of the brothers for possession of Rome, even down to the parallel claims of entitlement by reason of primogeniture. Stated alternatively, the narrowly averted armed conflict between Demetrius and Chiron images in small the narrowly averted civil broil between the factions of Saturninus and Bassianus. Even the language characterizing the contests is similar: as Tamora's sons are "woo[ers]" of and "competitors" for Lavinia (2.1.82, 77), so Caesar's are "suitors" of and "competitor[s]" for Rome (1.1.44, 63). In each case, moreover, the dispute is resolved by an intercessor who counsels concord and offers a politically expedient solution amenable to both rivals (Marcus, 1.1.18–48; Aaron, 2.1.103–31; note Aaron's appeal to "policy" [2.1.104]).

Lavinia, in fact, can be seen as an embodiment of Rome. Lavinia was the name of the wife of Aeneas who by her became the ancestor of Romulus, mythical founder of Rome. Further, her name "is the feminine form of Latinus, which derives from Latium, the area surrounding and including ancient Rome. So, connoted in Lavinia's name [are] the origin and identity of Rome itself. [Thus] [c]rimes against [Lavinia's] body are . . . crimes against the body of Rome."[61]

The extent to which *Titus* figures contemporary issues is further suggested by the play's more pertinent divergences from the prose tale:

(1) In the prose tale, the current Emperor remains alive. Absent, therefore, is the interregnum on which the play opens; the resulting factional struggle for the crown; the competing issues of primogeniture, nomination, and election; the threat of civil war; and Titus's disastrous nomination of Saturninus. Titus himself is never a candidate for the throne.

(2) In the prose tale, Lavinia is betrothed not to the Emperor's brother but to his only son. Consequently, she is never a political pawn.

(3) Although Attava and the Moor have a blackamoor child, the Emperor knows of the birth from the outset, and the Moor harbors no dynastic aspirations. Lacking, therefore, is any reference to the Moor's firstborn son and heir and any attempt to exchange offspring.

(4) The Moor of the prose tale, while wicked, does not originate Lavinia's rape. Also absent are his desire for Rome's ruin, his advocacy of policy and force, and his identification with the law of primogeniture and with a monastery.

(5) Except for a few scattered references to heaven, hell, and the Queen's "Devilish Designs," the prose tale is devoid of the play's theological overlay. Absent, for instance, are references to holy water, monasteries, Pius, and Catholic ceremony; the "impious" sacrifice of Alarbus; Lavinia's "martyrdom"; the Christlike connotations surrounding Bassianus; and allusions to the Apocalypse. Allusions to Elizabeth—to Astraea and Virgo, for example (*Tit* 4.3.4, 64)—are also absent.

(6) Finally, no Lucius (or comparable figure) appears in the prose tale. What is Lucius's function in the play?

Rome's accord with the Goths, and the extirpation of popish tyranny embodied in Saturninus, Aaron, and Tamora, combine to suggest the deliverance of England from papal oppression. Lucius prefigures *Lear*'s Edgar and *Macbeth*'s Malcolm, the Christlike saviors who return to restore order, heal division, and deliver the realm from the forces of darkness. Besides being suggestive of light, Lucius's name recalls Rome's first Christian king, who, according to John Foxe, established the true Christian faith in Britain, ridding the realm of idolatry and superstition and, by virtue of being labelled God's vicar by pope Eleutherius, proving that spiritual jurisdiction lay with the king.[62] "The Goths who accompany Lucius, we may then say, are there to secure the Protestant succession."[63]

Other Christlike allusions appear in Lucius's conquest of "the devil" (5.1.145) by means of his symbolically righteous army; his salvation of the realm that had consigned him to probable death; and the scars, attesting to his truth, that he offers to show the unbelieving:

> I am the turned-forth . . .
> That hath preserved [Rome's] welfare in my blood
> And from her bosom took the enemy's point,
> Sheathing the steel in my adventurous body.
> Alas, you know I am no vaunter, I;
> My scars can witness, dumb although they are,
> That my report is just and full of truth.
>
> (5.3.109–15)

Lucius's salvific role is further manifested in an act that attests the purgation of his Catholic impulses and that brings the play full circle. His sparing of the firstborn son of the captive, Aaron, in deference to Aaron's pleas for mercy, counters his slaying of Alarbus, the firstborn son of the captive, Tamora, in deafness to her pleas. The act augurs the end of popish "ceremony," barbarity, and injustice, and of the revenge cycle the slaying initiated.[64]

Although Lucius (i.e., a Protestant) ultimately rules Rome (i.e., England), Shakespeare strongly implies that the future is by no means assured. The foreign threat is arrested, not eradicated; it continues in Aaron's son, who remains alive and well and who—ironically exceeding even Aaron's earlier hopes for him—will be reared in the imperial court. A reembodiment of his militaristic father (Aaron would raise him as a warrior and commander), the child is potentially a foreign invader:[65] aided by Moorish sympathizers who have gained a foothold in Rome (the allegorical equivalents of such pro-Spanish subversives as the Jesuits), he could one day lay claim to the realm—particularly in view of his theoretical right to the throne conferred by his royal lineage.

Titus, then, fuses political allegory with Platonic political theory to project the consequences of the Elizabethan succession crisis. In the play, an unsettled succession results in a factious interregnum, which enables the seizure of power by a tyrant, the naturalization of his foreign queen, and the intrusion of a second foreign element, the queen's paramour. The situation paves the way for the state's subversion, for dynastic infiltration and extinction, and for bondage to a foreign-dominated regime. Integrally linked to these events is a constitutional decline that moves from the destabilized monarchy on which the play opens, to democracy (figured in the submission of the election decision to the people, who must also ratify Titus's nominee), to tyranny (the regime of Saturninus). Lavinia, like Lucrece a synecdoche for Rome/England, images both literally and figuratively the larger political situation:[66] consequent on monarchic collapse, she becomes the supreme political prize, the chaste, spotless bride whom the rival contenders (including Tamora's sons) strive to rape or possess. The legitimate betrothed of Protestantism (Bassianus), she is ravished by the combined forces of Spain (Aaron) and the Babylonian Whore. Protestantism (Bassianus) is annihilated, Catholicism is imposed under the aegis of a papal tyrant and his foreign queen (an embodiment of the Scots/Stuart dynasty) in league with another treacherous alien (Philip/Spain), and the fractured state lapses into barbarism. England's destruction could not be more complete.

Conclusion

THIS STUDY HAS SOUGHT TO SHOW THAT FOUR OF THE FIVE ROMAN works under discussion attest a sequence of constitutional decline replicating that posited by Plato in the *Republic*. As in Plato, this decline is precipitated by monarchic destabilization or failure, thereafter moving successively through oligarchy and democracy and concluding in tyranny. The study has further argued that this sequence is prefigured and substantially encapsulated in the fifth work; and that all five are oblique glosses on England's political milieu, projecting a decline in England analogous to that of Rome. The profound antirepublicanism these works attest reflects the deep-seated fear of the "headlessness" that had fostered England's own dynastic wars—a fear Platonically inculcated and scripturally reinforced. Hence the English antipathy to democracy and to what were widely perceived as the escalating democratic impulses fostered by the policies of both Elizabeth and James.

Did Shakespeare envision some sort of tetralogy when he began *Lucrece*? Problematizing the issue are the nonchronological composition of the four works in question, their mixed genres (three plays and a poem), and the fact that the constitutional decline they collectively encompass is not paralleled by a corresponding (i.e., allegorical) English decline. Nevertheless, their affinities are copious. All four—*Lucrece, Coriolanus, Julius Caesar,* and *Antony and Cleopatra*—concern the disastrous consequences of a failed or destabilized monarchy, consequences that include factiousness, schism, and the descent of the state into anarchy, civil war, and barbarism. In addition, these works collectively trace a continuous span of Roman history, which begins with the expulsion of the Tarquins and concludes with the triumph of Augustus. Each work encompasses one or more separate stages in the decline of Rome along with a corresponding growth in popular rule; and each concerns a continuing stage in a battle for supremacy waged by a new set of antagonists whose strife emanates from events in the preceding work. The stakes also progressively broaden, these works collectively moving from control of Rome to control of the world.

Additionally linking these works are characters, events, and verbal and structural parallels, which carry over from one work to one or more of the others. Brutus, in his various incarnations, is the works' common, largely pivotal denominator. All three Brutuses are putative champions of liberty, all are instrumental in advancing popular rule, and all are instigators of rebellion or revolution, deploying oratory to incite the people against the man they seek to destroy: against Tarquin in *Lucrece*, Marcius in *Coriolanus*, and Caesar in *Julius Caesar*. While *Antony and Cleopatra* contains no Brutus per se, Brutus's name is repeatedly mentioned, recalling his role in Caesar's killing, and Antony's role in Brutus's death. The Brutus of *Caesar* at once looks back to and reembodies the Brutus of *Lucrece*, whose antimonarchic mantle he assumes as he prepares to rid Rome of the man who "would be crowned"; thus did the earlier Brutus "from the streets of Rome / The Tarquin drive, when he was called a king" (*JC* 2.1.12, 53–54). Both *Caesar* and *Coriolanus* open on a disordered and volatile populace, contain a conspiracy devised by an envious, power-seeking rival, and depict the ritual slaughter of their titular hero. The mob's cry "Tear him to pieces" in *Coriolanus*, which precedes the slaughter of Marcius, occurs verbatim in *Julius Caesar* and precedes the slaughter of Cinna. In scope, consequence, and thematic import, moreover, Marcius's inconstancy parallels almost exactly that of Julius Caesar. Each man proclaims himself immovable, each believes that his constancy distinguishes him from the commoners he contemns, and each man's inconstancy leads to his death. In addition, Marcius's capitulation to Volumnia (3.2), in which Marcius reverses himself three times, parallels Caesar's capitulation to Decius (2.2), in which Caesar reverses himself twice, praise or flattery being the chief means of persuasion in both cases (*JC* 2.1.203–09, 2.2.83–91; *Cor* 3.2.109–12).

There are further parallels. In *Antony and Cleopatra*, Caesar and Caesarism reemerge in Octavius (now explicitly referred to as "Caesar"), Antony supplants Brutus as the Caesarean antagonist, and

Actium replaces Philippi as the battleground where the power struggle is played out. Antony's overriding of Enobarbus's saving military counsel at Actium parallels Brutus's overriding of Cassius's at Philippi, leading in each case to catastrophic defeat. Antony's suicide replicates Brutus's: each follows from a fall from power, each is preceded by a follower's refusal to assist in the deed, and each transpires on the field of battle. The fall of the conspirators in *Caesar* recalls that of the Tarquins in *Lucrece*: each ensues from an inflammatory oration accompanied by a public display of the protagonist's stabbed and bleeding corpse. *Caesar* and *Antony* are also structurally similar, Brutus's fall and Antony's rise in the one paralleling Antony's fall and Octavius's rise in the other.[1] The banishment of Tarquin in *Lucrece* prefigures that of Marcius in *Coriolanus*, in which play, moreover, we are twice reminded of Marcius's role in the routing of Tarquinius Superbus, Rome's king in *Lucrece*. Additionally common to all four works is the metamorphosis of one tyrant into another in the continuing battle for control of Rome, a battle invariably emanating from Rome's divided rule; and all four detail the collapse of a regime.[2]

Lending further weight to the notion of a tetralogy are the affinities of these works with Shakespeare's two English tetralogies. The English plays encompass a span of history politically analogous to Rome's, commencing, like *Lucrece*, with a kinsman's murder and a usurpation[3] and proceeding through the civil wars stemming from the divided claims to the throne—the analogue of the wars engendered by the battle for Rome's helm. The impotence of Henry VI, the imprudence of Richard II, and the tyranny of Lucius Tarquinius alike incur the collapse of order, unleashing faction, upheaval, and strife. In all three sets of works, the populace holds the key to power: in *Richard II*, as the tool of Bolingbroke; in *2 Henry VI*, as the tool of York (note, e.g., 3.1.355–59); in *Lucrece*, as the tool of Brutus; in *Coriolanus*, as the tool of the tribunes, the patricians, and Aufidius; and in *Caesar*, as the tool of the conspirators and the counterconspirators alike. Both sequences, Roman and English, conclude with the cessation of warfare and with national unification under one sovereign head, Bosworth Field replacing Actium as the site of the final power struggle.

Like the Roman works, the English ones center on the descent into lawlessness produced by monarchic failure. Henry VI's incompetence results in the loss of France, and in a battle for the Crown by a succession of opportunists who exploit court factionalism for their own ends—a succession culminating in the diabolically despotic Richard III. In *2 Henry VI*, popular unrest leads to Jack Cade's rebellion and to the banishment and death of the Duke of Suffolk; in *Coriolanus*, it leads to multiple uprisings, and to the banishment and death of Coriolanus. In both cases, the rulers are forced to capitulate to the people, a sign of escalating popular power and, concomitantly, of impending anarchy. The parallel executions of Suffolk and Coriolanus further the slide into chaos as the people take the law into their own hands. In the final play of each series, the state has lapsed into tyranny, Octavius like Richard achieving supremacy by annihilating every rival for power.

Additional parallels between *Caesar* and *2 Henry VI* include the killing of Cinna the Poet merely because his name is Cinna, which recalls the killing of the man who addresses Jack Cade by his true name instead of as "Lord Mortimer"; and the scenes of riot in both plays giving way to full-scale civil war.[4]

Yet a further parallel linking the three sets of plays resides in the figure of Lucrece: depicting a "red" and "white" battle for "sovereignty" (*Luc* 64–71), Lucrece's face images the War of the Roses, a war which, I have argued, becomes the work's governing metaphor. As for the nonchronological composition of the Roman works, it may be noted that the sequence of the English history plays departs equally radically from historical continuity: the tetralogy encompassing the period from Henry VI through Richard III substantially antedates that encompassing the period from Richard II through Henry V, *King John* is roughly concurrent with *Richard II*, and *Henry VIII* comes twenty years after *Richard III*.

Titus Andronicus differs from the other four works in being ahistorical. It is nevertheless allied with these works, most saliently through its political concerns. Central to *Titus* is the concern with the succession that informs both *Caesar* and *Lucrece*. Like Lucrece, Lavinia is a synecdoche for Rome, the rape in each instance imaging the larger political situation, and the woman being the object of rival factions. The rape and dismemberment of Lavinia by barbarous aliens parallels in small the rape and dismemberment of Rome by foreign powers. As in *Lucrece*, Rome is equated with Troy; Troy and Rome are equated with England; and Troy, Rome, and England are linked through political allegory. Like the other four works, *Titus* explores the consequences of monarchic collapse, consequences that include schism, power struggle, the chance afforded the unscrupulous opportunist to seize the crown, and the state's descent into tyranny, barbarism, and war. In its movement from monarchy to democracy to tyranny, *Titus* also encapsulates and prefigures a sequence of decline analogous to that collectively charted by the other four works.

The notion of unity as salvational is not confined to the Roman works; it informs much of Shakespeare's canon, including both tetralogies. Thus Henry V wins Agincourt—and France—because he is able to unite his commoners and nobles and meld his fractious and disparate subjects (represented by the Irish Macmorris, the English Gower, the Scottish Jamy, and the Welsh Fluellen) into a unified and concordant whole.[5] The French, conversely, are rent by rivalry and discord, which their camp scenes preceding the battle are calculated to illustrate. The French disunity is typically a manifestation of the ruling ethos: the king has dissociated himself from his commoners, who are deemed contemptible by him and an aristocracy who fail to discern the necessity of the parts to the whole. In the Constable's words, the common soldiers are "our superfluous lackeys and our peasants, / Who in unnecessary action swarm / About our squares of battle" (*H5* 4.2.26–28).[6]

Henry is Plato's philosopher king, embodying perhaps more fully than any other Shakespearean ruler the attributes of rational princeship. Unlike Antony and Cleopatra, who contemn the people; and Caesar, who professes superiority to "ordinary men"; and the French, who must "sort our nobles from our common men" lest "our vulgar drench their peasant limbs / In blood of princes" (4.7.73–77), Henry considers himself "a common man" (4.8.51), recognizing that only the surface trappings of kingship differentiate him from the rest of mankind (4.1.236–37, 257–78; see also 4.1.102–110).[7] This concept of the necessity of the parts to the whole was, as we have seen, not only Platonic; it was scripturally decreed. That is why Henry is "the mirror of all Christian kings" (2.0.6): at one with his subjects, with patrician and commoner alike, Henry manifests a union tantamount to a brotherhood of Christ.

Charles's favoring of the nobility, in contrast, proves disastrous. As opposed to the English, whose leadership accrues to a single, unifying head, the French leadership is relegated to a contentious multiplicity of heads as the nobles instead of the king take command. The result is military anarchy: an uncoordinated rush to the field, and defeat when victory were possible "If any order might be thought upon" (4.5.22). Plurality will similarly doom England under Henry VI, "Whose state so many had the managing, / That they lost France and made his England bleed" (Epilogue 11–12). *King Lear* is one of Shakespeare's more harrowing comments on divided rule, a division typically following on monarchic collapse, here in the form of abdication. Relatedly, *Troilus*'s Ulysses describes what ensues absent the "med'cinable eye" of a king—"What plagues and what portents, what mutiny, / What raging of the sea, shaking of earth, / Commotion in the winds, frights, changes, horrors, / Divert and crack, rend and deracinate / The unity and married calm of states / Quite from their fixure" (1.3.91–101). Here the "absent" leader is the feckless Agamemnon, whose impotence has fostered the "factions" (1.3.80) that confound the Greek army.

That Shakespeare condemned the masses is logical to conclude, given their generally unsavory depiction in these works. Yet, as we have repeatedly seen, the Shakespearean ruler who contemns or eschews his commoners rarely prospers. Shakespeare follows Plato in presenting the masses as unreasoning, fractious, and figuratively blind. They are not, however, uniformly bestial. As the Platonic analogue of the passions, they are a force for good or evil depending on how they are led. Ruled by a strong and enlightened head—the monarchic equivalent of reason—they are an ordered and constructive force conducing to the state's felicity; shorn of such leadership, they become a bestial and anarchic force conducing to the state's destruction. We have witnessed both facets of this principle in *Coriolanus*. We have only to juxtapose the "headless," bestial commoners of *Julius Caesar* against the king-led, heroic commoners of *Henry V* to grasp Shakespeare's use of this principle.

The anti-Catholic bias that I have alleged in *Titus Andronicus* must inevitably give rise to the question of Shakespeare's religion. As is well known, Shakespeare's religious preferences are notoriously difficult to determine. All we can say for certain is that he was writing for an audience, and an Establishment, that were predominantly Protestant and rampantly nationalistic and at the forefront of whose consciousness were Spain's recent attempted invasion of England, the Spanish atrocities in the Netherlands, the distinct possibility of those atrocities next being visited upon England, and the repeated papist attempts on Elizabeth's life. Hence the anti-Catholic tenor many of the plays arguably and perhaps necessarily evince.

But even if Shakespeare were Catholic, would he have championed England's subjection to Spain and a foreigner on England's throne? Very probably not. To quote Alison Plowden, English Catholics "could have accepted . . . the peaceful accession of Mary Stuart with clear consciences, but no one except the extreme right-wing lunatic fringe would for a moment have accepted Philip of Spain—despite his descent from John of Gaunt." It is perhaps worth noting in this regard that when news of the Armada's defeat was spread abroad, "the English students in the college at Rome cheered aloud at the news."[8] As for the most likely contender to succeed Elizabeth, James VI of Scotland, I have sought to show, in *Titus*, Shakespeare's antipathy to the succession of James, and, in *Antony* and *Coriolanus*, his continuing antipathy to the Scots king after his accession.

One final question remains: did Shakespeare know the *Republic* directly? In the absence of precise verbal correspondences, direct indebtedness is difficult to assess. Nevertheless, as I have tried to show, many of these works' Platonic elements that appear in the *Republic* are found in none of the works' known sources, suggesting that Shakespeare was governed by more than a secondhand familiarity with Plato's text.

Absent definitive authorial comment, whether Shakespeare ultimately intended these works as a tetralogy must similarly remain conjectural. What seems clear is that each work was occasioned by a political crisis that threatened the safety or the integrity of the state. In each work, Shakespeare equates the destruction of Rome with impending upheaval in England deriving from England's kindred political ills. As we have seen, *Titus*, *Lucrece*, and *Caesar* concern the unsettled succession, with its potential for civil war and mob rule. *Coriolanus* mirrors the Parliamentary (and thus national) fragmentation arising from James's contempt for the Commons' grievances, which led—as does the analogous oppression of the play's populace—to the Commons' escalating demands for political rights. This class struggle, as Shakespeare foresaw, would lay the ground for another civil war. *Antony and Cleopatra* addresses the dangers posed by James's absolutism and excess. Each work is thus a plea for provident rulership and a sound monarchy, sole bulwarks against the state's destruction—against, in short, England's going the political way of Rome.

What does emerge as reasonably indisputable is these works' common political concerns and the attendant constitutional decline that informs all five. If nothing else, this decline affords us another context for assessing these pieces of literature in the endless debate on what—if anything—unifies and defines the Roman works.

Notes

Chapter 1: Introduction

1. For details of the Urbino murder, see Harold Jenkins, ed., *Hamlet*, The Arden Shakespeare (London: Methuen, 1982), 102, 507–8. On Shakespeare's possible reason for changing Urbino to Vienna, see Leah S. Marcus, *Puzzling Shakespeare: Local Reading and Its Discontents* (Berkeley and Los Angeles: University of California Press, 1988), 162.

2. Whether *Hamlet* was in fact performed at court remains uncertain. On the play's possible topicality, see Bullough, 8:18–19, 40–45. Drama, of course, was not the sole venue for political criticism; it was, however, the most expedient, given the public and private audiences it was able to reach and—owing to its oratorical nature—to influence. On the relationship of the monarch to the staged performance and on acting as a form of oratory, see Stephen Orgel, *The Illusion of Power: Political Theater in the English Renaissance* (Berkeley and Los Angeles: University of California Press, 1975), 9–17.

3. F. Smith Fussner, *The Historical Revolution: English Historical Writing and Thought, 1580–1640* (London: Routledge, 1962), 9, 10; C. A. Patrides, *The Grand Design of God: The Literary Form of the Christian View of History* (London: Routledge, 1972), 70; Joseph Anthony Mazzeo, *Renaissance and Revolution: The Remaking of European Thought* (New York: Random House, Pantheon, 1965), 276.

4. D. R. Woolf, *The Idea of History in Early Stuart England: Erudition, Ideology, and 'The Light of Truth' from the Accession of James I to the Civil War* (Toronto: University of Toronto Press, 1990), 10, 17; Wallace K. Ferguson, *The Renaissance in Historical Thought: Five Centuries of Interpretation* (Cambridge: Houghton Mifflin, Riverside Press, 1948), 5, quoted in Fussner, *Historical Revolution*, 12.

5. Mazzeo, *Renaissance and Revolution*, 288–89.

6. Woolf, *Idea of History*, 142, 11.

7. Mazzeo, *Renaissance and Revolution*, 288; Herbert Weisinger, "Ideas of History during the Renaissance," in *Renaissance Essays*, ed. Paul Oscar Kristeller and Philip P. Wiener (New York: Harper & Row, 1968), 74–94, 85. Cf. Antony's reference to "the tide of times" (*JC* 3.1.259).

8. Woolf, *Idea of History*, 5.

9. Sir Thomas Elyot, *Governor*, 228–29, 10–11.

10. Woolf, *Idea of History*, 184. As Woolf here explains, Heylyn's *anacyclosis* entails a movement "from monarchy to tyranny, to aristocracy, to oligarchy, to a 'republicke,' to a democracy, and finally back to monarchy."

11. *The History of Florence,* in *The Works of Nicholas Machiavel, Secretary of State to the Republic of Florence. Newly Translated from the Originals* . . . . By Ellis Farneworth (London, 1762), 1:213–14, quoted in Weisinger, "Ideas," 86.

12. John N. King, *Milton and Religous Controversy: Satire and Polemic in* Paradise Lost (Cambridge: Cambridge University Press, 2000), 71; Roy Strong, *The Cult of Elizabeth: Elizabethan Portraiture and Pageantry* (1977; reprint, London: Pimlico, 1999), 115, 126–27.

13. David Norbrook, *Poetry and Politics in the English Renaissance,* rev. ed. (Oxford: Oxford University Press, 2002), 13; Bernard Capp, "The Political Dimension of Apocalyptic Thought," in *The Apocalypse in English Renaissance Thought and Literature,* ed. C. A. Patrides and Joseph Wittreich (Ithaca: Cornell University Press, 1984), 97. The providential view of history, imposed by Shakespeare's sources Holinshed and Hall on their accounts of English history and arguably informing Shakespeare's English tetralogies, is omitted from this study since it is not germane to the five works being considered.

14. The idea seems to have been something of a commonplace; compare Sir Thomas Elyot: history presents "as it were the mirror of man's life"; expressing "the beauty of virtue and the deformity and loathliness of vice," it teaches what is profitable and what is to be eschewed, to the end that "our wits may be amended and our personages . . . more apt to serve our public weal and our prince" (*Governor,* 231).

15. Richard Reynoldes, *Chronicle of all the noble Emperours of the Romaines* . . . (1571). The point and the quotation are those of T. J. B. Spencer, "Shakespeare and the Elizabethan Romans," *Shakespeare Survey* 10 (1957): 30. However, I question Spencer's assertion that the history of the Republic was less relevant than that of the Empire, although Spencer elsewhere takes the latter to include "the political events which allowed the rise and led to the fall of Julius Caesar and the conflict between Octavian and Mark Antony" (*William Shakespeare: The Roman Plays*: Titus Andronicus; Julius Caesar; Antony and Cleopatra; Coriolanus [n.p., Longmans, Green, 1963, 9]); I concur instead in Woolf's view (*Idea of History,* 172) that the Republic's history was more relevant.

16. Richard Grafton, *An Abridgement of the Chronicles of England* (1563), sig B2r (noted by Woolf, *Idea of History,* 10); Thomas Blundeville, *The True Order and Methode of Wryting and Reading Hystories* (1574), ed. Hugh G. Dick, in *Huntington Library Quarterly* 3 (1940): 154–55. On history as a guide for princes, see also Spencer, "Elizabethan Romans," 30.

17. See Spencer, "Elizabethan Romans," 29.

18. Woolf, *Idea of History,* 197, 172. Cf. Spencer, "Elizabethan Romans," 30.

19. To the Elizabethan, impotence and collapse were synonymous, both implying the absence of the rational, ordering principle by which the state's integrity is sustained.

20. Brents Stirling, "Anti–Democracy in Shakespeare: A Re-survey," *Modern Language Quarterly* 2 (1941): 495. The bulk of this paragraph is indebted to Stirling.

21. Molin, *C. S. P. Ven.,* 1603–1607, 219; Giustinian, *C. S. P. Ven.,* 1607–10, 8 (both cited by Stirling, "Anti-Democracy," 498). See Stirling for further examples.

22. Stirling, "Anti-Democracy," 493.

23. *Macbeth* illustrates the process within the soul. The incipient "murder" of "thought" or reason engendered by Macbeth's contemplated murder of Duncan

sunders his "single state" (1.3.140–41), plunging him into sleeplessness, hallucination, and terror, and a reign of carnage emblematic of the condition of tyranny to which his soul has sunk. As is typical in Shakespeare, the word "state" plays on two meanings: *condition* and *polity*.

24. Woolf, *Idea of History*, 178.

25. G. R. Elton, *England Under the Tudors*, 3d ed. (1955; London: Routledge, 1991), 396, 397.

26. Woolf, *Idea of History*, 176, 177.

27. Fulke Greville, *Of Monarchy*, in vol. 1 of *The Works of Fulke Greville, Lord Brooke*, ed. Alexander B. Grosart, 4 vols. (1870; reprint, New York: AMS Press, 1966), stanzas 592, 589; William Fulbecke, *An Historicall Collection of the Continuall Factions, Tumults, and Massacres of the Romans and Italians during the Space of One Hundred and Twentie Yeares Next before the Peaceable Empire of Augustus Caesar* (London, 1601). Both cited by Woolf, *Idea of History*, 177, 179–80.

28. Elyot, *Governor*, 10–11.

29. Ibid., 11, see also 7; Christopher Marlowe, trans., *The First Book of Lucan['s Pharsalia]*, in *The Works and Life of Christopher Marlowe*, gen. ed. R. H. Case (1931; reprint, New York: Gordian Press, 1966), 4:267, quoted in Clifford Ronan, "*Antike Roman*": *Power Symbology and the Roman Play in Early Modern England, 1585–1635* (Athens: University of Georgia Press, 1995), 79.

30. The concept informs *Romeo and Juliet*, for example, in which the filial disobedience of the lovers parallels the people's disobedience to the prince. Both alike incur factiousness, civil strife, and death.

31. J. Leeds Barroll, "Shakespeare and Roman History," *Modern Language Review* 53 (1958): 328–29.

32. See Paul Dean, "Tudor Humanism and the Roman Past: A Background to Shakespeare," *Renaissance Quarterly* 41 (1988): 107–8.

33. Ronan, *Antike Roman*, 80. The stereotype was, of course, not confined to drama; note, e.g., Elyot's comment (quoted above) on the "factions or seditions" that characterized republican Rome.

34. See Marie Axton, *The Queen's Two Bodies: Drama and the Elizabethan Succession*, Royal Historical Society Studies in History, no. 5 (London: Royal Historical Society, 1977).

35. Axton, *Queen's Two Bodies*, 3, 81. See Axton for devices writers employed to evade censure.

36. Thomas Heywood, *An Apology for Actors* (1612), ed. Richard H. Perkinson (New York: Scholars' Facsimiles & Reprints, 1941), F3.

37. Margot Heinemann, "Political Drama," in *The Cambridge Companion to English Renaissance Drama*, ed. A. R. Braunmuller and Michael Hattaway (Cambridge: Cambridge University Press, 1990), 177.

38. The original title of the *Republic* was *Politeia*, deriving from "polis" (Greek for "city-state"); hence Plato's title refers to the ordering of the state. The English title derives from the Latin *Respublica*, the title accorded the work by Cicero, who called his own treatise on the subject *De Republica* ("on the state"). The English title is thus a misnomer, implying, as it does, a republic or a nonmonarchic state—the antithesis of the ideal state of Plato's *Republic*.

39. James Holly Hanford, "A Platonic Passage in Shakespeare's *Troilus and Cressida*," *Studies in Philology* 13 (1916): 102. For related historical views, see

Spencer, "Elizabethan Romans"; Barroll, "Roman History"; and Wayne A. Rebhorn, "The Crisis of the Aristocracy in *Julius Caesar*," *Renaissance Quarterly* 43 (1990): 75–111. For further historical background, see James Emerson Phillips, *The State in Shakespeare's Greek and Roman Plays* (1940; reprint, New York: Octagon, 1972). Compare Elyot's definition of the state: "A public weal is a body living, compact or made of sundry estates and degrees of men, which is disposed by the order of equity and governed by the rule and moderation of reason" (*Governor*, 1).

40. Lester K. Born, trans., *The Education of a Christian Prince*, by Desiderius Erasmus (New York: Columbia University Press, 1936), 52, 54.

41. In addition to Hanford, see, e.g., I. A. Richards, "*Troilus and Cressida* and Plato," *Hudson Review* 1 (1948): 362–76; Paul Shorey, *Platonism Ancient and Modern* (Berkeley and Los Angeles: University of California Press, 1938), 180, 222; J. Churton Collins, *Studies in Shakespeare* (London: Constable, 1904), 35; Howard B. White, *Copp'd Hills towards Heaven: Shakespeare and the Classical Polity* (The Hague: Martinus Nijhoff, 1970), 113–33; and Paul A. Cantor, "Prospero's Republic: The Politics of Shakespeare's *The Tempest*," in *Shakespeare as Political Thinker*, ed. John Alvis and Thomas G. West (Durham: Carolina Academic Press, 1981), 239–55. Correspondences have also been discerned in isolated passages in *Julius Caesar*, most notably the soul/state analogy in Brutus's soliloquy, Antony's funeral oration, and the reference to the mob as multi-headed (respectively, *Rep.* 4.441–42, 6.493, and 9.588). See also J. L. Etty, "Studies in Shakespeare's History: VI—*Julius Caesar*," *Macmillan's Magazine* 87 (1903): 354, who views Brutus as the antithesis of Plato's philosopher king; and John Alvis, "Caesarian Honors, Brutus's Dilemma, and the Advent of Christianity," in *Shakespeare's Understanding of Honor* (Durham: Carolina Academic Press, 1990), 125–63, who argues that Plato's *First Alcibiades* underlies the ocular motif initiated at *JC* 1.2.51–53.

42. Francis MacDonald Cornford, trans., *The Republic of Plato* (1941; reprint, London: Oxford University Press, 1974), 221.

43. Karl Raimund Popper, *The Open Society and Its Enemies*, 4th ed., 2 vols. (1945; Princeton: Princeton University Press, 1963), 1:39, 40.

44. My summary follows Frederick Copleston, *Greece and Rome*, vol. 1, pt. 1, of *A History of Philosophy* (1946; Garden City: Doubleday, Image Books, 1962), 259.

45. For related views of these Roman works, see John R. Kayser and Ronald J. Lettieri, "'The Last of All the Romans': Shakespeare's Commentary on Classical Republicanism," *Clio* 9 (1979): 197–227; and Alvis, "Caesarian Honors," 149–52. Cf. Robert S. Miola, "*Julius Caesar* and the Tyrannicide Debate," *Renaissance Quarterly* 38 (1985): 271–89, who finds the play ambivalent concerning whether Caesar was a tyrant.

46. Whether Plato postulated a cyclical view of constitutional change is a matter of debate. See, e.g., Mazzeo, *Renaissance and Revolution*, 275, 281, and Patrides, *Grand Design of God*, 17, who conclude that he did (the list also includes Aristotle, who believed Book VIII of Plato's *Republic* taught such a cycle). Cf. G. W. Trompf, *The Idea of Historical Recurrence in Western Thought from Antiquity to the Reformation* (Berkeley and Los Angeles: University of California Press, 1970), 18–20, who observes that the *Republic* contains no reference to such a cycle, nor in any real sense does the *Laws*. It should be noted that Plato's theory of political decline is a variation of his law of universal decay, which holds that change, to which all things are

subject, entails ever-increasing, irreversible corruptibility. Such a view makes it unlikely that Plato would have subscribed to a cyclic theory of history, which assumes a return to an original, ideal state.

47. The play's rising-falling pattern is extensively analyzed by John W. Velz, "Undular Structure in 'Julius Caesar,'" *Modern Language Review* 66 (1971): 21–30. Velz argues that the tide motif, variously deployed throughout the play and epitomized by Brutus's equating of fortune in human affairs with a tide at flood stage, becomes a metaphor for the play's structure, which is comprised of a repetitive series of rises and falls. This motif, I submit, is another manifestation of Shakespeare's use of the tidal theory of history.

48. Studies of the Roman works often subordinate the question of unity to other considerations. Maurice Charney, e.g. (*Shakespeare's Roman Plays: The Function of Imagery in the Drama* [Cambridge: Harvard University Press, 1961]), focuses on imagery; Derek Traversi (*Shakespeare: The Roman Plays* [Stanford: Stanford University Press, 1963]), on character; and Coppélia Kahn (*Roman Shakespeare: Warriors, Wounds, and Women* [London: Routledge, 1997]), on gender ideology. For Vivian Thomas (*Shakespeare's Roman Worlds* [London: Routledge, 1989]), the works demonstrate Shakespeare's endorsement of such Roman values as constancy and valor; for Alexander Leggatt (*Shakespeare's Political Drama: The History Plays and the Roman Plays* [London: Routledge, 1988]), Shakespeare's interest in human behavior within political structures. Critics pursuing the question of unity include J. L. Simmons (*Shakespeare's Pagan World: The Roman Tragedies* [Charlottesville: University Press of Virginia, 1973]); John Alvis ("The Coherence of Shakespeare's Roman Plays," *Modern Language Quarterly* 40 [1979]: 115–34); Robert S. Miola (*Shakespeare's Rome* [Cambridge: Cambridge University Press, 1983]); Michael Platt (*Rome and Romans According to Shakespeare*, rev. ed. [Lanham, Md.: University Press of America, 1983]); and Paul A. Cantor (*Shakespeare's Rome: Republic and Empire* [Ithaca: Cornell University Press, 1976]), Simmons holding that the plays are unified by a Christian awareness of the limitations of pagan Rome; and Alvis, that *Caesar, Coriolanus,* and *Antony* show "the tragic costs of living for self–glory." Miola approaches the works chronologically rather than historically. Both Cantor and Platt explore Rome's passage from republic to empire. Platt sees *Lucrece* as initiating the series of "great lives and deeds" conducing to the Republic's glory; Cantor opposes the "public spiritedness" defining the Republic in *Coriolanus* to the "eros" defining the Empire in *Antony and Cleopatra*. No study approaches these works from the standpoint of the unifying influence of Plato's constitutional theory.

Given the number of studies on the Roman works, this list is not meant to be exhaustive. For a more comprehensive overview, including the various notions of what works the rubric "Roman" embraces, see Kahn, 21 n. 3.

49. *Cymbeline*, sometimes considered a Roman work, is omitted from this study because of its predominantly British setting.

50. Citations refer to *The Politics of Aristotle*, ed. and trans. Ernest Barker (1946; reprint, London: Oxford University Press, 1978); and *Ethica Nicomachea*, in *Introduction to Aristotle*, ed. Richard McKeon, Modern Library (New York: Random House, 1947).

51. Copleston, *Greece and Rome*, pt. 2, 96.

52. On scholars alleging the influence of Aristotle on Shakespeare, consult *Shakespeare and the Classical Tradition: An Annotated Bibliography, 1961–1991*, comp. Lewis Walker (New York: Routledge, 2002). See also Phillips, *State*.

53. Phillips, *State*, 20–21, 104.

54. T. W. Baldwin, *William Shakespere's Small Latine & Lesse Greeke*, 2 vols. (Urbana: University of Illinois Press, 1944), 2:661. See also Jonathan Bate, *Shakespeare and Ovid* (Oxford: Clarendon Press, 1993), 7; Charles and Michelle Martindale, *Shakespeare and the Uses of Antiquity: An Introductory Essay* (London: Routledge, 1990), 11; and H. P. Rickman, "Shakespeare and Plato," *Hermes: Zeitschrift für Klassische Philologie* 124 (1996): 378.

55. Ben Jonson may have owned a Ficino edition; see Stephen Medcalf, "Shakespeare on Beauty, Truth and Transcendence," in *Platonism and the English Imagination*, ed. Anna Baldwin and Sarah Hutton (Cambridge: Cambridge University Press, 1994), 118.

56. Russ McDonald, "'I Loved My Books': Shakespeare's Reading," in *The Bedford Companion to Shakespeare: An Introduction with Documents* (Boston: St. Martin's Press, Bedford Books, 1996), 103 (to which this account, including quotations, is closely indebted); Leonard Barkan, "What Did Shakespeare Read?", in *The Cambridge Companion to Shakespeare*, ed. Margreta de Grazia and Stanley Wells (Cambridge: Cambridge University Press, 2001), 34, 35. My account is necessarily only an outline; for a comprehensive investigation of Shakespeare's probable curriculum, see Baldwin, and the more economical studies of Barkan and McDonald. Grace Tiffany ("Shakespeare's Dionysian Prince: Drama, Politics, and the 'Athenian' History Play," *Renaissance Quarterly* 52 [1999]: 369 n) states that Plato's earlier and middle dialogues were commonly presented in grammar school, but I have so far been unable to confirm this.

57. McDonald, "Shakespeare's Reading," 103; see also Bate, *Shakespeare and Ovid*, 7–8.

58. Bate, *Shakespeare and Ovid*, 13; McDonald, "Shakespeare's Reading," 103.

59. On *Tmp*, Martindale, *Shakespeare and the Uses of Antiquity*, 33; Bate, *Shakespeare and Ovid*, 8–9. On *Tit*, J. A. K. Thomson, *Shakespeare and the Classics* (1952; reprint, Westport, Conn: Greenwood Press, 1978), 54–58.

60. Thomson, *Shakespeare and the Classics*, 43–44; McDonald, "Shakespeare's Reading," 103; Bate, *Shakespeare and Ovid*, 13, 24.

61. E. K. Chambers, *William Shakespeare: A Study of Facts and Problems*, 2 vols. (Oxford: Clarendon Press, 1930), I:312.

62. Baldwin, *Shakespere's Small Latine*.

63. See Walker, *Shakespeare and the Classical Tradition*. For earlier criticism, consult John W. Velz, *Shakespeare and the Classical Tradition: A Critical Guide to Commentary, 1660–1960* (Minneapolis: University of Minnesota Press, 1968).

64. Rickman, "Shakespeare and Plato," 378, who suggests that Shakespeare may have read the Greek text of *Phaedo*. That Falstaff is meant to recall Socrates has been variously alleged.

65. Barbara Tovey, "Shakespeare's Apology for Imitative Poetry: *The Tempest* and *The Republic*," *Interpretations* 11 (1983), 275–316. That Shakespeare read Ficino is suggested by (among others) White, *Copp'd Hills towards Heaven*, 13; Medcalf, "Shakespeare on Beauty," 118; and Collins, *Studies in Shakespeare*, 35, Collins argu-

ing that *MV* 5.1.63–65 derives beyond "reasonable doubt" from 10:610 of the Latin version of the *Republic*.

66. See Walker, *Shakespeare and the Classical Tradition*, and Velz, *Shakespeare and the Classical Tradition*. On the *Republic*, see, e.g., Cantor, *Shakespeare's Rome*, and n. 41 above.

67. Phillips, *State*, 32–33, 35.

68. Heinemann, "Political Drama," 164; Marcus, *Puzzling Shakespeare*, 152. See also Orgel, *Illusion of Power*, 9.

69. E. K. Chambers, *The Elizabethan Stage*, 4 vols. (Oxford: Clarendon Press, 1923), 1:325. See also Philip J. Finkelpearl, "The King's Men and the Politics of Beaumont and Fletcher," in *Court and Country Politics in the Plays of Beaumont and Fletcher* (Princeton: Princeton University Press, 1990), 245–47; and Stephen Orgel, "Making Greatness Familiar," in *Pageantry in the Shakespearean Theater*, ed. David M. Bergeron (Athens: University of Georgia Press, 1985), 19–25.

70. Heywood, *Apology for Actors*, Third Book, F3.

71. Woolf, *Idea of History*, 142–44. Compare Baldassare Castiglione, *The Book of the Courtier* (1528), trans. Sir Thomas Hoby (London: J. M. Dent; New York: E. P. Dutton, 1974): The ultimate aim of the courtier is to guide his prince—to teach him "what honour and profit shall ensue to him . . . by justice . . . and by the other vertues that belong to a good prince, and contrariwise what slander, and damage commeth of the vices contrarie to them" (261).

72. Sir Walter Ralegh, Preface to *The History of the World*, in *The Works of Sir Walter Ralegh, Kt., Now First Collected . . .* , 8 vols. (New York: Burt Franklin, 1965), 2:lxiii; Samuel Daniel, *The Tragedie of Cleopatra*, in Bullough, 5:112–14.

73. Dean, "Tudor Humanism," 87–88. Dean traces, from its beginnings to the Renaissance, the tradition of using Roman history as a medium for interpreting English history.

Chapter 2: *The Rape of Lucrece*

1. As Ernest Barker points out, Plato's ideal state is characterized by "a mind . . . under the control of the sovereign element of reason; and the constitution in which it issues, a constitution similarly marked by the predominance of wisdom over the other elements of the State, is termed by Plato both monarchy and aristocracy." *The Political Thought of Plato and Aristotle* (1918; reprint, New York: Dover Publications, 1959), 178.

2. Julia Annas, *An Introduction to Plato's* Republic (Oxford: Clarendon Press, 1981), 296.

3. Barker, *Political Thought*, 179–80.

4. Political interpretations of *Lucrece* include E. P. Kuhl, "Shakespeare's *Rape of Lucrece*," *Philological Quarterly* 20 (1941): 352–60, who contends that the work, reflecting the political discontent of the 1590s, expresses Shakespeare's censure of royal rule; and Michael Platt, "*The Rape of Lucrece* and the Republic for Which It Stands," *Centennial Review* 19 (1975): 59–79, who argues that the work is republican in sentiment, but stops short of terming it subversive. See also Ian Donaldson, "'A Theme for Disputation': Shakespeare's Lucrece," in *The Rapes of Lucretia: A*

Myth and Its Transformations (Clarendon: Oxford University Press, 1982), 104–17; Annabel Patterson, *Reading Between the Lines* (Madison: University of Wisconsin Press, 1993), 297–310; and James M. Tolbert, "The Argument of Shakespeare's *Lucrece*: Its Sources and Authorship," *Texas Studies in English* 29 (1950): 77–90.

5. See Kuhl, "Shakespeare's *Rape of Lucrece*," 352–55.

6. Ovid, *Fasti*, quoted in Kuhl, "Shakespeare's *Rape of Lucrece*," 353; Henry Bullinger, "Of the Third Precept of the Second Table, which is in Order the Seventh of the Ten Commandments . . . ," in *The Decades of Henry Bullinger*, trans. H. I., ed. Rev. Thomas Harding, Parker Society (Cambridge: Cambridge University Press, 1849), 1:417; Elyot, *Governor*, 10–11. Bullinger (1504–1575) was a Swiss reformer.

7. Donaldson, "Theme for Disputation," 108.

8. Raphael Holinshed, *Holinshed's Chronicles of England, Scotland, and Ireland* (London: J. Johnson, 1807–8), 3:422, cited by Kuhl, "Shakespeare's *Rape of Lucrece*," 355; Donaldson, 112.

9. See Kuhl, "Shakespeare's *Rape of Lucrece*," 354–56.

10. Donaldson, "Theme for Disputation," 118.

11. Ibid., 9.

12. See John W. Velz, "The Ancient World in Shakespeare: Authenticity or Anachronism? A Retrospect," *Shakespeare Survey* 31 (1978): 1–12. For further contemporary applications of the metaphor, see Susan Frye, *Elizabeth I: The Competition for Representation* (New York: Oxford University Press, 1993), 82–84.

13. David Willbern notes a kindred pattern of what he calls "shifting cross-identifications," in which Lucrece alternately represents Troy, Helen, Priam, and Hecuba; and Sinon represents Tarquin and Collatine ("Hyperbolic Desire: Shakespeare's *Lucrece*," in *Contending Kingdoms: Historical, Psychological, and Feminist Approaches to the Literature of Sixteenth-Century England and France*, ed. Marie-Rose Logan and Peter L. Rudnytsky [Detroit: Wayne State University Press, 1991], 213–14). See also John N. King, *Tudor Royal Iconography: Literature and Art in an Age of Religious Crisis* (Princeton: Princeton University Press, 1989), 261–62.

14. A hint of political intent appears as early as the Dedication, where Shakespeare refers to the work as a "pamphlet" (Kuhl, "Shakespeare's *Rape of Lucrece*," 356). It is perhaps noteworthy that despite the poem's sexually-charged content, Shakespeare's countryman Gabriel Harvey allied it not with *Venus and Adonis* (with its appeal to "the younger sort") but with the "tragedie of Hamlet"—a play about the killing of a king—on the ground that *Lucrece* and *Hamlet* were more amenable to "the wiser sort." (*Gabriel Harvey's Marginalia*, ed. G. C. Moore Smith [Stratford-upon-Avon: Shakespeare Head Press, 1913], 232.)

15. *OED*, s.v. "Cabinet" (*sb.*): "The private room in which the confidential advisors of the sovereign . . . meet; the council-chamber" (II.7.a).

16. See *OED*, s.v. "Seat," *sb.*, II.8.a, II.8.b; and Shakespeare's use of the term in *3H6* 1.1.26, 4.6.2; *H5* 1.1.89; and *Tit* 1.1.14.

17. Tacitus, *Dialogue of the Orators*; Davy Du Perron, *L'Avant Discours de Rhétorique ou Traitte de l'Eloquence*; Montaigne, "De la vanité des paroles." This paragraph, including quotations, follows Marc Fumaroli, "Rhetoric, Politics, and Society: From Italian Ciceronianism to French Classicism," in *Renaissance Eloquence: Studies in the Theory and Practice of Renaissance Rhetoric*, ed. James J. Murphy (Berkeley and Los Angeles: University of California Press, 1983), 253–57.

18. On the centrality of the rhetorical motif in the poem, see Richard A. Lanham, "The Ovidian Shakespeare: *Venus and Adonis* and *Lucrece*," in *The Motives of Eloquence: Literary Rhetoric in the Renaissance* (New Haven: Yale University Press, 1976), 82–110; and Nancy J. Vickers, "'This Heraldry in Lucrece' Face,'" *Poetics Today* 6:1–2 (1985): 171–84. See also Heather Dubrow, *Captive Victors: Shakespeare's Narrative Poems and Sonnets* (Ithaca: Cornell University Press, 1987), 439; and Rawdon R. Wilson, "Shakespearean Narrative: *The Rape of Lucrece* Reconsidered," *SEL* 28 (1988): 39–59.

19. Compare Shakespeare's related terms for *crown* or *kingship*: "golden round" (*Mac* 1.5.28); "golden rigol" (*2H4* 4.5.36); "golden circuit" (*2H6* 3.1.352); "golden sovereignty" (*R3* 4.4.329); and "golden crown" (*R2* 3.2.59, *R3* 4.4.140, *Cym* 3.1.60).

20. *The Discourses of Niccolò Machiavelli* (1950; reprint, London: Routledge, 1975), 1:464, quoted in G. W. Majors, "Shakespeare's First Brutus: His Role in *Lucrece*," *Modern Language Quarterly* 35 (1974): 344. The point is Majors'.

21. See *De Oratore*, in *Cicero*, trans. H. Rackham, 28 vols. (London: Heinemann, 1942): vols. 3 and 4, 1.28.128–130.

22. (*De Oratore* 3.59.223). Note the use of this axiom by Nestor, who "Mak[es] such sober action with his hand / That it beguiled attention, charmed the sight" (1403–4); and by Sinon, whose "borrowed tears" beguiled Priam, incurring the burning of Troy (1541–61). See also Thomas Wilson, *The Art of Rhetoric* (1560), ed. Peter E. Medine (University Park: Pennsylvania State University Press, 1994), 243–44. Wilson's treatise, which covers the full range of Ciceronian rhetoric, was widely influential.

23. Frances A. Yates, *Astraea: The Imperial Theme in the Sixteenth Century* (1975; reprint, London: Pimlico, 1993), 50–51. The Greville passage that follows (from *Caelica*, ed. U. Ellis-Fermor [Gregynog Press, 1936], 103) is quoted in Yates. See also Roy Strong, *The Cult of Elizabeth: Elizabethan Portraiture and Pageantry* (1977; reprint, London: Pimlico, 1999), 68, 139.

24. Coppélia Kahn, "The Rape in Shakespeare's *Lucrece*," *Shakespeare Studies* 9 (1976): 49.

25. Yates, *Astraea*, 76; Elizabeth Jenkins, *Elizabeth the Great* (New York: Coward-McCann, 1958), 292.

26. See, e.g., Yates's discussion of J. Case's *Sphaera civitatis* (1588), *Astraea*, 64–65.

27. Earl of Cumberland quoted in John Nichols, ed., *The Progresses and Public Processions of Queen Elizabeth* (London, 1823), 3:492 (the poem appears in Davison's "Poetical Rapsodie, 1611," 197); Davies quoted in Strong, *Cult of Elizabeth*, 53.

28. See Jenkins, *Elizabeth the Great*, 292–93. Shakespeare also possibly uses the moon/stars symbol to denote Elizabeth and her maids in *Tro* 5.2.94–95.

29. Strong, *Cult of Elizabeth*, 116.

30. Eric S. Mallin, "Emulous Factions and the Collapse of Chivalry: *Troilus and Cressida*," *Representations* 29 (1990): 154–55; see also Strong, *Cult of Elizabeth*, 116, 129–87.

31. *Anglorum Feriae, Englandes Hollydayes, celebrating the 17th of Novemb. last, 1595, beginning happyle the 38 yeare of the raigne of our soveraigne ladie Queene Elizabeth*; Works, 2: 287, quoted in Elkin C. Wilson, *England's Eliza* (1939; reprint, New York: Octagon, 1966), 178.

32. Only Livy has the men plight their faith regarding revenge; in Chaucer and Ovid, Lucrece makes no such request. In no source is the request framed in the context of knighthood and chivalry. Shakespeare's Tarquin is also a knight (*Luc* 197).

33. Kahn, "Rape in Shakespeare's *Lucrece*," 57.

34. Mallin, "Emulous Factions," 149.

35. See Mallin, "Emulous Factions"; James E. Savage, "*Troilus and Cressida* and Elizabethan Court Factions," *The University of Mississippi Studies in English* 5 (1964): 43–66; and A. L. Rowse, *Shakespeare's Southampton: Patron of Virginia* (New York: Harper & Row, 1965), 168–69.

36. Alan Gordon Smith, *William Cecil: The Power behind Elizabeth* (1934; reprint, New York: Haskell House, 1971), 244.

37. John Guy, *Tudor England* (Oxford: Oxford University Press, 1988), 443; Mallin, "Emulous Factions," 146.

38. Wallace T. MacCaffrey, *Elizabeth I: War and Politics, 1588–1603* (Princeton: Princeton University Press, 1992), 516. Essex's alleged purpose for the revolt was to get the Queen to oust the Cecilians.

39. Hist. MSS. Comm., Bath *Longleat* MSS., Devereux Papers, 1533–1659, p. 280; quoted in Mervyn James, *Society, Politics and Culture: Studies in Early Modern England* (Cambridge: Cambridge University Press, 1986), 423.

40. MacCaffrey, *War and Politics*, 473.

41. According to Elizabeth, the play was performed "40tie times in open streets and houses" under Essex's auspices. The day before his rebellion, Essex and some cohorts persuaded the Chamberlain's Men to perform a play about Richard's deposition and killing, presumably to promote popular support.

42. Robert Lacey, *Robert, Earl of Essex* (New York: Atheneum, 1971), 300.

43. J. E. Neale, *Queen Elizabeth I: A Biography* (1934; reprint, Garden City, N.Y.: Doubleday, Anchor Books, 1957), 388.

44. Jenkins, *Elizabeth the Great*, 319.

45. Everard Guilpin, "Satyre I," in *Skialetheia*, 1598 [by] Everard Guilpin, Shakespeare Association Facsimiles, no. 2 (London: Oxford University Press, 1931), sig. C3v.

46. Peter Ure, ed., *King Richard II*, The Arden Shakespeare, 5th ed. (London: Methuen, 1961), 42 n. 31.

47. "I am Richard II, know ye not that?" The comment was reportedly made in 1601 during a conversation with William Lambarde, Keeper of the Records in the Tower. Lily B. Campbell, *Shakespeare's "Histories": Mirrors of Elizabethan Policy* (San Marino, Calif.: Huntington Library, 1947), 169–81, and E. K. Chambers, *William Shakespeare: A Study of Facts and Problems* (Oxford: Clarendon, 1930), 1:353, discuss these analogies more fully.

48. Although published in 1597, it may have been written in 1595 or earlier. See Chambers, *Facts and Problems*, 1:354–55.

49. Robert Parsons [R. Doleman, pseud.], *A Conference about the Next Succession to the Crowne of Ingland* (1594), ed. D. M. Rogers, English Recusant Literature 1558–1640, vol. 104 (Menston, England: Scolar Press, 1972).

50. According to accounts of his cohorts, the revolt suffered from Essex's conflicting goals: to make himself king, to hasten James's installation, and to secure the court so that he could gain access to Elizabeth in order to make his case (Frye,

Elizabeth I, 106). Essex himself, having testified that he was simply seeking to disabuse Elizabeth of lies by the Cecil faction, subsequently proclaimed himself a traitor. Essex had in fact sought military support from James, but the plan never materialized.

51. Frye, *Elizabeth I*, 114, 124. This and the two following paragraphs are heavily indebted to Frye.

52. Frye, *Elizabeth I*, 118, 136.

53. Ibid., 138–39, q.v. for further details on how Cecil conveyed the idea of attempted rape.

54. Jenkins, *Elizabeth the Great*, 309–10; Neale, *Elizabeth I*, 374–77. Again, his purported aim was not her overthrow but the removal of his enemies from her presence.

55. Frye, *Elizabeth I*, 124, quoting John Nichols, ed., *The Progresses and Public Processions of Queen Elizabeth* (1823; reprint, New York: AMS Press, 1966), 3:232.

56. The parallels between the two are noteworthy. In deserting the Roman camp for Collatium, Tarquin neglects "His honor, his affairs, his friends, his state" (45–46). Essex's desertion of the English camp for Compiègne, which brought a stinging rebuke from the Privy Council, was similarly seen as a neglect of honor, affairs, and state. See Richard C. McCoy, *The Rites of Knighthood: The Literature and Politics of Elizabethan Chivalry* (Berkeley and Los Angeles: University of California Press, 1989), 81. On the Rouen desertion, see Neale, *Elizabeth I*, 335.

57. John Carpenter, *Liber Albus*, trans. H. T. Riley (London, 1861), 396, quoted in D. W. Robertson, Jr., "The Concept of Courtly Love as an Impediment to the Understanding of Medieval Texts," in *The Meaning of Courtly Love*, ed. F. X. Newman (Albany: State University of New York Press, 1972), 11; Anthea Hume, *Edmund Spenser: Protestant Poet* (Cambridge: Cambridge University Press, 1984), 147. In 1419 when he compiled his book, Carpenter was Clerk of the City.

58. S. K. Heninger, Jr., "The Tudor Myth of Troy-novant," *South Atlantic Quarterly* 61 (1962): 386–87; Strong, *Cult of Elizabeth*, 121, quoting from *The Works of George Peele*, ed. A. H. Bullen (London, 1888), 2:346–47.

59. Robertson, "Concept of Courtly Love," 11–12.

60. Mallin, "Emulous Factions," 165.

61. All quoted in Brents Stirling, "Anti-Democracy in Shakespeare: A Re-survey," *Modern Language Quarterly* 2 (1941): 495–97.

62. Campbell, *Shakespeare's "Histories,"* 172, 175. By 1580–81, the rumors concerning the Queen had become so vociferous that Parliament enacted new and stricter penalties for those who maligned her (Campbell, 173).

63. MacCaffrey, *War and Politics*, 473.

64. Ibid., 521.

65. The prince as a moral glass for his subjects was a commonplace notion. Compare King James's advice to his son and heir: "Let your owne life be a . . . mirrour to your people, that therein they may . . . see, by your image, what life they should leade" (*Basilikon Doron*, in Charles Howard McIlwain, *The Political Works of James I* [1918; reprint, New York: Russell & Russell, 1965], 43).

66. Edward II, Richard II, and Henry VI. Ure, introduction to *King Richard II*, lvii.

67. Neale, *Elizabeth I*, 336.

68. MacCaffrey, *War and Politics*, 533.

69. Wayne A. Rebhorn, "The Crisis of the Aristocracy in *Julius Caesar*," *Renaissance Quarterly* 43 (1990): 104–5.
70. See MacCaffrey, *War and Politics*, 525.
71. Ibid., 536.

Chapter 3: *Coriolanus*

1. Compare First Citizen's statement that the rulers "make edicts for usury to support usurers" (1.1.79–80). The element of usury, however, could also have derived from Plutarch's *Coriolanus*.
2. Compare *Cor* 1.1.14–23, 78–84.
3. For the sake of consistency, I refer to the titular character as "Marcius" throughout.
4. Quoted in Lawrence Stone, *The Causes of the English Revolution, 1529–1642* (New York: Harper & Row, 1972), 49.
5. Charles Howard McIlwain, introduction to *The Political Works of James I* (1918; reprint, New York: Russell & Russell, 1965), xxxiii.
6. James never wearied of reminding his recalcitrant Parliaments of the king/God equation. See David Harris Willson, *King James VI and I* (New York: Oxford University Press, 1956), 243, 257, 264; and Wallace Notestein, *The House of Commons, 1604–1610* (New Haven: Yale University Press, 1971), 67, 179, 282. The concept was a linchpin of his political philosophy; see McIlwain, *Works*, xxxviii–xxxix, xxxv, xl.
7. James held that all law derives from the king, who is thus "aboue the law, as both the author and giuer of strength thereto." *The Trew Law of Free Monarchies*, in McIlwain, *Works*, 63.
8. McIlwain, *Works*, xlii.
9. *Trew Law*, 62.
10. That *Coriolanus* is topically slanted, reflecting in particular the Midlands Insurrection and James's parliamentary conflicts, has been widely argued. Unexamined, however, is the role of these issues in the political decline, both Rome's and England's, that is the subject of this book. Topical studies pertinent to the present one include W. Gordon Zeeveld, "*Coriolanus* and Jacobean Politics," *Modern Language Review* 57 (1962): 321–34; Clifford Chalmers Huffman, *Coriolanus in Context* (Lewisburg, Pa: Bucknell University Press, 1971); E. C. Pettet, "*Coriolanus* and the Midlands Insurrection of 1607," *Shakespeare Survey* 3 (1950): 34–42; Andrew Gurr, "*Coriolanus* and the Body Politic," *Shakespeare Survey* 28 (1975): 63–69; Leah S. Marcus, *Puzzling Shakespeare: Local Reading and Its Discontents* (Berkeley and Los Angeles: University of California Press, 1988), 202–11; Annabel M. Patterson, *Shakespeare and the Popular Voice* (Cambridge, Mass.: Basil Blackwell, 1989), 120–53; Stephen Coote, "*Coriolanus* and Seventeenth-Century Politics," in *William Shakespeare: Coriolanus*, ed. Bryan Loughrey, Penguin Critical Studies (London: Penguin, 1992), 86–97; R. B. Parker, introduction to *The Tragedy of Coriolanus*, The Oxford Shakespeare (Oxford: Clarendon Press, 1994); and Shannon Miller, "Topicality and Subversion in William Shakespeare's *Coriolanus*," *SEL* 32 (1992): 287–310. Miller, going beyond previous topical studies, argues a series of parallels between Coriolanus and James I that include treason. See also Clifford Davidson,

"*Coriolanus*: A Study in Political Dislocation," *Shakespeare Studies* 4 (1968): 263–74; D. J. Gordon, "Name and Fame: Shakespeare's *Coriolanus*," in *The Renaissance Imagination*, ed. Stephen Orgel (Berkeley and Los Angeles: University of California Press, 1975), 206–7; and James Emerson Phillips, "Violation of Order and Degree in *Coriolanus*," in *The State in Shakespeare's Greek and Roman Plays* (1940; reprint, New York: Octagon, 1972), 147–71.

11. Huffman, *Coriolanus in Context*, 150, q.v. regarding reasons for the disaffection. Another fissure was simultaneously developing owing to James's efforts to impose conformity on the Puritans, who turned to Parliament "while the bishops turned to the King" (Willson, *James VI and I*, 210). A considerable majority of the Commons had Puritan leanings, and Puritans were the clerical and secular leaders of the opposition both in and out of Parliament (Notestein, *Commons*, 255; Stone, *Causes*, 103).

12. These included such issues as purveyance and wardship. On these and other grievances, consult Notestein, *Commons*, 85–106, 160–202. Purveyance was "the right of the king's agents to set low values on goods commandeered in his name for the support of his household" (Alvin Kernan, *Shakespeare, the King's Playwright: Theater in the Stuart Court, 1603–1613* [New Haven: Yale University Press, 1995], 125); abuses involved paying prices for commodities, including corn, often at less than one-fourth of their true value (Notestein, *Commons*, 99, 102). The play's opening scene appears to conflate allusions to this abuse and to the Midland riots as the Citizens propose to kill Marcius so they can procure "corn at [their] own price" (1.1.10–11).

13. Quoted in Huffman, *Coriolanus in Context*, 150.

14. Wallace Notestein, *The Winning of the Initiative by the House of Commons*, Proceedings of the British Academy (London: Oxford University Press, 1924), 49–50; Zeeveld, "Jacobean Politics," 327, 328; Stone, *Causes*, 116.

15. D. A. Traversi, *Shakespeare: The Roman Plays* (Stanford: Stanford University Press, 1963), 214. Traversi uses these words in connection with Marcius's refusal to defer to his inferiors.

16. Other reasons for the Commons' rise to power are adduced by Notestein, *Initiative*; see also George Macaulay Trevelyan, *History of England* (London: Longmans, 1926), 401–3. Shakespeare, however, makes rhetorical proficiency the determining factor, not only in *Coriolanus* but in *Lucrece* and *Caesar*.

17. Zeeveld, "Jacobean Politics," 333. Studies containing rhetorical considerations of the play include D. J. Enright, "*Coriolanus*: Tragedy or Debate?" *Essays in Criticism* 4 (1954): 1–19; G. Thomas Tanselle and Florence W. Dunbar, "Legal Language in *Coriolanus*," *Shakespeare Quarterly* 13 (1962): 231–38; and Leonard Tennenhouse, "*Coriolanus*: History and the Crisis of Semantic Order," in *Drama in the Renaissance: Comparative and Critical Essays*, ed. Clifford Davidson, C. J. Gianakaris, and John H. Stroupe (New York: AMS Press, 1986), 217–35. See also Harry Levin, introduction to *Coriolanus*, in *William Shakespeare: The Complete Works*, gen. ed. Alfred Harbage (New York: Viking, Penguin, 1969), 1213; Paul A. Cantor, *Shakespeare's Rome: Republic and Empire* (Ithaca: Cornell University Press, 1976), 110–16; and Parker, *Tragedy of Coriolanus*, 73–77.

18. Tennenhouse, "Semantic Order," 219.

19. Both quoted in G. R. Elton, *England Under the Tudors*, 3d ed. (London: Routledge, 1991), 400.

20. *Apology of the House of Commons, made to the King, touching their Privileges*, in *The Parliamentary History of England, from the earliest period to the year 1803* . . . , 36 vols. (London: 1806–1820), 1:1033.

21. Compare Menenius's reference to the citizens as "incorporate" (1.1.129).

22. 1 Cor. 12.21–22; compare First Citizen's designation as a "toe" (1.1.154). The corporate variant posited the "state as a corporate organism, symbolised in parliament with the king as head and lords and commons as 'members'" (Gurr, 63). The Platonic variant derives from *Rep.*, book 4; the Christian from 1. Cor. 12. See also 1 Cor. 12.12–25: "For as the bodie is one, and hathe many membres, and all the membres of the bodie, which is one, thogh they be many, yet are but one bodie: even so is Christ. For by one Spirit are we all baptized into one bodie. . . . God hathe tempered the bodie together . . . [so that] there shulde be [no] diuision in the bodie: but that the members shulde haue the same care one for another."

23. *Apology*, 1035, 1036.

24. In addition to the organ of digestion and excretion, the term meant a cesspool, a sewage conduit, and a gathering place for vice and corruption (*OED*, s.v. "sink," *sb.*), the senses in which writers conventionally used it. See, e.g., *An Homilie against Disobedience and Willful Rebellion*, which calls rebellion "the whole puddle and sinke of all sinnes against God and man"; and *FQ* 1.1.22, which describes the "hellish sinke" of Errour's womb.

25. Note, e.g., Menenius's epicurean reputation (2.1.47–49, 80–82), his comment at 5.1.52–58 (which further belies the spare diet he alleges for the patriciate), and his aversion to soldiership (3.2.34–37). Compare Plato's contention that oligarchical rulers lead lives of "luxury and idleness" and are generally averse to and unfit for battle (*Rep.* 8.556, 551; see also 556).

26. Compare James's claim that all law derives from "himselfe, or his predecessours; and so the power flowes alwaies from him selfe" (*Trew Law*, 63). Hence his statement to the Commons in 1603, when they protested his interference in the Goodwin-Fortescue election, that "since they derived all matters of priviledge from him, and by his grant, he expected they should not be turned against him" (*Apology*, 1002).

27. An opposing body of interpretation holds that in *Coriolanus* Shakespeare criticizes the metaphor of the body politic as an outmoded fiction. See, e.g., James Holstun, "Tragic Superfluity in *Coriolanus*," *ELH* 59 (1983): 485–507; Arthur Riss, "The Belly Politic: *Coriolanus* and the Revolt of Language," *ELH* 59 (1992): 53–75; and Gurr, "Body Politic." Cf. Zvi Jagendorf, "*Coriolanus*: Body Politic and Private Parts," *Shakespeare Quarterly* 41 (1990): 455–69.

28. E.g., "proceed," "resolved," "assembly," "petition," "dissolved."

29. Compare Marcius's speech to his troops before Corioles with Henry V's to his before Harfleur. Marcius's divides; Henry's unites. Both speeches reflect the leadership qualities of their speakers and amply demonstrate why Marcius loses Rome and Henry wins France.

30. See chapter 2 above.

31. Like Volumnia, the Tribunes enlist the visual component of rhetoric along with the aural to manipulate the people.

32. For an extended analysis of divided military command in Shakespeare's plays, see Paul A. Jorgensen, *Shakespeare's Military World* (1956; reprint, Berkeley and Los Angeles: University of California Press, 1973), 35–62.

33. These stratagems are simply variants of those she urges on Marcius at 3.2.74–79 and which she now calculatedly practices on her recalcitrant son: the hat "in . . . hand" of 3.2.75 has become the child "in . . . hand" of 5.3.23–24, and "Thy knee bussing the stones" (3.2.77) has become the kneeling, enjoined by Volumnia, of every member of her group, including young Marcius (5.3.54–57, 75, 169, 175).

34. While "infantlike" here refers to the initial power of the Tribunes, they and the people are thematically interchangeable; note, e.g., Sicinius's statement that the people are "The commoners, for whom we stand" (2.1.226).

35. "Proceedings and speeches at close of Parliament, 2 January 1567," in *Proceedings in the Parliaments of Elizabeth I*, ed. T. E. Hartley, Vol 1: 1558–1581 (Wilmington, Del.: Michael Glazier, 1981), 168–69.

36. Eugene M. Waith, "The Herculean Hero," in *Modern Critical Interpretations: William Shakespeare's* Coriolanus, ed. Harold Bloom (New York: Chelsea House, 1988), 11, reprinted from Eugene M. Waith, *The Herculean Hero in Marlowe, Chapman, Shakespeare and Dryden* under the title "Shakespeare" (New York: Columbia University Press, 1962); see also Huffman, *Coriolanus in Context*, 188. For an extreme form of this view, see Geoffrey Miles, *Shakespeare and the Constant Romans* (Oxford: Clarendon Press, 1996), 149–68, who argues that Marcius embodies the steadfastness of the Senecan Stoic hero.

37. Willson, *James VI and I*, 165.

38. Notestein, *Commons*, 60; Robert Ashton, ed., *James I by His Contemporaries* (London: Hutchinson, 1969), 56; see also Willson, *James VI and I*, 165.

39. Arthur Wilson, *The History of Great Britain, being the Life and Reign of King James the First* (1653), 668, quoted in Ashton, *James I*, 64; compare *Cor* 1.1.163–221.

40. *Cal. St. P. Venetian, 1603–1607*, 509–14, quoted in Ashton, *James I*, 10.

41. Willson, *James VI and I*, 178.

42. Kernan, *King's Playwright*, 107–8; Ashton, *James I*, 10.

43. Roger B. Manning, *Village Revolts: Social Protest and Popular Disturbances in England, 1509–1640* (Oxford: Clarendon Press, 1988), 232.

44. *Trew Law*, 55.

45. Willson, *James VI and I*, 246.

46. Speech in Parliament, 1609–10, McIlwain, *Works*, 529.

47. *Apology*, 1048.

48. The triumph of Aufidius that concludes the play departs notably from Plutarch (Shakespeare's principal source), who ends with the Romans conquering the Volscians and slaying Aufidius in battle.

Chapter 4: *Julius Caesar*

1. *Brutus*, 188. References to Plutarch (*Caesar, Brutus, Antonius, Cicero*) are to *Plutarch's Lives of the Noble Grecians and Romans Englished by Sir Thomas North* (1579), ed. W. E. Henley, The Tudor Translations, vols. 5 and 6 (London: David Nutt, 1895–96). For a summary of critical positions on this soliloquy, see Ernest Schanzer, *The Problem Plays of Shakespeare: A Study of* Julius Caesar, Measure for Measure, Antony and Cleopatra (New York: Schocken, 1963), 40.

2. These characteristics are substantially Shakespeare's additions. In Plutarch, Caesar is, except for a proneness to headaches and the falling sickness, physically and mentally unimpaired; and as to the falling sickness, Plutarch states that Caesar "yeelded not" to the disease "to make it a cloke to cherishe him withall [cf. 1.2.268–73], but contrarilie, tooke the paines of warre, as a medicine to cure" it. (*Caesar*, 17–18; see also 54). Elsewhere he cites Caesar's "great wisedom, power, and fortune" (*The Comparison of Dion with Brutus*, 239).

3. Caesar, of course, was traditionally perceived as an opportunistic populist. The point here is Caesar's association with what the populace represents: "basest metal."

4. Cf. *Caesar*, 62, and *Antonius*, 13.

5. See Irving Ribner, "Political Issues in *Julius Caesar*," *Journal of English and Germanic Philology* 56 (1957): 10–22.

6. This speech is Shakespeare's addition to Plutarch's narrative. Cf. Plutarch: "So when he [Caesar] was set, the conspirators flocked about him, and . . . presented one Tullius Cimber, who made humble sute for the calling home againe of his [banished] brother. . . . They all made as though they were intercessors for him . . . and kissed his head and brest. Caesar at the first, simplie refused their kindnesse and intreaties: but afterwardes, perceiving they still pressed on him, he violently thrust them from him" (*Brutus*, 197).

7. This, again, is Shakespeare's addition. In Plutarch, Calpurnia dreams that "Caesar was slaine" and that she saw a broken pinnacle atop Caesar's house. The next morning, she begs Caesar to remain at home and "to adjorne the session of the Senate, untill an other day." Not only is the dream different, but Decius states merely that were Caesar to return to the Senate "when Calpurnia shoulde have better dreames: what would his enemies . . . say, and how could they like of his frendes wordes?" (*Caesar*, 65–66).

8. Cf. Plutarch's contention that "Caesar was not . . . fickle headed" (*Antonius*, 6).

9. The concept of the brute mentality of the populace also derives ultimately from Plato, who terms them "a mighty . . . beast" and "the great brute" (*Rep.* 6.493). The concept was a Renaissance commonplace. Cf. Frederick Tupper, Jr., "The Shaksperean Mob," *PMLA* 27 (1912): 486–523.

10. Francis MacDonald Cornford, *The Republic of Plato* (1941; reprint, London: Oxford University Press, 1974), 264.

11. Pompey's son; he also attempted to kill Pompey (see *Caesar*, 37–48, 56–57). Pompey was Caesar's son-in-law through marriage to Caesar's daughter Julia.

12. Jan H. Blits, *The End of the Ancient Republic: Essays on* Julius Caesar (Durham: Carolina Academic Press, 1982), 23. The wolf image as well as the lion image discussed below are Shakespeare's additions.

13. Compare Plutarch: "[T]he chiefest cause that made [Caesar] mortally hated, was the covetous desire he had to be called king: which first gave the people just cause . . . to beare him ill will." And: "[T]hey could not abide the name of a king, detesting it as the utter destruction of their liberty" (*Caesar*, 60; *Antonius*, 13). On the Republican equation of king and tyrant, see Rebecca W. Bushnell, *Tragedies of Tyrants: Political Thought and Theater in the English Renaissance* (Ithaca: Cornell University Press, 1990), 144–46. See also John Velz, "Clemency, Will, and

Just Cause in 'Julius Caesar,'" *Shakespeare Survey* 22 (1969): 109–18, on the distinction between tyrants and kings.

14. The seizure and its attendant speech are Shakespeare's addition. While Plutarch reports instances of Caesar's falling sickness (*Caesar*, 17, 54), the occasion of his being offered the crown is not one of them. Cf. *Caesar*, 61–62.

15. The Platonic correspondence between ruler and state is a standard notion in Shakespeare. Compare *Hamlet*, in which Denmark's "rottenness" reflects that of Claudius; and *Macbeth* (esp. 2.4), in which the myriad, gross perversions in nature reflect those in Macbeth's soul.

16. The monster as symbol for perversion of the natural order was another standard concept. See James Emerson Phillips, *The State in Shakespeare's Greek and Roman Plays* (1940; reprint, New York: Octagon, 1972), 65–66; and chapter 2 above.

17. Socrates explains that each of the soul's faculties has its characteristic desire: reason seeks after truth, will after power and fame, and appetite after gain (9.580–81). To these correspond three classes of men, depending on which element predominates: the philosophic, the ambitious, and the lover of gain. In Elizabethan psychology, the will is responsible for translating thought into action, ideally serving reason by choosing the good. In the unregenerate man, however, the will follows the blind guide of the appetites. In the case of Caesar, Shakespeare appears to be fusing the two contexts. Elsewhere he identifies Caesar (i.e., the tyrant) with the appetites and passions (i.e., with their correlative, the mob). In all three instances, however, the point remains the same: reason is enslaved by the lower faculties.

18. See the related study of Bernard R. Breyer, "A New Look at *Julius Caesar*," in *Essays in Honor of Walter Clyde Curry*, comp. John W. Stevenson, Vanderbilt Studies in the Humanities 2 (Nashville: Vanderbilt University Press, 1954), 175–76. For a non-Platonic interpretation of the will/tyranny relationship, see Velz, "Just Cause," who argues that Caesar, acting *in voluptatem*, reflects the tyrant of Seneca's *De Clementia*.

19. Cornford, *Republic*, 264.

20. Brents Stirling, "'Or else were this a savage spectacle,'" in *Unity in Shakespearian Tragedy: The Interplay of Theme and Character* (New York: Columbia University Press, 1956), 47.

21. Plutarch's account is the antithesis: "[T]hey durst not acquaint Cicero with their conspiracie, although he was a man whome they loved dearelie, and trusted best: for they were affrayed that he being a coward by nature, and age also having increased his feare, he woulde quite turne and alter all their purpose, and quench the heate of their enterprise" (*Brutus*, 191–92; see also *Cicero*, 358).

22. *Antonius*, 15; see also *Brutus*, 201, and *Cicero*, 358. Cf. Schanzer, *Problem Plays*, 43, who believes Antony's character and oration derive from Appian.

23. Cf. John W. Velz, "Caesar's Deafness," *Shakespeare Quarterly* 22 (1971): 400–401; and Douglas L. Peterson, "'Wisdom Consumed in Confidence': An Examination of Shakespeare's *Julius Caesar*," *Shakespeare Quarterly* 16 (1965): 19–28. Both argue that Caesar here speaks figuratively, Velz suggesting that Caesar's deafness derives from Plutarch's *Life of Alexander the Great*.

24. James Holly Hanford, "A Platonic Passage in Shakespeare's *Troilus and Cressida*," *Studies in Philology* 13 (1916): 107, quoting *Rep.* 9.572.

25. Gary B. Miles, "How Roman Are Shakespeare's 'Romans'?" *Shakespeare Quarterly* 40 (1989): 279.

26. See *OED*, s.v. "Caesar," 2.

27. Both Plutarch and Shakespeare cite Brutus's pursuit of philosophy. Plutarch states that Brutus "framed his ... life by the rules of vertue and studie of Philosophie" and that "he loved Platoes sect best" (*Brutus*, 182, 183; see also 221, 222). Shakespeare notes Brutus's study of philosophy at 4.3.144–45 and 5.1.104–11.

28. Cf. Plutarch: "For by flattering of him [Brutus], a man coulde never obteyne any thing at his handes, nor make him to doe that which was unjust" (*Brutus*, 187). The seeming nobility of the enterprise rather than Cassius's flattery is what seduces Plutarch's Brutus, although Plutarch also refers elsewhere to Brutus's ambition (*Caesar*, 63).

29. Shakespeare's addition; the speech has no corollary in Plutarch.

30. In a related study ("The Metaphor of Alchemy in *Julius Caesar*," *Costerus* 5 [1972]: 135–51), William B. Toole explores the play's alchemical motif, arguing that it illuminates, through irony, key aspects of plot and character. Toole views Cassius's soliloquy in the context of this motif but concludes, as I do not, that while Cassius succeeds in seducing Brutus, he fails to transform Brutus's character. The repeated connection between character and metal is also noted by T. S. Dorsch in his Arden edition of the play (London: Methuen, 1955), lxvii–lxviii, who additionally considers the play's recurring *metal/mettle* pun. See also Cumberland Clark, "The Art of the Alchemist," in *Shakespeare and Science* (Birmingham, England: Cornish, 1929), 63, who analyzes the alchemical motif in Shakespeare's works in the context of Elizabethan scientific views.

31. I base this meaning on the *OED* definition of "Humour," *v.*, 5: "To give a particular character or style to." Such working or "humoring" of metal is a recurring motif in the play; note, e.g., Brutus's statement to Cassius: "What you would work me to, I have some aim" (1.2.163), and Brutus's profoundly ironic reference to "th' insuppressive mettle of our spirits" (2.1.134). *Metal* and *mettle* were interchangeable spellings, *metal* having the additional meaning of "the 'stuff' of which a man is made, with reference to character" (*OED*, s.v. "Metal," *sb.*, 1.f). Shakespeare plays on both meanings throughout, the two senses conceivably having been suggested by the *Republic*, in which they are similarly fused. The phrase "honorable metal" may also derive from the *Republic*, i.e., from Socrates' tenet that those whose souls are composed of gold "have the greatest honour" (6.492).

32. Brutus's analogy derives from *Rep.* 4.441–44, the passage in which Socrates likens the soul to the State. In the soul as in the State, vitiation of the ordained hierarchy produces chaos. The concept was a Renaissance commonplace, and Shakespeare need not have gotten it from the *Republic* directly.

33. All noted by Dorsch, *Julius Caesar*, xli. Brutus's pomposity, as Dorsch points out, has little or no basis in Plutarch. Brutus's tyranny is extensively explored in Gordon Ross Smith's seminal "Brutus, Virtue, and Will," *Shakespeare Quarterly* 10 (1959): 67–79, which argues that Brutus uses his putative virtue to cloak his relentlessly egotistical willfulness.

34. G. R. Elton, *England under the Tudors*, 3d ed. (1955; reprint, London: Routledge, 1962), 469.

NOTES TO CHAPTER 4

35. Wallace T. MacCaffrey, *Elizabeth I: War and Politics, 1588–1603* (Princeton: Princeton University Press, 1992), 520; John Guy, *Tudor England* (Oxford: Oxford University Press, 1988), 439.

36. See J. E. Neale, *Queen Elizabeth I: A Biography* (1934; reprint, Garden City, N. Y.: Doubleday, Anchor Books, 1957), 362; MacCaffrey, *War and Politics*, 517.

37. On the Parsons book and the Essex/Bolingbroke identification, see chapter 2 above.

38. Andrew Gurr, ed., *King Richard II*, The New Cambridge Shakespeare (Cambridge, England: Cambridge University Press, 1984), 6; Lily B. Campbell, *Shakespeare's "Histories": Mirrors of Elizabethan Policy* (San Marino, Calif: Huntington Library, 1947), 190. Hayward's dedication was in Latin.

39. Neale, *Elizabeth I*, 367; MacCaffrey, *War and Politics*, 522; cf. MacCaffrey, 523.

40. Guy, *Tudor England*, 524; Neale, *Elizabeth I*, 368.

41. MacCaffrey, *War and Politics*, 522, quoting William Camden, *Annals of Queen Elizabeth* (London, 1675).

42. MacCaffrey, *War and Politics*, 526; Neale, *Elizabeth I*, 369; Howard Nenner, *The Right to be King: The Succession to the Crown of England, 1603–1714* (Chapel Hill: University of North Carolina Press, 1995), 265 n. 65.

43. The point and the quotation are Neale's, *Elizabeth I*, 369.

44. MacCaffrey, *War and Politics*, 526.

45. Neale, *Elizabeth I*, 371; Elton, *England under the Tudors*, 473.

46. Neale, *Elizabeth I*, 374.

47. Guy, *Tudor England*, 447.

48. Ibid., 448, quoting *Calendar of State Papers, Domestic, 1598–1601*, 453–55.

49. Guy, *Tudor England*, 448; Neale, *Elizabeth I*, 375. See also MacCaffrey, *War and Politics*, 525, 533–36.

50. On this passage and the Queen's domination by favorites, see chapter 2 above.

51. *OED*, s.v. "Broached," 2.

52. The Caesar faction may be taken to include those who favor Caesar's supremacy, including the senators about to make him king. Note Brutus's reference to the conspirators as "the faction" (2.1.77).

53. David Daniell, ed., *Julius Caesar*, The Arden Shakespeare, Third Series (Walton-on-Thames: Thomas Nelson, 1998), 23.

54. Guy, *Tudor England*, 443.

55. The phrase is Elton's, *England under the Tudors*, 469. Compare the comment of William Camden: the Earl sought to outshine "both his equals and superiours, to detract from the praise of all which were not at his devotion, [and] to frowne upon others which had any power or grace with the Queene" (*Annals of Queen Elizabeth*, quoted in Richard C. McCoy, *The Rites of Knighthood: The Literature and Politics of Elizabethan Chivalry* [Berkeley and Los Angeles: University of California Press, 1989], 84).

56. Elton, *England under the Tudors*, 469.

57. Compare Plutarch's account, in which Cassius hates Caesar because Caesar had preferred Brutus for the Praetorship and, reportedly, had confiscated his lions but more probably because "even from his cradell [he] could . . . abide [no] maner of tyrans" (*Brutus*, 189; see also *Caesar*, 63–64, and *Antonius*, 13). Cassius's depiction of Caesar is Shakespeare's invention.

58. On Naunton as well as other parallels adduced by Elizabethans between the two, see Wayne A. Rebhorn, "The Crisis of the Aristocracy in *Julius Caesar*," *Renaissance Quarterly* 43 (1990): 102–3. Caesar's adulation by "the vulgar" (1.1.70) finds a parallel in an anonymous 1603 poem, which cites Essex's admiration by "the vulgar sorte," q.v. chapter 2 above.

59. Shakespeare seems to have gone out of his way to stress Caesar's decline. Besides adding such details as deafness (perhaps additionally suggestive of advanced age) and a fever contracted in Spain, Shakespeare makes Caesar a poor swimmer, effectively inverting the account in Plutarch: Plutarch's Caesar escapes from the Egyptians by leaping from a boat "into the sea, with great hazard.... [H]olding divers bookes in his hand, he did never let them go, but kept them alwayes upon his head above water, and swamme with the other hand, notwithstanding that they shot marvelously at him, and was driven somtime to ducke into the water: howbeit the boate was drowned presently" (*Caesar*, 51). Caesar's "falling sickness," while not added, is augmented. That Caesar can figure more than one personage is entirely plausible; Shakespeare is again employing the "mirrors-more-than-one" device, q.v. chapter 2 above.

60. Daniell, *Julius Caesar*, 163 n. The issue's prominence is noted by Daniell. Strictly speaking, of course, Caesar was not childless; according to Plutarch, he had a daughter (Julia, already noted, who died in 54 B.C.), and a son (Caesarion, by Cleopatra) killed by Octavius in 30 B.C. possibly because, as Caesar's child, he was seen by Octavius as a potential rival.

61. Nenner, *Right to be King*, 23 (see also 22–25), representatively quoting Peter Wentworth, *A Pithie Exhortation to Her Majestie for Establishing Her Successor to the Crowne* (1587, pub. 1598), 8.

62. Roy Strong, *The Cult of Elizabeth: Elizabethan Portraiture and Pageantry* (1977; reprint, London: Pimlico, 1999), 125–26.

63. See Robert Lacey, *Robert, Earl of Essex* (New York: Atheneum, 1971), 56–57; Guy, *Tudor England*, 439. Ironically, her indecision did not include her adamancy about naming a successor.

64. Both cited by Strong, *Cult of Elizabeth*, 48; Daniell, *Julius Caesar*, 25. Daniell (22–29) adduces further parallels.

65. This last point is made by Norman Sanders, "The Shift of Power in *Julius Caesar*," *Review of English Literature* 5 (1964): 35. Further parallels between the two Caesars are noted by Sanders.

66. See Barbara L. Parker, "The Whore of Babylon and Shakespeare's *Julius Caesar*," *SEL* 35 (1995): 265–66.

Chapter 5: *Antony and Cleopatra*

1. Paul A. Cantor, *Shakespeare's Rome: Republic and Empire* (Ithaca: Cornell University Press, 1976), 130.

2. "As becomes clear in [2.6.]15–19, the motive for Pompey's rebellion is that the three triumvirs have taken over the power which should belong to the Senate and have achieved the kind of political dominance for which Julius Caesar was assassinated." John Wilders, ed., *Antony and Cleopatra*, The Arden Shakespeare, Third Series (London: Routledge, 1995), 155 n.

3. On the pervasive bawdy punning and phallic overtones in the play, see Philip J. Traci, *The Love Play of Antony and Cleopatra: A Critical Study of Shakespeare's Play* (The Hague: Mouton, 1970), 78–95, 155–60. Traci persuasively argues that the movement of the play is a sustained metaphor of the love-act.

4. Margot Heinemann, "'Let Rome in Tiber melt': Order and Disorder in 'Antony and Cleopatra,'" in *Antony and Cleopatra*, ed. John Drakakis, New Casebooks (New York: St. Martin's Press, 1994), 170.

5. Antony's veto of prudent military counsel at Actium parallels Brutus's veto of such counsel preceding Phillipi and incurs the same disastrous consequences. Brutus's action likewise signified a descent into tyranny, q.v. chapter 4 above.

6. Cantor, *Shakespeare's Rome*, 201.

7. Nicholas P. White, *A Companion to Plato's Republic* (Indianapolis: Hackett Publishing, 1979), 220.

8. Rebecca W. Bushnell, *Tragedies of Tyrants: Political Thought and Theater in the English Renaissance* (Ithaca: Cornell University Press, 1990), 53. The description equally defines Tarquin.

9. White, *Companion*, 25.

10. Ernest Barker, *The Political Thought of Plato and Aristotle* (1918; reprint, New York: Dover, 1959), 181–82. Cf. Cantor's use of the concept of eros in *Shakespeare's Rome*.

11. Sir Thomas Elyot, *Of the Knowledge Which Maketh a Wise Man*, ed. Edwin Johnston Howard (Oxford, Ohio: Anchor Press, 1946), 206, 209. Bushnell (*Tragedies of Tyrants*, 52–53) provides further examples; see also 10, 26–29. Largely owing to Stuart absolutism, the psychological concept of the tyrant eventually gave way to a legalistic one, applied to anyone who would deprive another of his liberty or property (Bushnell, 76).

12. This does not preclude her from also being a tyrant; as indicated above, Eros was by definition a tyrant, living lawlessly within the soul and leading it on "as a tyrant leads a State" (*Rep.* 9.575).

13. Thomas B. Stroup, "The Structure of *Antony and Cleopatra*," *Shakespeare Quarterly* 15 (1964): 295.

14. David Kaula, "The Time Sense of *Antony and Cleopatra*," *Shakespeare Quarterly* 15 (1964): 217.

15. The judgment of history preoccupies the characters generally. Antony will fight Caesar so that "I and my sword will earn our chronicle" (3.13.178). Cleopatra dies to preserve her image of greatness; her suicide will earn her "A nobleness in record" (4.14.99). Enobarbus ponders "earn[ing] a place i' the story" through fidelity to Antony (3.13.46); dying, he asks to be adjudged "A master-leaver and a fugitive" (4.9.24–25). Other Shakespearean characters concerned with history's judgment include Brutus and Cassius (*JC* 3.1.112–20), who, like Cleopatra contemplating the lovers' "revels," predict the future staging of their deeds; Cressida (*Tro* 3.2.183–95); and Henry V (*H5* 4.3.40–60).

16. Heinemann, "Let Rome in Tiber melt," 171.

17. Cantor, *Shakespeare's Rome*, 194–95.

18. The identification of Cleopatra with serpents occurs at 1.5.26; 2.5.41, 78–80, 97; 2.7.26, 27, 42, 49 (the crocodile was also considered a serpent); 4.15.26; and 5.2.243–311 passim. Note also the Clown's account of the asp as "the pretty worm of Nilus" (compare Cleopatra as Antony's "serpent of Old Nile" [1.5.26]),

which "kills and pains not" and "is not to be trusted . . . , for indeed there is no goodness in the worm" (5.2.243–67). The description at once refers to the asp and Cleopatra.

19. Cf. Plutarch 6:87, in which she does not kiss Iras, and reportedly dies of a snakebite to her arm. Roy Battenhouse points out that a woman with serpents at her breasts was a common medieval emblem for Luxuria (*Shakespearean Tragedy: Its Art and Its Christian Premises* [Bloomington: Indiana University Press, 1969], 424 n. 50).

20. "Those whom God hath joined together, let no man put asunder." "The Form of Solemnization of Matrimony," in *Liturgical Services: Liturgies and Occasional Forms of Prayer Set Forth in the Reign of Queen Elizabeth*, ed. William Keatinge Clay, Parker Society (Cambridge: Cambridge University Press, 1847), 219.

21. On the homoeroticism in the play, see also Jonathan Gil Harris, "'Narcissus in thy face': Roman Desire and the Difference it Fakes in *Antony and Cleopatra*," *Shakespeare Quarterly* 45 (1994): 408–25.

22. A prevalent critical view, exemplified by Janet Adelman (*The Common Liar: An Essay on* Antony and Cleopatra [New Haven: Yale University Press, 1973]), insists on the play's moral ambiguity. Conceding that Shakespeare is deliberately seeking to draw us into the act of judging, Adelman nonetheless argues that we are simultaneously shown the folly of judging since the truth cannot be known. Similarly, Mark Rose contends that, unlike the other tragedies, the play "provides no final 'truth,' no moral point of reference from which the action may be judged" (Introduction, *Twentieth Century Interpretations of* Antony and Cleopatra [Englewood Cliffs, N.J.: Prentice-Hall, 1977], 4). In addition to the evidence adduced above, the play contains pervasive moral signposts—mythological, iconographical, scriptural, and imagistic—to the contrary. See, e.g., Battenhouse, *Shakespearean Tragedy*, 161–83, 425 n. 50; Clifford Davidson, "*Antony and Cleopatra*: Circe, Venus, and the Whore of Babylon," *Bucknell Review* 15 (1980): 31–55; Gordon P. Jones, "The 'Strumpet's Fool' in *Antony and Cleopatra*," *Shakespeare Quarterly* 34 (1983): 62–68; J. Leeds Barroll, "Enobarbus' Description of Cleopatra," *Texas Studies in English* 37 (1958): 61–78; and Daniel Stempel, "The Transmigration of the Crocodile," *Shakespeare Quarterly* 7 (1956), 59–72. The difficulty of discernment is, I submit, deliberate on Shakespeare's part; on his possible reason for that difficulty, see Jeffrey Burton Russell, "The Devil and the Reformers," in *The Prince of Darkness: Radical Evil and the Power of Good in History* (Ithaca: Cornell University Press, 1988), 183–84. Russell focuses on Hamlet, but his argument is equally pertinent to *Ant*; see also his comments on Milton's Satan (189). On the play's political dimension, see also Paul Lawrence Rose, "The Politics of *Antony and Cleopatra*," *Shakespeare Quarterly* 20 (1969): 379–89; and Marilyn Williamson, "The Political Context in *Antony and Cleopatra*," *Shakespeare Quarterly* 21 (1970): 241–51.

23. Cantor, *Shakespeare's Rome*, 148.

24. Alvin Kernan, *Shakespeare, the King's Playwright: Theater in the Stuart Court, 1603–1613* (New Haven: Yale University Press, 1995), 121. On James I as Augustus, see Howard Erskine-Hill, *The Augustan Idea in English Literature* (London: Edward Arnold, 1983), esp. 164–69; and H. Neville Davies, "Jacobean *Antony and Cleopatra*," *Shakespeare Studies* 17 (1985): 124–26.

25. David Harris Willson, *King James VI and I* (New York: Oxford University Press, 1956), 178.

26. Ibid., 185.

27. Lucy Hutchinson, *Memoirs of the Life of Colonel Hutchinson*, ed. J. Hutchinson and Rev. C. H. Frith (London, 1848), 84, quoted in Kernan, *King's Playwright*, 111.

28. Francis Osborne, *Historical Memoirs on the Reigns of Queen Elizabeth and King James* (1658), 274; in *Secret History of the Court of James the First*, ed. Walter Scott (Edinburgh, 1811), vol. 1. Quoted in Kernan, *King's Playwright*, 119.

29. Kernan, *King's Playwright*, 111, 115–16.

30. Ibid., 120. *Antony and Cleopatra* was not the only court-staged play to denounce James's debauchery. See Stephen Orgel, *Pageantry in the Shakespearean Theater*, 24; and chapter 1 above.

31. James Emerson Phillips, *The State in Shakespeare's Greek and Roman Plays* (1940; reprint, New York: Octagon, 1972), 195.

32. *The Complete Works of John Webster*, ed. F. L. Lucas, 4 vols. (1927; reprint, New York: Gordian Press, 1966): vol. 2. See also Stempel, "Transmigration," 62–64; Phillips, *State*, 194–99; and Stephen Orgel, *The Illusion of Power: Political Theater in the English Renaissance* (Berkeley and Los Angeles: University of California Press, 1975), 42–43. Compare the Ghost's account of his murder in *Hamlet*, in which the poison coursing through the "alleys of the body" to curdle "The thin and wholesome blood" (1.5.68–71), microcosmically replicates the poisoning of the Danish body politic.

33. Williamson, "Political Context," 243; Stempel, "Transmigration," 64.

34. References are to Samuel Daniel, *The Tragedie of Cleopatra*, in Bullough, 5:436. Figures in parentheses refer to line numbers.

35. Cf. Kernan (129), who argues that although the play concerns Stuart court corruption, it transmutes Whitehall's profligacy and waste into magnificence and generosity.

36. This last point is Kaula's, "Time Sense," 217.

37. Compare Octavia's observation regarding Antony and Caesar: "no midway / Twixt these extremes at all" (3.4.19–20).

38. Robert P. Kalmey, "Shakespeare's Octavius and Elizabethan Roman History," *SEL* 18 (1978): 278–80, italics Kalmey's. See also David Bevington, introduction to *Antony and Cleopatra*, The New Cambridge Shakespeare (Cambridge: Cambridge University Press, 1990), 5–6.

39. Maurice Charney, *Shakespeare's Roman Plays: The Function of Imagery in the Drama* (Cambridge: Harvard University Press, 1961), 90.

40. Tacitus, *The Annals of Imperial Rome*, trans M. Grant (1964), 29–31, quoted in Heinemann, "Let Rome in Tiber melt," 177.

Chapter 6: *Titus Andronicus*

1. Jonathan Bate, ed., introduction to *Titus Andronicus*, The Arden Shakespeare, Third Series (London: Routledge, 1995), 16.

2. T. J. B. Spencer, "Shakespeare and the Elizabethan Romans," *Shakespeare Survey* 10 (1957): 32.

3. T. S. Eliot, "Seneca in Elizabethan Translation," in *Selected Essays, 1917–1932* (New York: Harcourt Brace, 1932), 67.

4. Bate, *Titus Andronicus*, 1. A number of these points have been anticipated by or are indebted to Bate.

5. Ibid., 20–21.

6. Ibid.; R. B. Wernheim, *After the Armada: Elizabethan England and the Struggle for Western Europe, 1588–1595* (Oxford: Clarendon Press, 1984), 453.

7. Howard Nenner, *The Right to be King: The Succession to the Crown of England, 1603–1714* (Chapel Hill: University of North Carolina Press, 1995), 13, 26.

8. Sir Thomas Craig, *The Right of Succession to the Kingdom of England, In Two Bookes; Against the Sophisme of Parsons the Jesuite, Who assum'd the Counterfeit Name of Doleman; By which he endeavours to overthrow not only the Rights of Succession in Kingdoms, but also the Sacred Authority of Kings themselves* (London, 1703), 64, 48, quoted in Nenner, *Right to be King*, 43. Points in this paragraph are indebted to Nenner, 43.

9. Nenner, *Right to be King*, 7, 22, 17.

10. William C. Carroll, introduction to *William Shakespeare, Macbeth: Texts and Contexts*, The Bedford Shakespeare Series (Boston: Bedford/St. Martin's, 1999), 8.

11. Marie Axton, *The Queen's Two Bodies: Drama and the Elizabethan Succession*, Royal Historical Society Studies in History, no. 5 (London: Royal Historical Society, 1977), 35.

12. Ibid., 94; see also 26–36.

13. Robert Parsons [R. Doleman], *A Conference about the Next Succession to the Crown of England, Divided into Two Parts* (1594), excerpted in Carroll, *Macbeth*, 195–200, 199. Unlike many Catholics, however, Parsons, a Jesuit, wished to exclude James because of his professed Protestantism, promoting instead the Catholic Isabella, daughter of Philip of Spain. On Parsons, see also James Emerson Phillips, *Images of a Queen: Mary Stuart in Sixteenth-Century Literature* (Berkeley and Los Angeles: University of California Press, 1964), 206–7.

14. Florence Sandler, "*The Faerie Queene*: An Elizabethan Apocalypse," in *Apocalypse in English Renaissance Thought and Literature*, ed. C. A. Patrides and Joseph Wittreich, 162.

15. Axton, *Queen's Two Bodies*, 76.

16. Wernham, *After the Armada*, 459; Wallace T. MacCaffrey, *Elizabeth I: War and Politics, 1588–1603* (Princeton: Princeton University Press, 1992), 313. See also Axton, *Queen's Two Bodies*, 76.

17. Arnold Oskar Meyer, *England and the Catholic Church under Queen Elizabeth*, trans. J. R. McKee (1916; reprint, London: Routledge & Kegan Paul, 1967), 375; see also Wernheim, *After the Armada*, 456. On James's possible Catholic leanings, see also G. F. Warner, "James VI and Rome," *English Historical Review* 20 (1905): 124–26.

18. Axton, *Queen's Two Bodies*, 76.

19. See Carroll, *Macbeth*, 271–72, 288.

20. Axton, *Queen's Two Bodies*, 32, 101. On the crown-as-corporation, see Axton, 12. The argument could also be made that Scotland was not a foreign realm, q.v. Axton, 33–35.

21. Ibid., 101.

22. Ibid., 106.

23. The terms "king" and "emperor" are used interchangeably throughout the play.

24. "A modern critic has blamed Titus for choosing the arrogant Saturninus instead of the amiable Bassianus; but any Elizabethan would regard it as natural and right for him to support the elder son rather than the younger" (Bullough, 6:21).

25. *Calendar of State Papers, Domestic, 1591–1594*, pp. 445–46, quoted in Lily B. Campbell, *Shakespeare's "Histories": Mirrors of Elizabethan Policy* (San Marino, Calif.: Huntington Library, 1947), 141.

26. Meyer, *England and the Catholic Church*, 85; Philip Hughes, *Rome and the Counter-Reformation in England* (London: Burns, Oates, 1942), 188.

27. Thomas Becon, "The Displaying of the Popish Mass," in *Prayers and Other Pieces of Thomas Becon*, ed. John Ayre, Parker Society (Cambridge: Cambridge University Press, 1844), 258–59; John Jewel, *Controversy with M. Harding*, in *The Works of John Jewel*, ed. John Ayre, Parker Society (Cambridge: Cambridge University Press, 1847), 2:452.

28. Compare Article 31 of the Thirty-Nine Articles of Religion: "[T]he sacrifices of Masses, in the which it was commonly sayde, that the Priestes did offer Christ for the quicke and the dead, to haue remission of paine or gylt, were blasphemous fables. . . ."

29. Becon, "Displaying of the Popish Mass," 267–68.

30. See, e.g., John Foxe, *The Acts and Monuments of John Foxe: with a Life of the Martyrologist, and Vindication of the Work, by the Rev. George Townsend, M.A.*, 8 vols. (New York: AMS Press, 1965), 1:69. Thus the religion of Rome in *Titus* becomes synonymous in both name and substance with what Protestants termed "the Romish religion" of Catholicism and "the Roman Church"—the sense invoked and epitomized by, e.g., Lucius's reference to "our Roman rites."

31. Bate, *Titus Andronicus*, 263 n.

32. John N. King, *Milton and Religious Controversy: Satire and Polemic in* Paradise Lost (Cambridge: Cambridge University Press, 2000), 70–71, 74. On the Roman Church as mother, see also Foxe, *Acts and Monuments*, 1:6.

33. *The HarperCollins Encyclopedia of Catholicism*, ed. Richard P. McBrien (n.p., HarperCollins, 1995), s.v. "indulgences."

34. Jewel, *The Defense of the Apology of the Church of England*, in *Works*, 4:689.

35. *Sermons and Miscellaneous Pieces of Archbishop Sandys*, ed. John Ayre, Parker Society (Cambridge: Cambridge University Press, 1841), 272. See also Foxe, *Acts and Monuments*, 1:6.

36. Jaroslav Pelikan, "Some Uses of Apocalypse in the Magisterial Reformers," in *Apocalypse in English Renaissance Thought and Literature*, ed. C. A. Patrides and Joseph Wittreich, 84.

37. J. C. Maxwell, introduction to *Titus Andronicus*, The Arden Shakespeare, Second Series, 3d ed. (London: Methuen, 1961), xxx; Bate, *Titus Andronicus*, 125 n. 28.

38. Thomas Rogers, *The Catholic Doctrine of the Church of England, An Exposition of the Thirty-Nine Articles*, ed. J. J. Perowne, Parker Society (Cambridge: Cambridge University Press, 1854), 179. John Jewel, voicing a similar sentiment, states that in Rome there is "little difference between wife and harlot" (*A Reply to M. Harding's Answer*, in *Works*, 2:707).

39. John N. King, *Spenser's Poetry and the Reformation Tradition* (Princeton: Princeton University Press, 1990), 115, see also 140; Richard Mallette, *Spenser and the Discourses of Reformation England* (Lincoln: University of Nebraska Press, 1997),

156. Spenser's Duessa (*FQ*, book 5) is another figuration of Mary. Published, like *Titus*, after Mary's death, book 5 charges the Scots queen with incontinence, bloodshed, sedition, "foule Adulterie," "lewd Impietie," and murder (*FQ* 5.9.48). The depiction, apparently printed with the approval of Elizabeth's government, elicited a vehement protest from James, who no doubt construed it as an attack on his right to succeed to the English throne (Phillips, *Images of a Queen*, 202–3).

40. The phrase is from John Bale, *The Image of Both Churches, Being an Exposition of the Most Wonderful Book of Revelation . . .* , in *Select Works of John Bale*, ed. Henry Christmas, Parker Society (Cambridge: Cambridge University Press, 1849), 494.

41. Mallette, *Discourses of Reformation England*, 156–57.

42. My discussion of the Two Churches in this paragraph is indebted to Sandler, "Elizabethan Apocalypse," 158–67.

43. Ibid., 163.

44. Ibid., 160.

45. Compare *LLL* 5.2.602: "Judas was hanged on an elder." The above-noted description of Bassianus (2.3.227) curiously echoes in *H8* (2.3.78–79) in the description of the future Elizabeth as "a gem / To lighten all this isle."

46. Thomas Rogers, *An Historical Dialogue touching Antichrist* (1589); cited by Bernard Capp, "The Political Dimension of Apocalyptic Thought," in *Apocalypse in English Renaissance Thought and Literature*, 97. The ideas in this paragraph follow Capp.

47. Titus, in his sacrifice of Alarbus, his slaughter and dismemberment of the Queen's sons, his perpetration of cannibalism, and his killing of Tamora and two of his own children, exceeds even Aaron in the number of murders he commits. A moral equivalence between the two characters is thus implied, which is reinforced by the parallel scope of their atrocities; e.g., the dismemberment and rape of Lavinia is paralleled by the dismemberment and burning of Alarbus.

48. Bullough, 5:39.

49. King, *Spenser's Poetry*, 85.

50. Bale, *Image of Both Churches*, 486; King, *Spenser's Poetry*, 85, 85 n.

51. Harold John Grimm, *The Reformation Era, 1500–1650* (New York: Macmillan, 1954), 438; Elizabeth Jenkins, *Elizabeth the Great* (New York: Coward-McCann, 1958), 243.

52. Mallette, *Discourses of Reformation England*, 158–59, quoting George Gifford, "Epistle Dedicatory," in *Sermons Vpon the Whole Booke of Revelation* (London, 1596), sigs. A3r, A4r.

53. In *Henry V* Shakespeare personifies England as "a weak, frightened, 'open' female that 'shook and trembled' at the violent inroads of the male Scots, who have penetrated her defenses with 'hot assays'"—attempted rapes averted only by English virtue (Carroll, *Macbeth*, 277).

54. William Harrison, *An Historicall Description of the Iland of Britaine . . .* in Raphael Holinshed, *Holinshed's Chronicles of England, Scotland, and Ireland* (1587), ed. Henry Ellis, 6 vols. (London: J. Johnson, 1807–8), 1:10; cited by Francesca T. Royster, "White-limed Walls: Whiteness and Gothic Extremism in Shakespeare's *Titus Andronicus*," *Shakespeare Quarterly* 51 (2000): 450.

55. Susan Frye, *Elizabeth I: The Competition for Representation* (New York: Oxford University Press, 1993), 82–83, 177 n. 62. Compare Spenser's allegorical depiction of Spain's sacking of Belgium, *FQ* 5.10.6–30.

56. Richard Vennar, *A Prayer for the prosperous Successe of hir Majestie's Forces in Ireland* (ca. 1600), quoted in Roy Strong, *Cult of Elizabeth*, 183.

57. Bate, *Titus Andronicus*, 20. The term "martyr," including its variants, occurs only twelve times in Shakespeare, four of them in *Titus*. Cf. *Tit* 5.2.180, which suggests a parodic martyrdom springing from a parodic Eucharist. While Catholics also referred to their persecuted faithful as martyrs, the context surrounding the motif of martyrdom in the play strongly discourages a pro-Catholic reading.

58. On the Moor/Jew association, see Ania Loomba, *Shakespeare, Race, and Colonialism*, Oxford Shakespeare Topics (Oxford: Oxford University Press, 2002), 146–48.

59. Mallette, *Discourses of Reformation England*, 152, 158. Compare Aaron's advocacy of "stratagem" and "force." Cf. Robert S. Miola, "'An alien people clutching their gods'?: Shakespeare's Ancient Religions," *Shakespeare Survey* 54 (2001): 34, who identifies Aaron with Protestantism.

60. Mallette, *Discourses of Reformation England*, 160.

61. Robin L. Bott, "'O Keep Me from Their Worse Than Killing Lust': Ideologies of Rape and Mutilation in Chaucer's *Physician's Tale* and Shakespeare's *Titus Andronicus*," in *Representing Rape in Medieval and Early Modern Literature*, ed. Elizabeth Robertson and Christine M. Rose (New York: St. Martin's Press, Palgrave, 2001), 201. Reference kindly pointed out by Michele Cortese.

62. Foxe, *Acts and Monuments*, 1:305, 308–10.

63. Bate, *Titus Andronicus*, 21.

64. The theme of spiritual rebirth through suffering and/or exile occurs elsewhere in Shakespeare; compare Edgar in *Lear*, Prospero in *Tempest*, and Claudio in *Ado*.

65. Royster, "White-limed Walls," 449. On the Moorish threat in the play, see Royster, 451.

66. On the Elizabethan equating of England and Rome, see chapters 1 and 2 above.

Conclusion

1. For further parallels, see Emrys Jones, *Scenic Form in Shakespeare* (London: Oxford University Press, 1971), 260–61.

2. These recurring characters and events suggest Shakespeare's subscription to the cyclical view of history, q.v. chapter 1 above.

3. "Lucius Tarquinius . . . caused his own father-in-law Servius Tullius to be cruelly murdered, and, contrary to the Roman laws and customs, not requiring or staying for the people's suffrages, . . . possessed himself of the kingdom" (*Luc*, Arg.).

4. Jones, *Scenic Form in Shakespeare*, 108.

5. Exemplifying this potentially lethal fractiousness is Williams's striking of Fluellen, who wears on his helmet the king's glove—the companion of the one Henry gave Williams when Williams challenged him to a duel and in answer to Williams's question, "How shall I know thee again?" Unreasoningly pugnacious, Williams represents "The blind and bloody soldier" (*H5* 3.3.34), whose proclivity to anarchy must be continually restrained by the analogue of reason, the king.

Hence Fluellen, "hot as gunpowder" and quick to requite an injury (4.7.177–78), and Macmorris's emblematic threat, "I will cut off your head" (3.2.132). Properly ordered, however, these fractious elements become ennobled, a constructive force conducing to the good of the whole. Thus Henry's command to his brawling soldiers to be friends (4.8.61) prompts the chastened Fluellen, in charity, to give Williams money to mend his shoes, and the beleaguered but united army succeeds, against all odds, in defeating France.

6. See also 3.5.38–52, in which Charles exhorts his men to vanquish the English. The speech, addressed exclusively to his nobles, is the counterpart of Henry's speech to his troops (3.1.17–34), which is addressed to both nobles and commoners.

7. Compare Lear, who discovers his elemental humanity only after shedding his royal trappings: his garments, his retainers, and his crown. See also Elyot: "If thou be a governor, . . . know that thou art verily a man compact of soul and body, and in that all other men be equal unto thee. . . . Ye shall know alway yourself, . . . remembering that your body be subject to corruption, as all other be, . . . and . . . that in nothing but only in virtue ye are better than another inferior person" (*Governor*, 165–66).

8. Alison Plowden, *Danger to Elizabeth: The Catholics under Elizabeth I*, rev. ed. (Phoenix Mill, England: Sutton, 1999), 237, 239.

Bibliography

Primary Sources

Apology of the House of Commons, made to the King, touching their Privileges. In *The Parliamentary History of England, from the earliest period to the year 1803.* . . . Vol. 1. London, 1806.

Aristotle. *Ethica Nicomachea.* In *Introduction to Aristotle.* Ed. Richard McKeon. New York: Random House, Modern Library, 1947.

———. *The Politics of Aristotle.* Ed. and trans. Ernest Barker. 1946. Reprint, London: Oxford University Press, 1978.

Bale, John. *The Image of Both Churches, Being an Exposition of the Most Wonderful Book of Revelation.* . . . In *Select Works of John Bale,* ed. Henry Christmas. Parker Society. Cambridge: Cambridge University Press, 1849.

Becon, Thomas. "The Displaying of the Popish Mass." In *Prayers and Other Pieces of Thomas Becon.* Ed. John Ayre. Parker Society. Cambridge: Cambridge University Press, 1844.

Blundeville, Thomas. *The True Order and Methode of Wryting and Reading Hystories* (1574). Ed. Hugh G. Dick. *Huntington Library Quarterly* 3 (1940): 149–70.

The Book of Common Prayer, 1559: The Elizabethan Prayer Book. Ed. John E. Booty. Charlottesville: University Press of Virginia, 1976.

Bullinger, Henry. "Of the Third Precept of the Second Table, which is in Order the Seventh of the Ten Commandments. . . ." In *The Decades of Henry Bullinger,* trans. H. I., ed. Rev. Thomas Harding, vol. 1. Parker Society. Cambridge: Cambridge University Press, 1849.

Castiglione, Baldassare. *The Book of the Courtier* (1528). Trans. Sir Thomas Hoby. London: J. M. Dent; New York: E. P. Dutton, 1974.

Cicero, Marcus Tullius. *De Oratore.* In *Cicero,* trans. H. Rackham. Vols. 3 and 4. London: Heinemann, 1942.

Daniel, Samuel. *The Tragedie of Cleopatra.* In *Narrative and Dramatic Sources of Shakespeare,* ed. Geoffrey Bullough. Vol. 5. London: Routledge and Kegan Paul; New York: Columbia University Press, 1964.

Elyot, Sir Thomas. *The Book Named the Governor.* Ed. S. E. Lehmberg. London: Dent; New York: Dutton, 1962.

———. *Of the Knowledge Which Maketh a Wise Man.* Ed. Edwin Johnston Howard. Oxford, Ohio: Anchor Press, 1946.

"The Form of Solemnization of Matrimony." In *Liturgical Services: Liturgies and Occasional Forms of Prayer Set Forth in the Reign of Queen Elizabeth*, ed. William Keatinge Clay. Parker Society. Cambridge: Cambridge University Press, 1847.

Foxe, John. *The Acts and Monuments of John Foxe: with a Life of the Martyrologist, and Vindication of the Work, by the Rev. George Townsend, M.A.* Vol. 1. New York: AMS Press, 1965.

The Geneva Bible (1560). Facsimile edition with introduction by Lloyd E. Berry. Madison: University of Wisconsin Press, 1969.

Greville, Fulke. *Of Monarchy.* In *The Works of Fulke Greville, Lord Brooke*, ed. Alexander B. Grosart. Vol. 1. 1870. Reprint, New York: AMS Press, 1966.

Guilpin, Everard. "Satyre I." In *Skialetheia, 1598 [by] Everard Guilpin*. Shakespeare Association Facsimiles, no. 2. London: Humphrey Milford, Oxford University Press, 1931.

Harvey, Gabriel. *Gabriel Harvey's Marginalia.* Ed. G. C. Moore Smith. Stratford-upon-Avon: Shakespeare Head Press, 1913.

Heywood, Thomas. *An Apology for Actors* (1612). Ed. Richard H. Perkinson. New York: Scholars' Facsimiles & Reprints, 1941.

An Homilie against Disobedience and Willful Rebellion. In *Certaine sermons or Homilies, appointed to be read in churches, in the time of Queen Elizabeth I, 1547–1571*. With introduction by Mary Ellen Rickey and Thomas B. Stroup. 2 vols. in 1. Gainesville, Fla.: Scholars' Facsimiles & Reprints, 1968.

James I. *The Trew Law of Free Monarchies.* In *The Political Works of James I*, ed. Charles Howard McIlwain. 1918. Reprint, New York: Russell & Russell, 1965.

———. *Basilikon Doron.* In *The Political Works of James I*, ed. Charles Howard McIlwain. 1918. Reprint, New York: Russell & Russell, 1965.

Jewel, John. *Controversy with M. Harding.* In *The Works of John Jewel*, ed. John Ayre, vol. 2. Parker Society. Cambridge: Cambridge University Press, 1847.

———. *The Defense of the Apology of the Church of England.* In *The Works of John Jewel*, ed. John Ayre, vol. 4. Parker Society. Cambridge: Cambridge University Press, 1847.

———. *A Reply to M. Harding's Answer.* In *The Works of John Jewel*, ed. John Ayre, vol. 2. Parker Society. Cambridge: Cambridge University Press, 1847.

Parsons, Robert [R. Doleman]. *A Conference about the Next Succession to the Crowne of Ingland* (1594). Ed. D. M. Rogers. English Recusant Literature 1558–1640, vol. 104. Menston, England: Scolar Press, 1972.

———. *A Conference about the Next Succession to the Crown of England, Divided into Two Parts* (1594). Excerpted in *William Shakespeare,* Macbeth*: Texts and Contexts*, ed. William C. Carroll, 195–200. Boston: Bedford/St. Martin's, 1999.

Plato. *The Republic.* In *The Dialogues of Plato*, trans. B. Jowett. 3d ed. Vol. 1. 1892. Reprint, New York: Random House, 1937.

Plutarch. *Plutarch's Lives of the Noble Grecians and Romans Englished by Sir Thomas North* (1579). Ed. W. E. Henley. The Tudor Translations. Vols. 5 and 6. London: David Nutt, 1895–96.

Proceedings in the Parliaments of Elizabeth I. Ed. T. E. Hartley. Vol. 1: 1558–1581. Wilmington, Del.: Michael Glazier, 1981.

Ralegh, Sir Walter. Preface to *The History of the World*. In *The Works of Sir Walter Ralegh, Kt., Now First Collected.* . . . Vol. 2. New York: Burt Franklin, 1965.

Rogers, Thomas. *The Catholic Doctrine of the Church of England, An Exposition of the Thirty-Nine Articles.* Ed. J. J. S. Perowne. Parker Society. Cambridge: Cambridge University Press, 1854.

Sandys, Edwin. *Sermons and Miscellaneous Pieces of Archbishop Sandys.* Ed. John Ayre. Parker Society. Cambridge: Cambridge University Press, 1841.

Shakespeare, William. *The Complete Works of Shakespeare.* Ed. David Bevington. Updated 4th ed. New York: Addison Wesley Longman, 1997.

Spenser, Edmund. *The Faerie Queene.* Ed. Thomas P. Roche, Jr. 1978. Reprint, London: Penguin, 1987.

Thirty-Nine Articles. *Articles whereupon it was agreed by the Archbyshops and Byshops of both prouinces and the whole cleargie, in the conuocation holden at London in the yeere of our Lord* GOD *1562 . . . for the stablishing of consent touching true religion.* London, 1581.

Webster, John. *The Complete Works of John Webster.* Ed. F. L. Lucas. Vol. 2. 1927. Reprint, New York: Gordian Press, 1966.

Wilson, Thomas. *The Art of Rhetoric* (1560). Ed. Peter E. Medine. University Park: Pennsylvania State University Press, 1994.

SECONDARY SOURCES

Adelman, Janet. *The Common Liar: An Essay on* Antony and Cleopatra. New Haven: Yale University Press, 1973.

Alvis, John. "Caesarian Honors, Brutus's Dilemma, and the Advent of Christianity." In *Shakespeare's Understanding of Honor.* Durham: Carolina Academic Press, 1990.

———. "The Coherence of Shakespeare's Roman Plays." *Modern Language Quarterly* 40 (1979): 115–34.

Annas, Julia. *An Introduction to Plato's* Republic. Oxford: Clarendon Press, 1981.

Ashton, Robert, ed. *James I by His Contemporaries.* London: Hutchinson, 1969.

Axton, Marie. *The Queen's Two Bodies: Drama and the Elizabethan Succession.* Royal Historical Society Studies in History, no. 5. London: Royal Historical Society, 1977.

Baldwin, T. W. *William Shakespere's Small Latine & Lesse Greeke.* Vol. 2. Urbana: University of Illinois Press, 1944.

Barkan, Leonard. "What Did Shakespeare Read?" In *The Cambridge Companion to Shakespeare*, ed. Margreta de Grazia and Stanley Wells. Cambridge: Cambridge University Press, 2001.

Barker, Ernest. *The Political Thought of Plato and Aristotle.* 1918. Reprint, New York: Dover Publications, 1959.

Barroll, J. Leeds. "Enobarbus' Description of Cleopatra." *Texas Studies in English* 37 (1958): 61–78.

———. "Shakespeare and Roman History." *Modern Language Review* 53 (1958): 327–43.
Bate, Jonathan. Introduction to *Titus Andronicus*. The Arden Shakespeare, Third Series. London: Routledge, 1995.
———. *Shakespeare and Ovid*. Oxford: Clarendon Press, 1993.
Battenhouse, Roy. *Shakespearean Tragedy: Its Art and Its Christian Premises*. Bloomington: Indiana University Press, 1969.
Bevington, David. Introduction to *Antony and Cleopatra*. The New Cambridge Shakespeare. Cambridge: Cambridge University Press, 1990.
Blits, Jan H. *The End of the Ancient Republic: Essays on Julius Caesar*. Durham: Carolina Academic Press, 1982.
Born, Lester K., trans. *The Education of a Christian Prince*, by Desiderius Erasmus. New York: Columbia University Press, 1936.
Bott, Robin L. "'O Keep Me from Their Worse Than Killing Lust': Ideologies of Rape and Mutilation in Chaucer's *Physician's Tale* and Shakespeare's *Titus Andronicus*." In *Representing Rape in Medieval and Early Modern Literature*, ed. Elizabeth Robertson and Christine M. Rose. New York: St. Martin's Press, Palgrave, 2001.
Breyer, Bernard R. "A New Look at *Julius Caesar*." In *Essays in Honor of Walter Clyde Curry*, comp. John W. Stevenson. Vanderbilt Studies in the Humanities 2. Nashville: Vanderbilt University Press, 1954.
Bullough, Geoffrey, ed. *Narrative and Dramatic Sources of Shakespeare*. Vols. 5 and 6. London: Routledge and Kegan Paul; New York: Columbia University Press, 1964, 1966.
Bushnell, Rebecca W. *Tragedies of Tyrants: Political Thought and Theater in the English Renaissance*. Ithaca: Cornell University Press, 1990.
Campbell, Lily B. *Shakespeare's "Histories": Mirrors of Elizabethan Policy*. San Marino, Calif.: Huntington Library, 1947.
Cantor, Paul A. "Prospero's Republic: The Politics of Shakespeare's *The Tempest*." In *Shakespeare as Political Thinker*, ed. John Alvis and Thomas G. West. Durham: Carolina Academic Press, 1981.
———. *Shakespeare's Rome: Republic and Empire*. Ithaca: Cornell University Press, 1976.
Capp, Bernard. "The Political Dimension of Apocalyptic Thought." In *Apocalypse in English Renaissance Thought and Literature*, ed. C. A. Patrides and Joseph Wittreich. Ithaca: Cornell University Press, 1984.
Carroll, William C. Introduction to *William Shakespeare, Macbeth: Texts and Contexts*. Bedford Shakespeare Series. Boston: Bedford/St. Martin's, 1999.
Chambers, E. K. *The Elizabethan Stage*. Vol. 1. Oxford: Clarendon Press, 1923.
———. *William Shakespeare: A Study of Facts and Problems*. Vol. 1. Oxford: Clarendon Press, 1930.
Charney, Maurice. *Shakespeare's Roman Plays: The Function of Imagery in the Drama*. Cambridge: Harvard University Press, 1961.
Clark, Cumberland. "The Art of the Alchemist." In *Shakespeare and Science*. Birmingham, England: Cornish, 1929.

Collins, J. Churton. *Studies in Shakespeare*. London: Constable, 1904.

Coote, Stephen. "*Coriolanus* and Seventeenth-century Politics." In *William Shakespeare: Coriolanus*, ed. Bryan Loughrey. Penguin Critical Studies. London: Penguin, 1992.

Copleston, Frederick. *A History of Philosophy*. Vol. 1, Pts. 1 and 2. *Greece and Rome*. New rev. ed. Garden City, N.Y.: Doubleday, Image Books, 1962.

Cornford, Francis MacDonald, trans. *The Republic of Plato*. 1941. Reprint, London: Oxford University Press, 1974.

Daniell, David, ed. *Julius Caesar*. The Arden Shakespeare, Third Series. Walton-on-Thames: Thomas Nelson, 1998.

Davidson, Clifford. "*Antony and Cleopatra*: Circe, Venus, and the Whore of Babylon." *Bucknell Review* 15 (1980): 31–55.

———. "*Coriolanus*: A Study in Political Dislocation." *Shakespeare Studies* 4 (1968): 263–74.

Davies, H. Neville. "Jacobean *Antony and Cleopatra*." *Shakespeare Studies* 17 (1985): 123–58.

Dean, Paul. "Tudor Humanism and the Roman Past: A Background to Shakespeare." *Renaissance Quarterly* 41 (1988): 84–111.

Donaldson, Ian. "'A Theme for Disputation': Shakespeare's Lucrece." In *The Rapes of Lucretia: A Myth and Its Transformations*. Clarendon: Oxford University Press, 1982.

Dorsch, T. S. Introduction to *Julius Caesar*. The Arden Shakespeare, Second Series. London: Methuen, 1955.

Dubrow, Heather. *Captive Victors: Shakespeare's Narrative Poems and Sonnets*. Ithaca: Cornell University Press, 1987.

Eliot, T. S. "Seneca in Elizabethan Translation." In *Selected Essays, 1917–1932*. New York: Harcourt Brace, 1932.

Elton, G. R. *England under the Tudors*. 3d ed. London: Routledge, 1991.

Enright, D. J. "*Coriolanus*: Tragedy or Debate?" *Essays in Criticism* 4 (1954): 1–19.

Erskine-Hill, Howard. *The Augustan Idea in English Literature*. London: Edward Arnold, 1983.

Etty, J. L. "Studies in Shakespeare's History: VI—*Julius Caesar*." *Macmillan's Magazine* 87 (1903): 350–60.

Finkelpearl, Philip J. "The King's Men and the Politics of Beaumont and Fletcher." In *Court and Country Politics in the Plays of Beaumont and Fletcher*. Princeton: Princeton University Press, 1990.

Frye, Susan. *Elizabeth I: The Competition for Representation*. New York: Oxford University Press, 1993.

Fumaroli, Marc. "Rhetoric, Politics, and Society: From Italian Ciceronianism to French Classicism." In *Renaissance Eloquence: Studies in the Theory and Practice of Renaissance Rhetoric*, ed. James J. Murphy. Berkeley and Los Angeles: University of California Press, 1983.

Fussner, F. Smith. *The Historical Revolution: English Historical Writing and Thought, 1580–1640*. London: Routledge, 1962.

Gordon, D. J. "Name and Fame: Shakespeare's *Coriolanus*." In *The Renaissance Imagination*, ed. Stephen Orgel. Berkeley and Los Angeles: University of California Press, 1975. Originally published as "Name and Fame," in *Papers Mainly Shakespearean*, ed. G. I. Duthie (Aberdeen University Studies, 1964).

Grimm, Harold John. *The Reformation Era, 1500–1650*. New York: Macmillan, 1954.

Gurr, Andrew. "*Coriolanus* and the Body Politic." *Shakespeare Survey* 28 (1975): 63–69.

———, ed. *King Richard II*. The New Cambridge Shakespeare. Cambridge: Cambridge University Press, 1984.

Guy, John. *Tudor England*. Oxford: Oxford University Press, 1988.

Hanford, James Holly. "A Platonic Passage in Shakespeare's *Troilus and Cressida*." *Studies in Philology* 13 (1916): 100–109.

The HarperCollins Encyclopedia of Catholicism. Ed. Richard P. McBrien. N.p.: HarperCollins, 1995.

Harris, Jonathan Gil. "'Narcissus in thy face': Roman Desire and the Difference it Fakes in *Antony and Cleopatra*." *Shakespeare Quarterly* 45 (1994): 408–25.

Heinemann, Margot. "'Let Rome in Tiber melt': Order and Disorder in 'Antony and Cleopatra.'" In *Antony and Cleopatra*, ed. John Drakakis. New Casebooks. New York: St. Martin's Press, 1994.

———. "Political Drama." In *The Cambridge Companion to English Renaissance Drama*, ed. A. R. Braunmuller and Michael Hattaway. Cambridge: Cambridge University Press, 1990.

Heninger, S. K., Jr. "The Tudor Myth of Troy-novant." *South Atlantic Quarterly* 61 (1962): 378–87.

Holstun, James. "Tragic Superfluity in *Coriolanus*." *ELH* 59 (1983): 485–507.

Huffman, Clifford Chalmers. *Coriolanus in Context*. Lewisburg, Pa: Bucknell University Press, 1971.

Hughes, Philip. *Rome and the Counter-Reformation in England*. London: Burns, Oates, 1942.

Hume, Anthea. *Edmund Spenser: Protestant Poet*. Cambridge: Cambridge University Press, 1984.

Jagendorf, Zvi. "*Coriolanus*: Body Politic and Private Parts." *Shakespeare Quarterly* 41 (1990): 455–69.

James, Mervyn. *Society, Politics and Culture: Studies in Early Modern England*. Cambridge: Cambridge University Press, 1986.

Jenkins, Elizabeth. *Elizabeth the Great*. New York: Coward-McCann, 1958.

Jenkins, Harold, ed. *Hamlet*. The Arden Shakespeare, Second Series. London: Methuen, 1982.

Jones, Emrys. *Scenic Form in Shakespeare*. London: Oxford University Press, 1971.

Jones, Gordon P. "The 'Strumpet's Fool' in *Antony and Cleopatra*." *Shakespeare Quarterly* 34 (1983): 62–68.

Jorgensen, Paul A. *Shakespeare's Military World*. 1956. Reprint, Berkeley and Los Angeles: University of California Press, 1973.

Kahn, Coppélia. "The Rape in Shakespeare's *Lucrece*." *Shakespeare Studies* 9 (1976): 45–72.

———. *Roman Shakespeare: Warriors, Wounds, and Women*. London: Routledge, 1997.

Kalmey, Robert P. "Shakespeare's Octavius and Elizabethan Roman History." *SEL* 18 (1978): 275–87.

Kaula, David. "The Time Sense of *Antony and Cleopatra*." *Shakespeare Quarterly* 15 (1964): 211–23.

Kayser, John R., and Ronald J. Lettieri. "'The Last of All the Romans': Shakespeare's Commentary on Classical Republicanism." *CLIO* 9 (1979): 197–227.

Kernan, Alvin. *Shakespeare, the King's Playwright: Theater in the Stuart Court, 1603–1613*. New Haven: Yale University Press, 1995.

King, John N. *Milton and Religious Controversy: Satire and Polemic in* Paradise Lost. Cambridge: Cambridge University Press, 2000.

———. *Spenser's Poetry and the Reformation Tradition*. Princeton: Princeton University Press, 1990.

———. *Tudor Royal Iconography: Literature and Art in an Age of Religious Crisis*. Princeton: Princeton University Press, 1989.

Kuhl, E. P. "Shakespeare's *Rape of Lucrece*." *Philological Quarterly* 20 (1941): 352–60.

Lacey, Robert. *Robert, Earl of Essex*. New York: Atheneum, 1971.

Lanham, Richard A. "The Ovidian Shakespeare: *Venus and Adonis* and *Lucrece*." In *The Motives of Eloquence: Literary Rhetoric in the Renaissance*. New Haven: Yale University Press, 1976.

Leggatt, Alexander. *Shakespeare's Political Drama: The History Plays and the Roman Plays*. London: Routledge, 1988.

Levin, Harry. Introduction to *Coriolanus*. In *William Shakespeare: The Complete Works*, gen. ed. Alfred Harbage. New York: Viking, Penguin, 1969.

Loomba, Ania. *Shakespeare, Race, and Colonialism*. Oxford Shakespeare Topics. Oxford: Oxford University Press, 2002.

MacCaffrey, Wallace T. *Elizabeth I: War and Politics, 1588–1603*. Princeton: Princeton University Press, 1992.

Majors, G. W. "Shakespeare's First Brutus: His Role in *Lucrece*." *Modern Language Quarterly* 35 (1974): 339–51.

Mallette, Richard. *Spenser and the Discourses of Reformation England*. Lincoln: University of Nebraska Press, 1997.

Mallin, Eric S. "Emulous Factions and the Collapse of Chivalry: *Troilus and Cressida*." *Representations* 29 (1990): 145–79.

Manning, Roger B. *Village Revolts: Social Protest and Popular Disturbances in England, 1509–1640*. Oxford: Clarendon Press, 1988.

Marcus, Leah S. *Puzzling Shakespeare: Local Reading and Its Discontents*. Berkeley and Los Angeles: University of California Press, 1988.

Martindale, Charles, and Michelle Martindale. *Shakespeare and the Uses of Antiquity: An Introductory Essay*. London: Routledge, 1990.

Maxwell, J. C. Introduction to *Titus Andronicus*. 3d ed. The Arden Shakespeare, Second Series. London: Methuen, 1961.

Mazzeo, Joseph Anthony. *Renaissance and Revolution: The Remaking of European Thought*. New York: Random House, Pantheon, 1965.

McCoy, Richard C. *The Rites of Knighthood: The Literature and Politics of Elizabethan Chivalry.* Berkeley and Los Angeles: University of California Press, 1989.

McDonald, Russ. "'I Loved My Books': Shakespeare's Reading." In *The Bedford Companion to Shakespeare: An Introduction with Documents.* Boston: St. Martin's Press, Bedford Books, 1996.

McIlwain, Charles Howard. Introduction to *The Political Works of James I.* 1918. Reprint, New York: Russell & Russell, 1965.

Medcalf, Stephen. "Shakespeare on Beauty, Truth and Transcendence." In *Platonism and the English Imagination,* ed. Anna Baldwin and Sarah Hutton. Cambridge: Cambridge University Press, 1994.

Meyer, Arnold Oskar. *England and the Catholic Church under Queen Elizabeth.* Trans. J. R. McKee. 1916. Reprint, London: Routledge & Kegan Paul, 1967.

Miles, Gary B. "How Roman Are Shakespeare's 'Romans'?" *Shakespeare Quarterly* 40 (1989): 257–83.

Miller, Shannon. "Topicality and Subversion in William Shakespeare's *Coriolanus.*" *SEL* 32 (1992): 287–310.

Miola, Robert S. "'An alien people clutching their gods'?: Shakespeare's Ancient Religions." *Shakespeare Survey* 54 (2001): 31–45.

———. "*Julius Caesar* and the Tyrannicide Debate." *Renaissance Quarterly* 38 (1985): 271–89.

———. *Shakespeare's Rome.* Cambridge: Cambridge University Press, l983.

Neale, J. E. *Queen Elizabeth I: A Biography.* 1934. Reprint, Garden City, N.Y.: Doubleday, Anchor Books, 1957.

Nenner, Howard. *The Right to be King: The Succession to the Crown of England, 1603–1714.* Chapel Hill: University of North Carolina Press, 1995.

Nichols, John, ed. *The Progresses and Public Processions of Queen Elizabeth.* Vol. 3. London, 1823.

Norbrook, David. *Poetry and Politics in the English Renaissance.* Rev. ed. Oxford: Oxford University Press, 2002.

Notestein, Wallace. *The House of Commons, 1604–1610.* New Haven: Yale University Press, 1971.

———. *The Winning of the Initiative by the House of Commons.* Proceedings of the British Academy. London: Oxford University Press, 1924.

Orgel, Stephen. *The Illusion of Power: Political Theater in the English Renaissance.* Berkeley and Los Angeles: University of California Press, 1975.

———. "Making Greatness Familiar." In *Pageantry in the Shakespearean Theater,* ed. David M. Bergeron. Athens: University of Georgia Press, 1985.

Parker, Barbara L. "'A Thing Unfirm': Plato's *Republic* and Shakespeare's *Julius Caesar.*" *Shakespeare Quarterly* 44 (1993): 30–43.

———. "The Whore of Babylon and Shakespeare's *Julius Caesar.*" *SEL* 35 (1995): 251–69.

Parker, R. B. Introduction to *The Tragedy of Coriolanus.* The Oxford Shakespeare. Oxford: Clarendon Press, 1994.

Patrides, C. A. *The Grand Design of God: The Literary Form of the Christian View of History*. London: Routledge, 1972.

Patrides, C. A., and Joseph Wittreich, eds. *The Apocalypse in English Renaissance Thought and Literature: Patterns, Antecedents and Repercussions*. Ithaca: Cornell University Press, 1984.

Patterson, Annabel M. *Reading Between the Lines*. Madison: University of Wisconsin Press, 1993.

———. *Shakespeare and the Popular Voice*. Cambridge, Mass.: Basil Blackwell, 1989.

Pelikan, Jaroslav. "Some Uses of Apocalypse in the Magisterial Reformers." In *Apocalypse in English Renaissance Thought and Literature*, ed. C. A. Patrides and Joseph Wittreich. Ithaca: Cornell University Press, 1984.

Peterson, Douglas L. "'Wisdom Consumed in Confidence': An Examination of Shakespeare's *Julius Caesar*." *Shakespeare Quarterly* 16 (1965): 19–28.

Pettet, E. C. "*Coriolanus* and the Midlands Insurrection of 1607." *Shakespeare Survey* 3 (1950): 34–42.

Phillips, James Emerson. *Images of a Queen: Mary Stuart in Sixteenth-Century Literature*. Berkeley and Los Angeles: University of California Press, 1964.

———. *The State in Shakespeare's Greek and Roman Plays*. 1940. Reprint, New York: Octagon, 1972.

Platt, Michael. "*The Rape of Lucrece* and the Republic for which it stands." *Centennial Review* 19 (1975): 59–79.

———. *Rome and Romans According to Shakespeare*. Rev. ed. Lanham, Md.: University Press of America, 1983.

Plowden, Alison. *Danger to Elizabeth: The Catholics under Elizabeth I*. Rev. ed. Phoenix Mill, England: Sutton, 1999.

Popper, Karl Raimund. *The Open Society and Its Enemies*. 4th ed. Vol. 1. 1945. Reprint, Princeton: Princeton University Press, 1963.

Rebhorn, Wayne A. "The Crisis of the Aristocracy in *Julius Caesar*." *Renaissance Quarterly* 43 (1990): 75–111.

Ribner, Irving. "Political Issues in *Julius Caesar*." *Journal of English and Germanic Philology* 56 (1957): 10–22.

Richards, I. A. "*Troilus and Cressida* and Plato." *Hudson Review* 1 (1948): 362–76.

Rickman, H. P. "Shakespeare and Plato." *Hermes: Zeitschrift für Klassische Philologie* 124 (1996): 378.

Riss, Arthur. "The Belly Politic: *Coriolanus* and the Revolt of Language." *ELH* 59 (1992): 53–75.

Robertson, D. W., Jr. "The Concept of Courtly Love as an Impediment to the Understanding of Medieval Texts." In *The Meaning of Courtly Love*, ed. F. X. Newman. Albany: State University of New York Press, 1972.

Ronan, Clifford. *"Antike Roman": Power Symbology and the Roman Play in Early Modern England, 1585–1635*. Athens: University of Georgia Press, 1995.

Rose, Paul Lawrence. "The Politics of *Antony and Cleopatra*." *Shakespeare Quarterly* 20 (1969): 379–89.

Rose, Mark. Introduction to *Twentieth Century Interpretations of* Antony and Cleopatra. Englewood Cliffs, N.J.: Prentice-Hall, 1977.

Rowse, A. L. *Shakespeare's Southampton: Patron of Virginia*. New York: Harper & Row, 1965.

Royster, Francesca T. "White-limed Walls: Whiteness and Gothic Extremism in Shakespeare's *Titus Andronicus*." *Shakespeare Quarterly* 51 (2000): 432–55.

Russell, Jeffrey Burton. "The Devil and the Reformers." In *The Prince of Darkness: Radical Evil and the Power of Good in History*. Ithaca: Cornell University Press, 1988.

Sanders, Norman. "The Shift of Power in *Julius Caesar*." *Review of English Literature* 5 (1964): 24–35.

Sandler, Florence. "*The Faerie Queene*: An Elizabethan Apocalypse." In *Apocalypse in English Renaissance Thought and Literature*, ed. C. A. Patrides and Joseph Wittreich. Ithaca: Cornell University Press, 1984.

Savage, James E. "*Troilus and Cressida* and Elizabethan Court Factions." *The University of Mississippi Studies in English* 5 (1964): 43–66.

Schanzer, Ernest. *The Problem Plays of Shakespeare: A Study of* Julius Caesar, Measure for Measure, Antony and Cleopatra. New York: Schocken, 1963.

Shorey, Paul. *Platonism Ancient and Modern*. Berkeley and Los Angeles: University of California Press, 1938.

Simmons, J. L. *Shakespeare's Pagan World: The Roman Tragedies*. Charlottesville: University Press of Virginia, 1973.

Smith, Alan Gordon. *William Cecil: The Power behind Elizabeth*. 1934. Reprint, New York: Haskell House, 1971.

Spencer, T. J. B. "Shakespeare and the Elizabethan Romans." *Shakespeare Survey* 10 (1957): 27–38.

———. *William Shakespeare: The Roman Plays:* Titus Andronicus; Julius Caesar; Antony and Cleopatra; Coriolanus. N.p.: Longmans, Green, 1963.

Stempel, Daniel. "The Transmigration of the Crocodile." *Shakespeare Quarterly* 7 (1956): 59–72.

Stirling, Brents. "Anti-Democracy in Shakespeare: A Re-survey." *Modern Language Quarterly* 2 (1941): 487–502.

———. "'Or else were this a savage spectacle.'" In *Unity in Shakespearian Tragedy: The Interplay of Theme and Character*. New York: Columbia University Press, 1956.

Stone, Lawrence. *The Causes of the English Revolution, 1529–1642*. New York: Harper & Row, 1972.

Strong, Roy. *The Cult of Elizabeth: Elizabethan Portraiture and Pageantry*. 1977. Reprint, London: Pimlico, 1999.

Stroup, Thomas B. "The Structure of *Antony and Cleopatra*." *Shakespeare Quarterly* 15 (1964): 289–98.

Tanselle, G. Thomas, and Florence W. Dunbar. "Legal Language in *Coriolanus*." *Shakespeare Quarterly* 13 (1962): 231–38.

Tennenhouse, Leonard. "*Coriolanus*: History and the Crisis of Semantic Order." In *Drama in the Renaissance: Comparative and Critical Essays*, ed. Clifford Davidson, C. J. Gianakaris, and John H. Stroupe. New York: AMS Press, 1986.

Thomas, Vivian. *Shakespeare's Roman Worlds.* London: Routledge, 1989.

Thomson, J. A. K. *Shakespeare and the Classics.* 1952. Reprint, Westport, Conn.: Greenwood Press, 1978.

Tiffany, Grace. "Shakespeare's Dionysian Prince: Drama, Politics, and the 'Athenian' History Play." *Renaissance Quarterly* 52 (1999): 366–83.

Tolbert, James M. "The Argument of Shakespeare's *Lucrece*: Its Sources and Authorship." *Texas Studies in English* 29 (1950): 77–90.

Toole, William B. "The Metaphor of Alchemy in *Julius Caesar.*" *Costerus* 5 (1972): 135–51,

Tovey, Barbara. "Shakespeare's Apology for Imitative Poetry: *The Tempest* and *The Republic.*" *Interpretations* 11 (1983): 275–316.

Traci, Philip J. *The Love Play of* Antony and Cleopatra: *A Critical Study of Shakespeare's Play.* The Hague: Mouton, 1970.

Traversi, Derek A. *Shakespeare: The Roman Plays.* Stanford: Stanford University Press, 1963.

Trevelyan, George Macaulay. *History of England.* London: Longmans, Green, 1926.

Trompf, G. W. *The Idea of Historical Recurrence in Western Thought from Antiquity to the Reformation.* Berkeley and Los Angeles: University of California Press, 1970.

Tupper, Frederick, Jr. "The Shaksperean Mob." *PMLA* 27 (1912): 486–523.

Ure, Peter, ed. *King Richard II.* 5th ed. The Arden Shakespeare, Second Series. London: Methuen, 1961.

Velz, John W. "The Ancient World in Shakespeare: Authenticity or Anachronism? A Retrospect." *Shakespeare Survey* 31 (1978): 1–12.

———. "Caesar's Deafness." *Shakespeare Quarterly* 22 (1971): 400–401.

———. "Clemency, Will, and Just Cause in 'Julius Caesar.'" *Shakespeare Survey* 22 (1969): 109–18.

———. *Shakespeare and the Classical Tradition: A Critical Guide to Commentary, 1660–1960.* Minneapolis: University of Minnesota Press, 1968.

———. "Undular Structure in 'Julius Caesar.'" *Modern Language Review* 66 (1971): 21–30.

Vickers, Nancy J. "'This Heraldry in Lucrece' Face.'" *Poetics Today* 6, no. 1–2 (1985): 171–84.

Waith, Eugene M. "The Herculean Hero." In *Modern Critical Interpretations: William Shakespeare's* Coriolanus, ed. Harold Bloom. New York: Chelsea House, 1988. First published in Eugene M. Waith, *The Herculean Hero in Marlowe, Chapman, Shakespeare and Dryden* under the title "Shakespeare," 112–43. (New York: Columbia University Press; London: Chatto & Windus, 1962).

Walker, Lewis, comp. *Shakespeare and the Classical Tradition: An Annotated Bibliography, 1961–1991.* New York: Routledge, 2002.

Warner, G. F. "James VI and Rome." *English Historical Review* 20 (1905): 124–26.

Weisinger, Herbert. "Ideas of History during the Renaissance." In *Renaissance Essays,* ed. Paul Oscar Kristeller and Philip P. Wiener. New York: Harper & Row, 1968.

Wernheim, R. B. *After the Armada: Elizabethan England and the Struggle for Western Europe, 1588–1595.* Oxford: Clarendon Press, 1984.

White, Howard B. *Copp'd Hills towards Heaven: Shakespeare and the Classical Polity.* The Hague: Martinus Nijhoff, 1970.

White, Nicholas P. *A Companion to Plato's* Republic. Indianapolis: Hackett Publishing, 1979.

Wilders, John, ed. *Antony and Cleopatra.* The Arden Shakespeare, Third Series. London: Routledge, 1995.

Willbern, David. "Hyperbolic Desire: Shakespeare's *Lucrece.*" In *Contending Kingdoms: Historical, Psychological, and Feminist Approaches to the Literature of Sixteenth-Century England and France,* ed. Marie-Rose Logan and Peter L. Rudnytsky. Detroit: Wayne State University Press, 1991.

Williamson, Marilyn. "The Political Context in *Antony and Cleopatra.*" *Shakespeare Quarterly* 21 (1970): 241–51.

Willson, David Harris. *King James VI and I.* New York: Oxford University Press, 1956.

Wilson, Elkin C. *England's Eliza.* 1939. Reprint, New York: Octagon, 1966.

Wilson, Rawdon R. "Shakespearean Narrative: *The Rape of Lucrece* Reconsidered." *SEL* 28 (1988): 39–59.

Woolf, D. R. *The Idea of History in Early Stuart England: Erudition, Ideology, and 'The Light of Truth' from the Accession of James I to the Civil War.* Toronto: University of Toronto Press, 1990.

Yates, Frances A. *Astraea: The Imperial Theme in the Sixteenth Century.* 1975. Reprint, London: Pimlico, 1993.

Zeeveld, W. Gordon. "*Coriolanus* and Jacobean Politics." *Modern Language Review* 57 (1962): 321–34.

Index

Antichrist, 17, 121, 123, 125. *See also* Whore of Babylon
Antony and Cleopatra, 21, 24–25, 91–109; and eros, 94–95; political allegory in, 105–8; and tyranny, 92–109. *See also* Rome
Apology of the House of Commons . . . touching their Privileges, 152 nn. 20, 23, 26
Aristotle, 34; constitutional theory of, compared with Plato's, 26; *Nichomachean Ethics*, 26; *Politics*, 22, 26
Axton, Marie, 21, 115

Baldwin, T. W., 28
Bale, John, *Image of Both Churches*, 17, 121, 164 n. 50
Bate, Jonathan, 110, 118
Becon, Thomas, 117; "The Displaying of the Popish Mass," 163 n. 27
Bevington, David, 75
Bible: Geneva, 120; I Corinthians, 57, 152 n. 22; Matthew, 20; Revelation, 17, 120, 124
Blundeville, Thomas, *True Order and Methode of Wryting and Reading Hystories*, 18
Bullinger, Henry, *Lucretia*, 32

Campbell, Lily B., 50
Cantor, Paul A., 143 n. 48
Cecil, Robert, 49
Cecil, William, Lord Burghley, 51

Chambers, E. K., 29
Chapman, George: and Essex, 42
Charney, Maurice, 143 n. 48
Chaste Woman Clothed with the Sun, 17
Cicero, 27, 39, 63
Comedy of Errors, The, 28
constitutional change: classical theory of, 16–17
Coriolanus, 20–21, 23–25, 49, 54–73, 107; growth of democracy in, 60–65, 72, 74; parable of the belly in, 57–58; political allegory in, 54–57, 70–72; topicality in, 150 n. 10. *See also* oligarchy; Rome
Craig, Sir Thomas, 112; *The Right of Succession to the Kingdom of England*, 162 n. 8
Cymbeline, 143 n. 49

Daniel, Samuel, *The Tragedie of Cleopatra*, 30, 107–8
Daniell, David, 89
Davies, Sir John, 90; *Orchestra*, 41
democracy, 23, 130: as constitution, 24, 92; growth of, in *Coriolanus*, 60–65, 72, 74; passage of, into tyranny, 24, 74, 77–78, 92; in *Titus Andronicus*, 129
Devereux, Robert, second Earl of Essex, 19; and the Cecils, 43, 86; contemporary perception of, 44–46, 50–51, 86–88; and Henry Boling-

179

broke, 43–45, 50, 86, 148 n. 41; and *Henry V*, 88; Irish campaign, 86–88; and James VI, 51; and *Julius Caesar*, 86–90; militarism of, 42–43, 47, 51–52; Rouen desertion, 47, 149 n. 56; and Southampton, 87–88; as Tarquin in *Lucrece*, 42–52; and *Troilus*, 42, 48; treason of, 43–44, 87, 148 nn. 38, 50; —, as rape, 46–47
Dowland, John, 90
drama: and censorship, 29–30; function of, 30; as political criticism, 15, 20–22
Dudley, Robert, Earl of Leicester, 18, 49
Du Perron, Davy, 34

Eliot, T. S., 110
Elizabeth I, 130; as apocalyptic Bride, 122; as chivalric heroine, 41–42; as double Tudor Rose, 40; and Essex, 50, 86–89; and *Faerie Queene*, 46–47, 126; as God's handmaiden, 17; and *Julius Caesar*, 86–90; and Leicester, 49; as Lucrece, 40–42, 49–50; moon a symbol of, 40–41, 90; and Richard II, 45; ruled by favorites, 49–50; and the Succession, 18, 21, 29, 90, 111; and Troy, 48. *See also* Elizabethan Succession Crisis
Elizabethan Succession Crisis, 111–112, 129; and James VI, 112; and the Spanish threat, 111, 115, 124–26. *See also* Elizabeth I
Ellesmere, Lord Thomas, 56
Elyot, Sir Thomas, 27, 95; on constitutional decline, 16–17, 20, 32; definition of State, 142 n. 39; on democracy, 67; *The Governor*, 140 n. 14, 166 n. 7; *Of the Knowledge Which Maketh a Wise Man*, 159 n. 11
Erasmus, Desiderius, 27; *Education of a Christian Prince*, 30
eros: Cleopatra as, 95; and tyranny, 94, 159 n. 12
Essex, Earl of. *See* Devereux, Robert, second Earl of Essex

Ficino, Marsilio: and *Republic*, 27, 144 n. 55
"Form of Solemnization of Matrimony, The," 160 n. 20
Foxe, John, *Acts and Monuments* ("Book of Martyrs"), 121, 125, 128, 163 n. 30
Frye, Susan, 46
Fulbecke, William, 20

Gascoigne, George, *The Spoyle of Antwerp*, 124
Grafton, Richard, 18
Greene, Robert, *Friar Bacon and Friar Bungay*, 115
Gregory XIII (pope), 114
Greville, Fulke: *Caelica*, 40; *Of Monarchy*, 19–20
Guilpin, Everard, 44; *Skialetheia*, 148 n. 45

Hamlet, 15, 139 n. 2, 155 n. 15
Hanford, James Holly, 22, 82
Harrison, William, *An Historicall Description of the Iland of Britaine*, 124, 164 n. 54
Harvey, Gabriel: on *Rape of Lucrece*, 146 n. 14
Hayward, John, 49; *The First Part of the Life and Raigne of King Henry IIII*, 45, 86
Heinemann, Margot, 22
Henry V, 23, 29, 166 n. 6; and Essex, 88; Plato's philosopher king in, 134; and rational kingship, 38, 134–35, 165–66 n. 5; and tyranny, 95
Henry VI (Part 2), 49, 132–33
Henry VIII, 133
Henry VIII, will of, 113–14
Heylyn, Peter: on *anacyclosis*, 139 n. 10; *Augustus*, 17
Heywood, Thomas, 22, 30; *An Apology for Actors*, 141 n. 36, 145 n. 70
history: apocalyptic view of, 17–18; —, in *Faerie Queene*, 122; —, in *Titus Andronicus*, 121–23; Augustinian view of, 15; cyclical theory of, 16; —, Plato and, 142 n. 46; —, Shake-

speare and, 24; function of, 15, 30; politicization of, 16–17; providential view of, 140 n. 13; Renaissance view of, 16–18; Roman, 18–21
Holinshed, Raphael, 33, 140 n. 13
Hooker, Richard, 57
hydra: in *Coriolanus*, 67–68, 80; in *Henry V*, 67–68; symbolic of kingless State, 67–68

Indulgences, Theology of, 119

James I (James VI of Scotland), 44, 130, 136; absolutism of, 19, 29, 71–72, 105, 152 n. 26; and *Antony and Cleopatra*, 105–6; as Caesar Augustus, 105; contemporary burlesque of, 29–30; and *Coriolanus*, 55, 70–72; debauchery of, 105–6, 161 n. 30; and Elizabethan Succession, 113, 115; and Parliament, 55–57, 71–72, 151 n. 11; and *pax Romana*, 105; political philosophy of, 55, 150 nn. 6 and 7
Jewel, John, 117, 120; *The Defense of the Apology of the Church of England*, 163 n. 34; *A Reply to M. Harding's Answer*, 163 n. 38
John of Salisbury, *Policraticus*, 30
Jonson, Ben, 27, 28, 144 n. 55; *Catiline*, 21; *Sejanus*, 21
Julius Caesar, 21, 24–25, 33, 37, 39–40, 49–50, 70, 72–91, 107; and Essex, 86–89; and Plutarch, 74–75, 89–90, 154–58; political allegory in, 86–91; and tyranny, 74–91. *See also* Rome; soul
justice: popish, 119; in the soul, 79; in the State, 23

Kahn, Coppélia, 143 n. 48
Kernan, Alvin, 71
king: as analogue of reason, 135, 165 n. 5; antithesis of tyrant, 95; as moral glass, 149 n. 65. *See also* monarchy; soul: state's, mirror of ruler's
King John, 133

King Lear, 20, 128, 135, 166 n. 7
Kyd, Thomas, *The Spanish Tragedy*, 115

Leggatt, Alexander, 143 n. 48
Leicester, Earl of. *See* Dudley, Robert, Earl of Leicester
Locrine (anon.), 116
Lopez, Roderigo, 19, 49
Lucrece, rape of: and political allegory, 32–33, 53
Luther, Martin, *Passional Christi und Antichristi*, 120
Lydgate, John, *The Serpent of Division*, 30

Macbeth, 128, 140 n. 23, 155 n. 15
MacCaffrey, Wallace, 43
Machiavelli, Niccolò, 16–17; *Discourses*, 38–39
Mallette, Richard, 124
Mallin, Eric, 41–42, 48
Marlowe, Christopher, 20, 123; *Edward II*, 106
Mary Queen of Scots: as Duessa, 121, 126, 164 n. 39; and Philip of Spain, 112; and Protestant Succession, 112–15; and *Titus Andronicus*, 114–15, 121–22; as Whore of Babylon, 121–22
mass: satire on, 117–19; Thirty-Nine Articles of Religion on, 163 n. 28
McDonald, Russ, 27–28
McIlwain, Charles, 55
Merchant of Venice, The, 23
Meyer, A. O., 117
Midsummer Night's Dream, A, 41
Miola, Robert S., 143 n. 48
monarchy: as best form of government, 23, 145 n. 1; collapse of, 140 n. 19; —, as prelude to civil war, 19, 130; —, in *Titus Andronicus*, 111, 129, 133; founded on reason, 23; passage of, into oligarchy, 23. *See also* king
monasteries, dissolution of, 123
Montaigne, Michel Eyquem de, 35
More, Sir Thomas, *Utopia*, 30

Naunton, Sir Robert, 89
Nenner, Howard, 112

oligarchy: and class conflict, 23, 54, 74; as constitution, 23–24, 54; in *Coriolanus*, 54–68, 72; passage of, into democracy, 24
Othello, 125
Ovid, 32; *Fasti*, 28; *Metamorphoses*, 28

Parsons, Robert (R. Doleman), 113, 162 n. 13; *A Conference about the Next Succession*, 45, 86
Paul IV (pope), 114
Peele, George: *Anglorum Feriae*, 48; *Edward I*, 115
Philip II (king of Spain), 112, 114, 118, 125
Phillips, James Emerson, 29, 106
Pius IV (pope), 114
Pius V (pope), 116; and *Regnans in Excelsis*, 114
Plato, 34; *Laws*, 22; *Phaedo*, 28; theory of universal decay, 142 n. 46. *See also* democracy; monarchy; oligarchy; *Republic*; soul; timocracy; tyranny
Platt, Michael, 143 n. 48
Plutarch: and *Julius Caesar*, 74–75, 89–90, 154–58
Polybius, 16–17

Ralegh, Sir Walter, *The History of the World*, 30
rape: assault on Queen's chambers as, 46–47; equated with invasion, 124; in *Henry V*, 124, 164 n. 53; and Protestant polemics, 124; in *Titus Andronicus*, 123–27, 129. *See also* Lucrece, rape of; *Rape of Lucrece, The*
Rape of Lucrece, The, 18, 24–25, 31–53, 72–73, 107, 146 n. 14, 165 n. 3; chivalric motif in, 41–42, 52, 148 n. 32; political allegory in, 33–53, 146 n. 14, 163 n. 28; and Southampton, 51; and timocracy, 31–32, 51–52, 54. *See also* Lucrece, rape of; Rome, history of
Republic: correspondence between ruler and State in, 23–24, 155 n. 15; influence of, 22; and Plato's theory of constitutional decline, 22–24; as *Politeia*, 141 n. 38; Shakespeare's knowledge of, 27–29, 136; translations of, 27. *See also* democracy; monarchy; oligarchy; soul; timocracy; tyranny
Reynoldes, Richard, 18; *Chronicle of all the noble Emperours of the Romaines*, 140 n. 15
rhetoric: Cicero on, 39, 63; in *Coriolanus*, 56, 59–60, 62–64, 65– 66, 151 n. 16; as political vehicle, 34–35; and *Rape of Lucrece*, 35, 39–40, 49, 147 nn. 18 and 22
Richard II, 34, 44–45, 51, 132–33
Richard III, 23, 133
Rogers, Thomas, 120, 123; *The Catholic Doctrine of the Church of England*, 163 n. 38; *An Historical Dialogue touching Antichrist*, 164 n. 46
Rome: as Antichrist, 17; as archetype of civil strife, 20–21; history of, 18–21. *See also* Whore of Babylon
Romeo and Juliet, 30, 141 n. 30

Sandler, Florence, 114, 122
Sandys, Edwin, 120
satire, anti–Catholic, 116–29, 163 n. 30. *See also* Antichrist; Whore of Babylon
Shakespeare, William: classical learning of, 27–29, 142 n. 41; and cyclical theory of history, 24; knowledge of *Republic*, 27–29, 136; and Plato's theory of constitutional decline, 24–25; religion of, 135–36; view of the masses, 135. *See also under individual works*
Simmons, J. L., 143 n. 48
Smith, Sir Thomas, 56
soul: contamination of, 75–76; in *Julius Caesar*, 75–77, 83–85; hierarchy of, 84, 93, 156 n. 32; justice in, 79; metallic composition of, 75, 156 n. 31; as microcosm of State, 19, 23, 58–59, 68, 94–95, 135, 156 n. 32;

in *Rape of Lucrece*, 33, 36–37; state's, mirror of ruler's, 80, 94, 106. *See also* state, hierarchy of
Southampton, Earl of, 18, 51, 88
Spain, 135, 164 n. 55; as epitome of evil, 18; and *Titus Andronicus*, 111, 114–15, 124–26
Spanish Armada: and apocalyptic view of history, 18
Spencer, T. J. B., 110
Spenser, Edmund: *The Faerie Queene*, 33, 46–48, 118, 121–22, 124, 126, 164 n. 39; *The Shepheardes Calender*, 40
state, hierarchy of, 23
Strong, Roy, 17
Stuart, Mary. *See* Mary Queen of Scots
succession, modes of, 112–13

Tacitus, 16, 34
Tempest, The, 23, 28
tetralogy: "Roman," defined, 25–26; Roman works as, 131–33; Shakespeare's English, 53, 132–33
Thomas, Vivian, 143 n. 48
timocracy: as constitution, 31–32; and *Rape of Lucrece*, 31–32, 51–52, 54
Titus Andronicus, 21, 25, 28, 33, 110–29, 133; as anti-Catholic satire, 116–29; democracy in, 129; and Elizabethan succession crisis, 111–116, 129; and James VI, 115; and Mary Queen of Scots, 114–15; and Spanish threat, 111, 114–15, 124–26, 129; tyranny in, 111, 128, 129; unsettled succession in, 110–11. *See also* Rome

Traversi, Derek, 143 n. 48
Troilus and Cressida, 22–23, 73; and Essex, 42, 48; and kingship, 135
Troy: Elizabeth and, 48; England as, 33, 47–48, 133
tyranny, 133; and *Antony and Cleopatra*, 92–109; as complete injustice, 108; as constitution, 31, 95; and emasculation, 94, 108; and eros, 94–95, 159 n. 12; and *Henry V*, 95; and *Julius Caesar*, 74–91; and mob rule, 74, 80–82; Plato on, 24; in *Titus Andronicus*, 111, 128–29. *See also* tyrant
tyrant: antithesis of king, 95; Antony as, 108; Brutus as, 84–85; Caesar as, 78–82; definition of, 77, 82, 94–95; and lust (eros), 108; Octavius as, 109; Saturninus as, 128–29; as slave, 79, 94, 108. *See also* tyranny

Velz, John W., 143 n. 47
Venus and Adonis, 146 n. 14

Waith, Eugene, 68
Wars of the Roses: and Lucrece, 33–34, 36, 53, 133
Watson, Thomas, 48
Webster, John, *The Duchess of Malfi*, 106
Whore of Babylon, 124; and Catholic Church, 17; and *Faerie Queene*, 122, 124; Mary Queen of Scots as, 121; Rome as, 120; and *Titus Andronicus*, 120–25. *See also* Antichrist; satire, anti-Catholic
Woolf, D. R., 30